Def
Jam,
Inc.

Russell Simmons,

Rick Rubin,

and the

Extraordinary Story

of the

World's Most

Influential

Hip-Hop Label

Def Jam, Inc.

Stacy Gueraseva

 One World · Ballantine Books · New York

Published in the United States by One World Books, an imprint of The Random House Publishing Group, a division of Random House, Inc., New York.

ONE WORLD is a registered trademark and the One World colophon is a trademark of Random House, Inc.

Photographs of LL Cool J (p. 65) and Slick Rick (p. 157) copyright © Glen E. Friedman, from the book *Fuck You Too*. Reprinted with permission of Burning Flags Press.

Library of Congress Cataloging-in-Publication Data

Gueraseva, Stacy.
Def Jam, Inc.: Russell Simmons, Rick Rubin, and the extraordinary story of the world's most influential hip-hop label / by Stacy Gueraseva.
p. cm.
Includes bibliographical references (p. 291) and discography (p. 299).
ISBN 0-345-46804-X
1. Def Jam Recordings—History.   2. Simmons, Russell.   3. Rubin, Rick.
4. Sound recording executives and producers—United States—Biography.
5. Rap (Music)—History and criticism.   I. Title.

ML427.D44G84 2005
782.421649'092'2—dc22
[B]   2004066261

Printed in the United States of America

www.oneworldbooks.net

9 8 7 6 5 4 3 2 1

First Edition

Design by Mercedes Everett

To Jules

Contents

Introduction

Why am I writing the introduction to this book? After all, I am only a tiny piece of this huge Def Jam mosaic that has inspired people around the world. Other than its obvious, ground-breaking recording artists, Def Jam developed a culture where an intern could one day become president of the company, where a messenger could become an A&R man, an unknown comedian, after appearing on *The Def Comedy Jam,* could go on to make $20 million a movie, where a graffiti artist could become one of the industry's most sought-after art directors, where a street corner poet could win a Tony for appearing on Broadway, and where a white DJ who started a record company out of his dorm room could become one of the most successful and prolific record producers of all time.

And by chance even me, the young, white, Jewish kid who Russell Simmons brought into his world and eventually recognized my unique abilities and enthusiasm for filmmaking, which gave me the break I needed. Russell saw something in me and exposed me to a life of hip-hop. He gave me the opportunity to shadow him during an important period in Def Jam's history. The experience taught me things that could not be found in any book or on even the most wise street corner. Def Jam's music and work aesthetic changed my life.

The first time I met Russell Simmons was in Washington Square Park, on the set of Run-DMC's "Run's House" video. It was 1987! I was sitting in my dorm room at NYU—I was a sophomore at the Tisch School for the Arts—when Glen Friedman called me and said I should go by the "Run's House" set to meet Russell. Glen was Def

Jam's primary photographer at that time, and had shot the album cover for a white rap group I was producing, Big Man On Campus (BMOC).

While shooting the BMOC cover at Harvard University, Glen had suggested that I should pick up a classic hooded Harvard Champion sweatshirt for Russell, who loved Champion sweatshirts. It seemed like a strange request, but being a seventeen-year-old wide-eyed rap fan, I thought that maybe when you meet someone in the rap business, you have to come bearing gifts. So when I gave the sweatshirt to Russell on the set, he looked at me like I was some obsessed fan. When, in fact, I really wasn't. I got mad at Glen for suggesting the sweatshirt, but the next time I ran into Russell, he remembered me for it.

I was out every night during college—Danceteria, Nell's, the Milk Bar—and started seeing Russell out all the time. One time he saw me with a gaggle of models, so of course he came over to say hi. He had a mini Cadillac stretch back then and invited me and the girls along for the ride, going from club to club, driven by his long-time driver Kenny Lee. We ended up at Save the Robots, an Alphabet City after-hours club that opened at 5 a.m. We left at about noon and continued on that schedule for as long as I can remember. It's a miracle that I even graduated from NYU.

My relationship with Russell was initially based on our mutual admiration for beautiful women, and I knew them all. But my real dream since I was eight years old was not to be going out every night to clubs but to be a film director. So whenever I would complete a student film, I would show it to Russell for his approval. He would watch and then say, "Great, now let's go out and chase some models!" Not that he wasn't interested in my work, but going out was definitely more interesting.

Lyor Cohen, however, took notice of the fact that I was in need of some attention when it came to my films. He was always going over to Russell's house to show him the latest Def Jam video (there were very few at the time), and Russell and Lyor would always ask for my opinion, too, whether it was because I was a film student or because I was always around. I had a feeling Lyor had no idea if a video was good or not, but it felt good that it was left up to Russell and me to decide. It was like another film school for me.

Russell always gets the credit for discovering me but it was Lyor who gave me my first directing job. He hired me to direct some public service announcements for Public Enemy on topics like black-on-black crime and safe sex—all part of his strategy to clean up Public Enemy's image after Professor Griff's anti-Semitic statements. The six PSA's I directed played constantly on The Box and BET, and I could tell that Russell was proud of me, but I was nervous about directing music videos for Def Jam. Would Russell still be my friend if I did a bad job?

In 1992, Russell and I decided to go to my hometown of Miami for a Public Enemy concert. We shared a room at The Marlin on South Beach. After the show, Russell and I went backstage, where Chuck D. mentioned that they were going to shoot a video for their new single, "Louder Than a Bomb." He recognized me as the director of their PSA's, and said to Russell, "Can Brett shoot the video?" Russell said, with me standing right by his side, "Brett who?" Chuck pointed to me and said, "Brett. White man Brett. Your friend." Russell reacted like the proudest father in the world. His face lit up and he said to me, "Do you wanna do it?" Of course I said, "Yes." Suddenly, I went from being the white kid Russell would go clubbing with to being his "Jewish son." From then on, Russell introduced me to everyone as his adopted son.

For the "Louder Than a Bomb" video, I followed Public Enemy on their tour with U2, city to city, through airports, arenas, and grocery shopping trips with Flavor Flav and his many kids. The video I shot was in black and white—the first of its kind for a documentary-style concert video. When it was finally delivered to MTV, they immediately added it to the rotation, and the strategic Bono cameo ensured continuous broadcasting. But something else happened when the video debuted that was even more defining for me, for other directors, and for the quality of future music videos. MTV credited the director of the video. And mine was the very first credit. What luck. All of a sudden, Russell started getting calls from artists, asking "Can Brett do my next video?" This time, he didn't have to ask, "Brett who?"

Erick Sermon called and asked me to direct the video for "Tonight's Da Night" from Redman's debut LP, *Whut? Thee Album*. The buzz on Redman was huge, and Def Jam needed a hit desperately. He suggested we shoot in front of his home in Newark, New Jersey, so that he didn't have to wake up too early. I got my film crew together one morning in a van and we set out for Newark, where Redman lived with his parents. While we waited for him to come out, we filmed shots of the Jewish cemetery right across the street. Hours later, Redman finally emerged with a huge tissue hanging from his nose. I was only able to get one take because he kept going, then got into his car and drove away. My crew jumped in the van and followed.

Around the corner from his house we met Redman's crew, the Pack Pistol Posse. He said, "Now I'm ready to shoot, white boy!" No makeup, no props, no wardrobe styling, just the clothes on their backs. Typical Def Jam artist—signed because of his talent, charisma, and star quality. There were no gimmicks.

The shoot then moved to Harlem, where 150 of Redman's closest friends were all standing in the cold waiting to be in his video. Redman got a last-minute idea to have a "white bitch" roll up and buy some weed. I said to him, "But Reg [short for Reggie, his real name], it's 3 a.m. There are no white bitches on the street in Harlem right now." He pointed off into the distance and said, "What about that 'white bitch'?" "That's my mom!" I said. He said, "So what?" And that's how my mom ended up being the "white bitch rolling up and buying some weed" in the Redman video.

Russell and Lyor each had their particular favorite Def Jam artists. Russell loved Bo$$, the South Central Cartel, and Pete Nice; Lyor favored Domino, Montell Jordan, and MC Serch. Of course, the videos I directed were for Russell's favorite artists. So if those records didn't sell, Lyor would blame me. When I was asked to direct LL Cool J's "Pink Cookies in a Plastic Bag (Getting Crushed by Buildings)" video, Lyor gave me the usual: "Don't ruin his career. The future of Def Jam is in your hands." While we were in the middle of directing the "Pink Cookies" video, LL's "Backseat of My Jeep" single started taking off on the radio instead, and Lyor realized we had done the video for the wrong single. So I suggested that we stop the song in the middle and cut in fifteen seconds of the hook of "Backseat of My Jeep" in order to tease the audience for what was coming. Teasers in videos would become standard practice after that.

Brian Grazer, a big Hollywood producer whom I met with Russell when Brian was doing *Boomerang* in New York, offered me a job around that time to be his assistant for $23,000 a year. I told him I appreciated the offer, but that I was a director not an assistant. So he offered me an extra $2,000. I said, "You don't understand. I'm a director like Ron Howard. I'm gonna be directing movies soon." He thanked me for coming in, and asked his assistant to bring in his next appointment. On my way out, he asked me to say "hi" to Russell for him. I said, "By the way, Russell has a great idea. He wants to do a black version of *The Nutty Professor.*" Brian immediately called Jerry Lewis in front of me and offered to buy the rights. Russell ended up with $600,000 as a producing fee and the soundtrack rights for Def Jam. Of course, I got to direct the videos for the soundtrack.

In the summer of 1997, I decided to move to L.A. to pursue my career in the movie business; Russell followed me and together we rented a house in the Hollywood Hills. The first feature I directed was *Money Talks,* starring Chris Tucker, whom I'd seen for the first time at one of the rehearsals for *The Def Comedy Jam.* I went on to direct *Rush Hour* and gave the soundtrack to Def Jam, of course, to distribute. But *Rush Hour* would never have happened if I hadn't been exposed to the living cultural experience that was, and still is, Def Jam.

Brett Ratner
Beverly Hills, March 28, 2005

Prologue

On September 5 of 2003 in New York City, a group of eleven men assembled in the same room for the first time in more than ten years. The occasion was a historic shoot for a "Def Jam Reunion," as the headline read, in *Vanity Fair* magazine's annual music issue. The three-page foldout spread looked at the people who'd started Def Jam Records, the most influential and longest-running hip-hop label. The men in the room were Def Jam's founders Rick Rubin and Russell Simmons; Def Jam's first artist, LL Cool J, who was still signed to the label; Lyor Cohen, former artist manager turned Def Jam's chief; Run and DMC of Run-DMC, and their former road manager Runny Ray; Chuck D. of Public Enemy, his sidekick Flavor Flav, as well as their former producer, Bomb Squad's Hank Shocklee. There was also Tom Araya of the heavy metal group Slayer, who were signed to Def Jam in 1986.

On a replica set of Rubin's old New York University dorm room, where he conceived the Def Jam logo and programmed his early beats, legendary photographer Annie Liebovitz was clicking away. No one in that room would have thought back in 1984, when Def Jam was officially founded as an independent label, that they would ever have the occasion to gather for its twentieth anniversary. "It felt incredible," recalled Lyor Cohen of that day. "All of us enjoyed it so much, it was so fun. There was no sadness, like, 'Oh, we miss . . .' It was all about optimism and sharing something really important."

But there *was* someone missing: Jam Master Jay, Run-DMC's DJ, who was a motivating and creative presence at Def Jam since the

beginning, and the founder of JMJ Records, home to one of Def
Jam's biggest groups, Onyx. He had been shot, execution-style, on
October 30, 2002, at the same Queens studio where he had recorded
for years. No one saw it coming. "Jay was the most proud of them
all," says Cohen. "If he was ever in trouble or in need of something,
he would never ask." His death was a staggering loss. Over at Def
Jam's offices on West Fiftieth Street, by the elevator bank of the executive floor, staff members arranged a set of tables draped in white
cloth, with a picture of Jay surrounded by flowers and a personal-
ized dedication. The arrangement remained there for more than
two weeks. As Chuck D. noted, "Jay really connected everyone
together."

Also missing from the picture were the Beastie Boys, Def Jam's
first platinum-selling group. Although they spent only three years at
the label, they left one of the most indelible marks on it. Mike D.,
MCA, and Ad-Rock were completely changed men from the young,
bratty, and wild kids who toured the country in 1987 with giant
Budweiser cans as stage props, a dancing girl in a cage, and an inflatable phallus. They had developed a varied repertoire as recording
artists for Capitol Records, to which they signed in 1989. These days,
they were family men.

Eighteen years after their multiplatinum phenomenon *Licensed to
Ill*, the Beasties were still recording and releasing new material. At the
time of the *Vanity Fair* shoot they were working on their eagerly anticipated sixth album, *To the Five Boroughs*, their first full-length release in seven years. Now considered the "elder statesmen" of rap
instead of the rebellious punk kids of their early years, the Beasties
had an entirely new generation of fans—many of whom were born
after the Beasties' first album was released.

Bill Adler, Def Jam's former publicist, had tried to convince the
Beasties to take part in the shoot, but to no avail. The trio simply refused to put aside their long-standing grudge against Rubin and Simmons over a royalties lawsuit, dating back to 1988. "Boy, they talk
about their newfound sense of being, and I thought that part of that

was about letting go and being positive," says Cohen. "They would have had a really great time."

Indeed, all those who were present were feeling elated. "Rubin and Simmons seemed like old friends who hadn't seen each other in a while," recalled Tom Araya. In the photograph, Simmons is leaning his head on Rubin's shoulder in the warm, familiar way of an old friend. "You could see that they were both very proud of the fact that they were able to do what they'd done. Big old smiles on their faces," says Araya. In fact, the idea to re-create the dorm room for the photo shoot—in a downtown warehouse—came from Rubin himself, who twenty years after creating the Def Jam logo was still exercising a kind of proud ownership. "I was looking at everybody, thinking, 'Damn, I didn't know we were a part of history in the making,' " Araya recalled. "I can't believe that we were at the beginning of something humongous. I just kinda sat there and looked at everybody: Chuck D., Flavor Flav, LL, the Run-DMC guys. Like, fuck."

So much had changed since those early days, most notably Russell Simmons, who was now a brand unto himself, with a hand in film, finance, fashion, and even politics. Rick Rubin had come to be regarded as one of the greatest rock producers of the century. His status in the music industry was almost mythical, as he produced such artists as Johnny Cash and the Red Hot Chili Peppers. LL Cool J had become a film and TV star; Public Enemy had severed ties with Def Jam in 2000 after fourteen years with the label and abandoned the traditional music distribution system.

But it was Def Jam Records itself that had gone through the most dramatic transformation. The Def Jam of the 1980s—when it was still a boutique-style, but fully operational, label with a small roster of artists and a handful of full-time staff who wore many hats around the office and had no clear job titles—was essentially obsolete. "The fact that we had any success at all is remarkable and a real testament to how good the work was, because everything else was poorly handled—out of ignorance and inexperience," Rubin recalled of the early days.

Def Jam was now the hip-hop arm of a new label known as Island Def Jam Group (Island Records is the rock and country arm), under the Universal Music Group, the world's largest record company.

From Tokyo to Berlin, London to Amsterdam, Island Def Jam has secured offices around the world and has become a true global empire in the new millennium. Its midtown Manhattan headquarters are a picture of corporate music at its most well-oiled, successful, and exciting: glass-paneled doors, shiny oak desks, luxury details like a juice/espresso bar with an adjacent magazine wall, breathtaking views of downtown Manhattan. It doesn't get much more corporate than occupying three floors in the towering Polygram building on Manhattan's West Fiftieth Street. Yet, despite going corporate, vestiges of Def Jam's creative spirit and do-it-yourself attitude remain. Most of the executives don't have MBA's or even college degrees; some had made their way to the top from humble beginnings like sweeping floors at a hair salon.

Like the greatest of American success stories, Def Jam's is about building a business, a dream, from the ground up. It is filled with many intriguing what-ifs. For example, before starting at NYU, Rick Rubin strongly considered going to the University of Chicago. What if he had gone there; would he have started Def Jam out of his dorm room, as he did at NYU? What if Def Jam had never signed a distribution deal with CBS Records, back in 1985; would they have died out like most hip-hop labels that started in the early and mid eighties? What if Rubin had never left the company in 1988; would it have gotten stronger, or dissolved?

Annie Leibovitz shot the final photo, and everyone went their separate ways. Within months, Cohen would be leaving Def Jam to become the chairman and chief executive officer of recorded music at Warner Music Group and a new chapter in the story would begin. He would be the last of the original executives to leave the label, and his departure would mark the end of an era—one of the most exciting times in music—but the beginning of a new chapter in Def Jam's constantly evolving story.

The emotional bond that Cohen, like so many other former employees, had forged with Def Jam was permanent. There is an old joke at Def Jam that "the company is like a cult," says Todd Moscowitz, a former staffer and now president of Asylum Records, a division of the Warner Music Group. But it really is true. As Cohen says, "We're *always* gonna be part of Def Jam."

Part One

Debut

1982–87

CHAPTER 1

The
Maverick

When New York University freshman Adam Dubin arrived on
campus in September of 1982 to move into his new home—
Weinstein Hall, at 5 University Place, in Greenwich Village—the
view that greeted him inside his tiny dorm room was uncanny. An
industrial-size Cerwin-Vega speaker stretched across the top of the
dressers; and both of the desks had been pushed together to hold two
turntables, a mixer, and a drum machine. The bookcases were stacked
with milk crates full of records; old magazines were scattered around
the floor. The only light source was a bandanna-draped lamp by his
roommate's bed (he had unscrewed all the other lightbulbs in the
room). It would turn out to be the roommate's second year in room
712, and he made it clear that this was his territory. "I noticed nothing in the room that let you know that there was any schoolwork to
be done," Dubin recalled. "No textbooks, notebooks, binders, loose-
leafs. Nothing."

"Where am I supposed to do my work?" he asked, a bit surprised.

"Work's to be done in the library," his new roommate announced
in a commanding baritone. "I like to do deejaying."

He introduced himself as Rick Rubin, a sophomore film and
video major, who, like Dubin and a large portion of NYU's student
body, came from Long Island. A heavyset kid with shoulder-length

brown hair and tinted eyeglasses, Rubin had on black jeans and a black T-shirt, topped with a biker-style leather jacket—his dress code on most days of the week. His friends had nicknamed him Rick Rock because of his passion for music and his rebel persona—similar to the "menacing aura of a character in an urban psycho-killer film," as one reporter wrote, that Rubin would cultivate several years later as one of music's most eccentric and visionary record producers.

Over the next few weeks, he took the time to show Dubin his world and seemed to enjoy playing the role of teacher. "It was important that I understood why he was gonna dominate the room," Dubin recalled. "He wanted to make sure that he didn't have some medical student for a roommate who's like, 'I can't study.'"

"What do you like to listen to?" he asked Dubin during their first conversation. "Led Zeppelin," said Dubin. Rubin frowned. "Rolling Stones," Dubin continued, and Rubin frowned again. He said that he was more excited by current sounds like a hard-core band from San Francisco called Flipper, which specialized in a subgenre of punk known as art-noise and was putting out records on an independent label. Rubin loved Flipper and their 1981 EP *Generic Flipper,* inspired him. The band had slowed down the superfast pace of hard-core for a few songs, chopping up each note. Their album cover was minimalist with black type on a yellow background, and a bar code that spelled out the name of the band instead of the usual numbers. The tracks on both sides of the record were listed as "Active Ingredients," and also came with quirky instructions like "Caution: If bleeding persists, contact your physician." *Generic Flipper* was "what Hose was trying to sound like," says Dubin. Hose was Rick's art-noise band, which he started during his freshman year at NYU.

One day Rubin showed his roommate an EP that he had recorded with Hose that past April of 1982. A fan of anything high-concept and cutting-edge, Rubin wanted Hose to be "more associated with an artistic movement," recalled Mike Espindle, a fellow student who would become the group's second lead singer. Rubin designed the professional-looking jacket after one of his favorite artists, Piet Mondrian, and his famous *Tableau II* painting. Just like the thick black intersecting lines and the red, whites, and yellows that fill the rectangles in Mondrian's painting, Rubin used bass and drums to create "a framework" for the song and "vocals and guitar to fill it with color," recalled Espindle. Along with original tracks there were covers, including Rick James's "Super Freak," but slowed down to its barest minimum. In his presentation of the band, Rubin made every attempt to avoid convention, even identifying the band members on the back of the album as Joel Horne, "Bash" (as in *bass*); Rick Rosen, "Truth" (vocals); and Rick Rubin, "Screech" (guitar). The black-and-yellow sticker on the EP advised, "This LP is to be played loud at 33⅓ RPMs."

The remarkable thing about the group was not its music, but how far Rubin had taken his passion. He didn't just record a demo and pass it around to friends, like most kids his age did; he actually finagled a distribution deal with the independent label 99 Records, owned by producer Ed Bahlman, who also operated a record store of the same name in the East Village. Rubin had been hanging out there since his senior year in high school and knew Bahlman well. "He kind of walked me through the process of how you go here to press the record, and you go here to have your labels made, and you go here to have your jacket covers made," Rubin recalled. Like a fledgling record executive, Rubin stopped by local record stores to keep track of how well his records were stocked. "I gotta check my inventory," he would say to Dubin, and together they made the rounds. "I had never met such a motivated nineteen-year-old," Dubin recalls of Rick.

Rubin applied the same level of commitment to any new endeavor he picked up. As a young boy, he had become obsessed with magic, practicing tricks for five hours a day in front of the mirror. He would commute into Manhattan from his Lido Beach, Long Island, home for the sole purpose of exploring his favorite magic stores, where he spent hours soaking up their atmospheres, and connecting with fellow magicians, most of whom were adults. "I'm a researcher by nature," he says. When his interest shifted to music in his early teens, Rubin picked up the guitar and became proficient with it within months. He started a punk band of his own, called The Pricks, and although he "wasn't the greatest [guitarist]," says Mike Espindle, "he did a lot with a little."

Rubin recalls having "mixed feelings" about his hometown, where he lived comfortably in a modern house with his parents, Mickey and Linda. "At the time, I wished that I was in Manhattan," he says. "But in retrospect, I think it very much played a role in who I am and gave me a different perspective." His suburban upbringing lacked the grittiness of city life and provided "a filter on what I got to see and hear," he says, "which probably led me to having more commercial taste."

Rick first became interested in hip-hop as a senior at Long Beach High School, a racially mixed school on Long Island, where Rubin was known as a music aficionado. (Next to his senior photo in the yearbook, Ricky, as he was called, had a quote: "I wanna play loud, I wanna be heard, I want all to know, I'm not one of the herd.") Rubin paid attention to the rap music his black classmates were listening to and noticed that their favorite groups changed weekly, depending on who had a new record out. Rubin liked their obsession with the newest and latest.

When he moved to Manhattan to attend NYU—where he originally enrolled as a philosophy major with the intention of going to law school—Rubin used the opportunity to navigate the hip-hop subculture and make important connections with key DJs around the city. He was one of the few white teenagers venturing into uptown hip-hop nightclubs like Harlem World or Disco Fever deep in the Bronx, which was known as a testing ground for new rappers. Negril—on Second Avenue and Tenth Street in Manhattan—had been one of Rubin's favorite nightspots, and the first club to bring hip-hop downtown. It was a small, dark space in the basement of an East Village restaurant, and Rubin went there for hip-hop night every Tuesday.

Within a few months the scene outgrew Negril, and the weekly party was moved to the Roxy, where Rubin would go to see rap groups like the Furious Five. He loved the immediacy of the contact between performers and the audience there. The Roxy had no proper stage back then, so when acts performed, the organizers would just rope off an area on the dance floor. Rubin observed the action intensely, sometimes dancing ("He was a good dancer," points out Dubin), but mostly just listening. "There was a lot of standing around on the side of the floor at the Roxy, and seeing if the beat worked or not," recalls college friend George Drakoulias. "And [Rubin] was bold," Espindle recalls. "He would go right up to the DJ tables and talk to them about their equipment and find out which records were hot." "Watch, and *learn,*" Rubin would say to his friends, only half-jokingly, as he would introduce himself to an important person at a club.

Rubin also loved the hip-hop slang he heard in the clubs and decided to attach a logo called Def Jam Records—which he also designed himself—on the Hose EP. "To emphasize it's about the DJ," he explains, Rubin made both of the first letters—the *D* and the *J*— bigger, chunkier, so that they stood out. *Def jam* was a phrase that hip-hoppers often used to describe the ultimate sound, the greatest "jam," or record. "For info, records, or criticism," a label on the back of the Hose record read, "send all mail to: Def Jam Recordings, 5 University Place, #712." It was important for Rubin to create the aura of a real company behind-the-scenes, even if Def Jam was still just an idea.

When he wasn't experiencing hip-hop live, Rubin was scouring record stores for the latest hip-hop releases. "I would buy them all," he recalled, "and most of them were terrible. None of them accurately portrayed what I heard when I went to Negril. There was nothing that was true to what hip-hop was, the real hip-hop scene." He was right: if you picked up any Sugar Hill record in 1982, you would hear a disco track with an MC rapping over it, with no basic song structure. "So as a fan, even though I would buy a rap record," said Rubin, "I still really couldn't wait to go to Negril next week."

Rick not only got access to all the edgiest clubs in the city by virtue of his endless networking, but going out with him was "always a blast," as Mike Espindle recalled. "He always knew the most interesting people." Those not invited to Rubin's outings felt sorely left out. One disgruntled Weinstein dorm resident even wrote a one-act play for his theater class about what it was like not to be invited out with Rick Rubin—"to sit around in the lobby of the dorm and know that me and Rick and a few other guys were out at this really cool thing, and how bad that made them feel," recalled Espindle.

When Rubin became interested in the new sounds of go-go—a percussion-based, jam-style music that used elements of hip-hop and funk—he called the manager of Trouble Funk, the most well-known go-go band at the time, and offered to book them at the Roxy. "It would have never dawned on me to try and call the guys and arrange this shit," says Dubin. "It seemed like something that people in the business do, but not nineteen-year-old kids."

•   •   •

Rubin liked staying up late and could often be found at Weinstein's reception desk at 3 a.m., hanging out with the night-shift desk clerks. Ric Menello, a graduate film student, was the head clerk, monitoring the reception area from midnight until eight in the morning. He and Rubin became close, spending many nights discussing movies, music, art, women, and ordering food from all-night restaurants like Cozy Soup'n'Burger and DeLion on Broadway. "I'll pay for it if you call in the order and make sure to get everything the way I like it," Rubin would often tell Menello, who would oblige. The two of them would stay up as late as 6 a.m. "philosophizing," as Menello called it.

By his sophomore year, academics had already taken a backseat to Rubin's real interest: music. Adam Dubin, who usually stayed up—and got up—late with him, learned by his second semester not to schedule any classes for the morning. Although he missed most of his classes, Rubin still got passing grades. One of the ways he managed to do this was by paying other students, like Ric Menello, to write papers for him.

The money came from Rubin's parents, who doted on their only child. "They were truly a remarkable family," recalled Mike Espindle of the close-knit Rubin clan. Mickey Rubin would often cook breakfast for his son and even collected tickets at a show Rick promoted in college. A self-made businessman in the wholesale shoe industry, Mickey understood the entrepreneural spirit well. Linda Rubin often drove her son to rock shows, waiting outside the club for him in her Cadillac until the show finished.

Access to money allowed Rubin to make mistakes without major consequences. The best example was a concert that he organized during his freshman year at NYU at the Hotel Diplomat near Thirty-fourth Street, called "Uptown Meets Downtown." Featuring a mix of hip-hop groups like the Treacherous Three and punk bands like Heart Attack and Liquid Liquid, it was one of the first live meldings of rap with punk. The show was even reviewed by the *Village Voice* and was referred to as a great fusion point in music. But Rubin's guest list outnumbered the ticket holders and the concert lost money as a result.

Rubin was not satisfied with just having a band; he also loved to deejay. Because he knew that dorm parties would provide him with a perfect opportunity to spin his records, Rubin convinced his friends to join the party committee. The Weinstein dorm had a long history of infamous parties and pranks. When the Ramones played there in the late 1970s, Dee Dee Ramone's girlfriend got kicked out for starting a vicious catfight; and once, there was a shooting at a student dance. The five-foot statue of the dorm's namesake, Joe Weinstein, was constantly being stolen and met its end one day when it was thrown off a roof, dangerously shattering into pieces. Students were also fond of pranks like "penning," in which coins, placed between the doorjamb and the door, resulted in the door being pushed in so tightly that the person inside couldn't get out. There was even a makeshift bar in the basement, called Joe's Pub (fourteen years later, another Joe's Pub would become a New York City hotspot).

Rubin was "a little rough around the edges" as a DJ, as college friend George Drakoulias recalled, but he wasn't trying to be Grandmaster Flash—he just wanted to mix good records. Since he had all the necessary party equipment right in his dorm room, he spent all the money the dorm party committee gave him on food—usually from White Castle—and alcohol (this was before the National Minimum Drinking Age Act of 1984, which changed the national legal drinking age from eighteen to twenty-one). Rubin was such a fan of White Castle that once he got their truck to deliver burgers right to his dorm.

With the Weinstein party committee at his disposal, Rubin threw parties every month. Sometimes he hired DJs that he had seen at the Roxy, but mostly he preferred to deejay himself. Rubin would only spin hip-hop, go-go, and some rock. "Anything but the conventional radio fare," recalled Dubin. If a student came up and requested a song like "Centerfold" by J. Giles Band, which was a big hit in 1982, Rubin would just stare at them with disdain out of his dark glasses.

He was fond of using his glasses as a tool of intimidation. During dinner with friends, Rubin took off the glasses when he started a meal, and put them back on when he was done, as if to say, "Hurry up." Rick was almost as passionate about food as he was about music. "Come down, we're gonna go eat," he would buzz his friends from the lobby each day. "Yo, but it's Empire Szechuan. It's your favorite bullshit," he would respond when there was any resistance. (The Rubin-coined phrase *favorite bullshit* was often used by him and his friends to describe something great.) It seemed that Rubin had a little more cash than his friends, and he often pitched in extra for meals. "Whatever I have, it always costs seven dollars, ten dollars more," he complained. But he still paid. If he ever wanted to do something, his parents usually gave him the money to make it happen. Still, he "wasn't the guy who was flashing a wad," recalled Espindle.

Rubin's elaborate sound system was a convenience when it came to deejaying Weinstein's parties, but it was a major nuisance for a few of his neighbors. His upstairs neighbor Nancy liked to go to bed at around 11 p.m., which was when Rubin's night usually got started. He and his friends would blast their music through the Cerwin-Vega speaker, waking up Nancy almost every night. When she would call

Rubin and yell at him or bang on the floor, he only turned the music up louder. "This is what I do! This is my art," he yelled back at her. "He really went out of his way to make her life miserable," Espindle recalled.

The conflict continued for months, and culminated one night in a near-fight. Rubin and his friends had just returned from a show amped and in the mood to party, so they sat around his room, laughing and listening to something really loud. Nancy started banging from above. Rubin increased the volume and, for added effect, started vacuuming the ceiling. Everyone was laughing hysterically, until suddenly the door blasted open, and there stood Nancy. "You motherfuckers!" she yelled, and ran into the room, wielding a small knife, according to Rubin. He made a quick getaway.

As a result of the incident, Rubin was threatened with being kicked out of the dorm. He appeared in the "Weinstein Court" to argue his case. "I am a punk rock musician, and volume is integral to the music," he said in his defense. "To have punk rock without volume is to diminish its artistic value and merit. Therefore, volume is a necessary part of me doing my art." He argued that when he listened to his music, he was studying, just as Nancy studied for her law classes. Rubin enlisted Menello to testify that he had heard few, if any, noise complaints about Rubin during his front-desk shift. "Someone has to have extrasensitive hearing like Superman to think it was too loud!" Menello proclaimed. Besides, there were noisemakers far worse than Rubin in the dorm, like one guy who liked to annoy his neighbor by hooking up his electric typewriter to stereo amps and typing so furiously that the keyboard produced gunshotlike sounds.

Rubin's defense worked. He was allowed to stay in the dorm— under some strict regulations. "I was the first person brought up on charges in the fifteen or twenty years that they had a court," Rubin remembered proudly. His upstairs neighbor Nancy moved soon after.

As long as he wasn't being punished, Rubin often encouraged and took part in the troublemaking. He could convince almost anyone to do almost anything for him. "You *gotta* do it," Rubin would insist.

"You *know* you want to." Back when he played with his high school band, The Pricks, Rubin frequently encouraged and got a real kick out of watching the lead singer jump into the crowd during a song, walk up to a person, stare at him intensely, and then just slap him for no good reason. During a summer tour with Hose in 1982, Rubin instructed one of the group members to set the sprinklers off in the club with a lighter right in the middle of their set. Sure enough, the sprinklers went off, but Rubin escaped getting blamed for the incident. "Which is also kind of Rick's personality," said George Drakoulias. "He was just fearless."

Rubin was not afraid to defy authority. A few months into his sophomore year, he decided that he wanted to replace his bed with a futon. The problem after he bought it was that he had both a bed and a futon in his room. "No problem for Rick," says Dubin. "He just threw [the bed] out into the hall." The dorm wrote them complaint letters about the bed's fire hazard in the hall, and one day the room-mates came home to find that maintenance put the bed back in their room. Rubin threw it back out in the hall, then appealed to the dorm to let them put the bed in storage. "He just wanted things his way," says Dubin. "His personal comfort was important to him. It wouldn't have occurred to me at that time to challenge the dorm as he did."

•   •   •

When not out at hip-hop clubs or throwing parties at Weinstein, Rubin and his friends went to see punk and rock shows at Manhattan clubs like Peppermint Lounge, Folk City, and the Continental Divide. On November 20, 1982, they attended a two-day benefit for a local punk label called RATcage at the legendary CBGB's venue. The first night had three local groups on the bill: the Beastie Boys, Reagan Youth, and The Young and the Useless. RATcage had recently put out *Polly Wog Stew,* the first EP by the Beastie Boys, which included Adam Yauch and Mike Diamond, as well as guitarist John Berry and future Luscious Jackson drummer Kate Schellenbach. None of them were older than sixteen. Their music was loud, energetic, and bold. The boys liked to jump around so wildly onstage that during the CBGB benefit show, Yauch—who was on bass—fell backward off the stage, landing on his back with the bass on top of him. Within seconds, however, he was back onstage, picking up the next song. He shrugged off his pain, screaming, "Fuck it! Fuck it!"

At that time, the "art-core" group The Young and the Useless—who had recently returned from a gig opening for Sex Pistol John Lydon's band PiL in Boston—was even more popular, and edgier, than the Beastie Boys. A downtown kid named Dave Skilken, who published a local fanzine, had founded the group and had recruited his best high school buddy, Adam Horovitz, to play guitar. "They had the potential to be larger than the Beastie Boys," recalled Dave Parsons, who put out The Young and the Useless's only known recording on the RATcage Records label, a 1982 EP called *Real Men Don't Floss.* "I can recall people calling from California wanting to book The Young and the Useless. They would have been the biggest punk band from New York. Everybody wanted to see them."

Among them was Rick Rubin and it wasn't long before he met Yauch, Horovitz, and Diamond, striking up a casual friendship.

By Rubin's junior year, Hose had changed lead singers—from Rick Rosen to Mike Epsindle—after "a sing-off" at CBGB's, and at least once a month the band managed to secure a gig. Sometimes they opened for hard-core bands like the Meat Puppets, at clubs like Folk City in Manhattan, City Gardens in Trenton, New Jersey, and Maxwell's in Hoboken. Espindle and Bell wrote a few songs with Rubin, and a few he wrote completely by himself, including "Happy," a love song.

A few weeks before summer vacation started—during which Rubin had planned a tour for Hose in the San Francisco region—Rubin brought home a hip-hop record called "It's Like That," backed with "Sucker MCs" by a new group, Run-DMC. From the moment he played it for Dubin, "Sucker MCs" was all he could talk about. He was excited about its beat-heavy and spare sound. "This is the real shit," he proclaimed, and then: "*I* could do this better."

CHAPTER 2

The Visionary

Robert Ford, a *Billboard* magazine staff writer, often traveled home to southeast Queens by subway, taking either the E or the F train. The year was 1978, and New York's subway cars were moving canvases, splashed with the vibrant, intricate art of graffiti writers. This was the best place for young kids who were part of the fledgling hip-hop scene to send a message, promote an event, or just express themselves. On those long, early-morning rides after a late night at the office or at a show, Ford started to notice a slew of impossible-to-peel-off stickers that advertised parties in Queens. They all bore the same logo: "Rush Productions."

Ford made a mental note to research who was behind the stickers, having been following the hip-hop subculture for *Billboard*. Luckily, he didn't have to search long, because one day while on the Q2 bus heading down Hollis Avenue, Ford saw a young boy putting up those same stickers on the bus. "Are you the guy who does Rush Productions?" he asked the boy. "No, that's my brother Russell," replied the boy, Joey Simmons. Ford asked him to give Simmons his card.

The next day, a hyper twenty-one-year-old Russell Simmons called Ford at the office. "He was a nervous wreck," recalled Ford. "Russell talked a mile a minute." They met in person at Ford's office the following day. It wasn't Simmons's appearance that got the attention of Ford and his office-mates—Simmons's wardrobe was typical of uptown hip-hoppers, consisting of a Kangol cap, knit sweater, wool pants, and sneakers—but his almost manic energy. "He was one of those guys who were just nonstop," says Ford. "He knew everything there was to know about rap music and understood what work went in to make it happen. That level of passion is incredible and you have to respect that."

"Welcome to Rush Town": 26-year-old Russell Simmons at his first Rush Management office, back when he dressed "like a substitute teacher," according to Rick Rubin.

Ford decided to include Simmons in a story he was writing on new black club owners and promoters. Two months later, Simmons helped Ford secure key interviews for a rap-related article he was writing: one was with Eddie Cheeba, who was on the bill of a party Simmons was promoting at Brooklyn's Restoration Plaza, and the other was with Kurtis Blow. Blow was the only rapper that Simmons could promote, because he was the only Harlem rapper who didn't mind working with Simmons, back when people from Harlem thought that their Queens counterparts were "soft." "So Russell obviously was a great advocate for Kurtis Blow for totally selfish reasons," points out Ford.

Simmons wanted to make a record with Kurtis Blow and to have Ford help him, because he didn't have any connections at record labels. But Ford did. Russell had been fixated on making a hip-hop record ever since he'd first heard The Fatback Band's "King Tut" at the Loft nightclub in the spring of 1979. *We're all gonna get paid now,* he was convinced. But Ford wasn't interested at first. He had no reason to make a record. Simmons persisted. "This was to be my first experience with Russell's unique gift for obsessive nagging when he really believes in something," recalled Ford, who finally agreed to collaborate. "I chose Kurtis Blow not for Kurtis Blow, but for Russell—he was my ambassador to rap," says Ford. "He was the only guy who knew everybody in rap."

Ford was thinking about what kind of song he would write, where he would record it, and how he would pay for it, when a *Billboard* ad salesman named Mickey Addy suggested doing a Christmas song. Ford shared the idea with another *Billboard* colleague and aspiring songwriter named J. B. Moore, and the two of them started brainstorming. "J.B. called my house late one night and read me the most perfect set of Christmas lyrics I could have imagined, that he called, simply enough, 'Christmas Rappin',' " Ford recalled. Moore said he was ready to invest his own money and experience in the studio into making a hip-hop record.

To come up with a melody for "Christmas Rappin', " Ford enlisted the help of R&B bass player Larry Smith, an old high-school friend. One late night, Smith, Simmons, Ford, and a keyboardist all showed up at Moore's tiny West Side apartment to begin work on the song. Russell was especially interested in the process of recording the song; he always wanted to be part of the action, learning, observing. "Go home now, Russell," Ford would say after a long night at Greene Street Recording in SoHo, where they recorded "Christmas Rappin' " in October of 1979.

After the single was finally mixed, Simmons launched Rush Management, with Kurtis Blow as his first artist. Now all that was left was to get the single on a record label and into stores. It would seem that Simmons's chances of finding a label were better than ever because, at the time, the Sugar Hill Gang's "Rapper's Delight" was selling well and the industry was responding to hip-hop. But when Ford and Moore tried shopping the record to other black industry executives, they were flat-out rejected "to the point of belligerence" by some, Ford recalled. Eventually, the partners signed a 12-inch deal with an album option with Polygram. "Christmas Rappin'," which came out during the first week of December of 1979, became the first hip-hop record to be released by a major label.

On the day that the record hit stores, Simmons started "running the track"—a term he used to describe his endless pursuit of every opportunity to promote his artists, and himself. "Robert, I'm at the [Paradise] Garage and the dance floor is full with faggots dancing to your record!" Simmons would scream into the phone at three in the morning. He would figure out ways to give influential DJs an incentive to play his records. One of the most important disco DJs at the time was Larry Levan, who was also openly gay. Once Levan asked Simmons whether Kurtis Blow was gay. "I don't know," Simmons replied coyly, "you'd have to ask him." Levan played the record, and Kurtis Blow was on his way to becoming an in-demand performer.

Simmons also took Kurtis to a boutique booking agency called Norby Walters that specialized in booking dance and funk acts like Kool & the Gang and Rick James. Norby booked Blow's very first date—in a New Haven, Connecticut, club for $350, and continued getting him dates at roller rinks and on tours like the Commodores. Working behind the reception desk at the agency was a young Bronx woman named Cara Lewis, who quickly bonded with the ever-present Simmons. The two of them started going out constantly—with Lewis always behind the wheel, since Simmons didn't drive—to Uptown clubs such as the Copa, Bond's, Disco Fever, and Paradise Garage. "Russell never shut up," Lewis recalls. "All he talked about was Kurtis Blow and [later] Run-DMC. Even before Run came out, I knew every lyric." But as much as Simmons liked to have fun, he was always business-minded and when it came to Rush Management and his artists, "there was definitely a plan," says Lewis. "It wasn't by accident."

The next step in his plan was to turn Kurtis Blow into a recording artist and get him an album deal.

The 12-inch agreement that Ford, Moore, and Simmons made with Polygram called for two singles from Blow, so they recorded another song called "The Breaks." It was an instant B-boy classic, with a catchy, crossover appeal. On the heels of its release in May of 1980, Moore and Ford started a record label called Prep Street Records; they moved into an office at 1133 Broadway, where they let Simmons rent a corner space.

A recent college graduate named Heidi Smith was hired as the assistant at Prep Street while Simmons was on the road with Kurtis Blow, essentially promoting "The Breaks" out of the back of a car. Blow was now one of the most popular rappers, so much so that the borough of Queens declared August 2, 1980, "Kurtis Blow Day." Smith realized that Russell must have been a person of importance after the number of calls he was receiving. One day, Simmons showed up at the office and "just kept talking—about records and music, and music and records," recalled Smith. "He was convinced that what he was saying was absolutely true, and he made people believe it." Part of Smith's job became keeping Simmons away from Prep Street's phones as much as possible so he couldn't run up their phone bills.

When Moore and Ford wouldn't make the more streetwise records he wanted with Kurtis Blow, Simmons started making them himself with his brother's group, Run-DMC. The idea for the group came to Simmons after he'd introduced Blow to his younger brother Joey, then thirteen years old. Nicknamed Run for "running at the mouth," Joey began deejaying for Kurtis Blow as "DJ Run Love, the son of Kurtis Blow" at area rap shows in the early eighties. He shared the tapes of his concert appearances with childhood friend Darryl McDaniels, whom Run coerced into performing onstage with him. Together with another boyhood friend from Hollis, Jason Mizell, the trio formed a rap group, and after going through a list of potential names, they reluctantly settled on Run-DMC, which was Russell's idea. At the time, they thought it couldn't have been worse. "You're killing us!" yelled Run. Over the next year, Russell used all of his experience with managing Kurtis Blow and his party promotion to mold Run-DMC into a marketable group.

In 1982, Prep Street released "Action" by the Rush-managed group Orange Krush, but folded the following year. That was going to leave Smith without a job, and Simmons without an office space. "Go to the realty office next door and see if you can get us an office," he told her. The two neighboring buildings—1133 Broadway and 1123 Broadway—were owned by the same management company. "If you just find us a small office somewhere in the building, I'll pay you when I can," he said. She did—a "tiny" space on the eleventh floor of 1133 Broadway—and was hired as his secretary. "But she was more like his partner," recalled former Def Jam artist Tashan. "Heidi was the one to take care of the details." Rush would remain there for the next two years. Along with Run-DMC, Rush Management handled the careers of more than ten artists, including Kurtis Blow and Jimmy Spicer.

The office was no bigger than a walk-in closet. To get to Simmons's desk, visitors had to practically climb over his secretary's desk. Or they could hang out on one of the thrift-store futons, "toy couches," as Simmons liked to call them. Inspired by a paint color she saw in a Bank of New York, Smith painted the walls burgundy for a more "professional" look. The only piece of office equipment was an old Smith Electric typewriter that would periodically break down.

To promote his artists, Simmons constantly threw parties. Every Wednesday night they hosted an event at Danceteria, but before being sent there, Rush artists had to pass the Disco Fever test. "Because if you got booed in the Fever, you wasn't gonna make it nowhere," recalled former Rush tour manager Tony Rome. "Once you made it in the Fever, then you start at Danceteria, 'cause the Danceteria was now a whole 'nother audience. This let us know if you had crossover appeal."

Hand-designing the numerous flyers and posters for Rush events was a former graffiti artist named Cey Adams, who wrote his tag "Cey" on subway trains and even appeared in the famed 1982 documentary *Style Wars* about the graffiti art subculture in New York City. He met Simmons through a mutual photographer friend who had worked with Run-DMC. Working virtually for no pay, Adams created all the artwork for Rush, including an office mural that said

"Welcome to Rush Town Management." Most of the time, Adams painted backdrops for shows, and the office would be permeated with spray-paint fumes. He would go down to Pearl Paint and buy a twenty-foot canvas, lay it out directly on the sidewalk, and paint it on the floor, "twister-style," he recalls. "And when you held it up, you just had to pray to God that it came out the way you wanted it to."

Adams thought Simmons was a laid-back boss, someone who "let you do your own thing." Sometimes he might yell, but it was never "out of control, seeing-red anger," recalled Heidi Smith. Simmons had a charm and sense of humor that made it impossible not to like him. "Russell always had a sense of adventure," confirms his older brother, Danny Simmons. Like Rick Rubin, Russell had a suburban upbringing, growing up in Jamaica, Queens, which was a mere thirty-minute drive from Rubin's hometown, Lido Beach, Long Island. And like Rubin, Simmons always had the unconditional moral and financial support of his family, which would ultimately contribute to his success as a businessman.

•   •   •

Although geographically part of New York City, Jamaica felt almost like the country, and the Simmons kids enjoyed a happy, almost idyllic childhood. With neighbors that had moved to Queens directly from the South, it was not uncommon to see chickens in backyards. The kids in Russell's neighborhood were fond of picking up some of the snakes they would find in the woods that surrounded the houses on Simmons's block, and bringing them back home to keep in aquariums. Sometimes, though, a snake would be so large that no one wanted to touch it—except Russell, who was bold enough to actually pick it up.

The Simmons family of four—the youngest, Joey, was not yet born—lived in a two-bedroom, two-story house, where Danny and Russell shared a room and a bunk bed. There was never a shortage of toys. "Our parents gave us a lot of stuff," Danny recalled. Evelyn and Daniel Senior had "good city jobs," and both were college-educated, having met at Howard University, so the family had a little more money than their neighbors. The boys' allowances were typically bigger than their friends', but they didn't mind sharing their wealth. "We were very generous," said Danny. Because both parents worked, the Simmons family had a housekeeper/babysitter who would come by several days a week.

Russell always had to be part of the action, often listening in on conversations that Danny would have with his friends. "It's him again!" they would exclaim upon discovering Russell crouching behind a couch, eavesdropping. On Saturday mornings, the brothers liked to watch Elvis Presley movies, like *Viva Las Vegas;* there seemed to be a new one on almost every Saturday on Channel 9. "Russell really, *really* loved Elvis Presley," recalled Danny. "He used to imitate him dancing and singing."

When Russell was seven, the family moved to Hollis, a quiet, middle-class community in the southeast section of Queens. But within a few short years, heroin flooded the streets of most black New York neighborhoods, including Hollis. "There was heroin all up and down Hollis Avenue," Danny remembered. "Every other kid was either on heroin or selling heroin, or both." The drug's explosion affected its quality and price. A bag of heroin sold for $2 in Harlem, and for $3 in Queens. Two kids would put in $1.50 for a bag and "get blasted," Danny said. Almost overnight, it seemed, "the vibe of Hollis became very dangerous." An ice cream parlor on Hollis Avenue, famous for its egg creams and sundaes, now became the drug dealers' turf.

But Russell, at least until he reached high school, was disinterested in drugs, focusing on sports like baseball with his junior high school team. Once he started at August Martin High in Jamaica (other famous alumni include disc jockey Ed Lover and Def Jam artist Kelly Price), sports took a backseat to the main attraction: getting "fly" for "little money," as Russell put it. He and his friends would "act older than we were," and try to be little "playboys," he recalls. "The right clothes, the right everything," he said. At night, the youngsters would go to the biggest club in Queens, Casablancas, or over to Nell Gwyn's in Times Square. "I loved music and used to go to parties all the time," said Russell.

The one person that Russell always looked up to was his father. Mr. Simmons had a "huge presence" in the neighborhood because he used to run a night center at a local high school with various activities (most New York City schools had night centers in the community). Russell "vibed off" his father's being well known and well liked by everyone, "even by criminals," said Danny. "They all respected my pops." "My father was slick," Russell recalled. "He used to be a good dresser, have his hat broke down to the side." Although Mr. Simmons supported education, he did not support elitism and used to refer to "bourgeois" black males as "fake, plastic-ass niggas," as Russell recalled, "which had a lot to do with being educated and still remaining the same person. He came from Baltimore and real, extreme poverty. Yet, after coming from the army, he was able to get educated, and his education didn't separate him from his history and his whole being." As an adult, Russell would apply his father's philosophy of being true to oneself to almost all of his endeavors.

Russell's rebellious older brother, Danny, meanwhile, developed a $50-a-day heroin habit and had started mainlining the drug, stealing from his mother's pocketbook to pay for his addiction. Eventually, his parents found out and sent him to live with his grandmother in St. Albans, Queens.

It wouldn't be long before Russell got sucked into Hollis's dangerous world as well. When his lung collapsed during a baseball game, Russell stopped playing sports altogether and got "caught up" with a local gang called the Seven Immortals. New York City in the late 1960s and early '70s was consumed by gangs. Most young people, if they weren't in a gang, knew someone who was a member.

One positive thing did come out of his gangbanging: Russell's serious, ten-year relationship with Pauline Minz—nicknamed Puppet—who was in the girls' division of the Seven Immortals. "She was very, very pretty, and she really had Russell's back," recalled Danny.

In fact, before he became famous, Russell was always a one-woman man, according to Danny. Only years later would Russell become involved with many women at the same time. "There was a period of time that he was a womanizer, because it was available. But it wasn't in his nature to chase a lot of women," said Danny.

Russell was a natural communicator. "He talked really well," Danny recalled. "And he was able to convince people of what he believed. He saw one thing, and he followed it, and he pushed. He was very dedicated and determined." Russell didn't become genuinely interested in music until high school, but once he did, "there was nothing else that he wanted to talk about," recalls Danny. "Anybody who's that driven is going to be successful."

Russell attended the Harlem branch of City College in 1974, commuting from his parents' house in Queens. Like Danny, he majored in sociology but paid little attention to his studies. Instead, he spent most afternoons in the school's big and bustling student lounge, where students would sit around smoking pot and playing cards. "There was always a section of the lounge for Russell and his friends and party people," Danny recalled.

Simmons was given the nickname Rush in college and soon started sporting a large medallion around his neck with that name. He fell in with a group of aspiring party promoters during his freshman year, including Curtis Walker, soon to be known as DJ and rapper Kurtis Blow. They called themselves The Force and gave parties in Harlem at clubs like Small's Paradise and Charles Gallery. However, "hip-hop did not make Russell start promoting parties," noted Danny. "Russell started promoting because of the group of friends he was hanging out with, and before hip-hop came on the scene. Russell was promoting different kinds of records: disco records, party records. Then hip-hop hit." "He's wrong," Simmons countered. "It *was* hip-hop, one hundred percent. Seeing [Harlem rapper] Eddie Cheeba."

When the competition in Harlem forced Simmons to expand into other boroughs, he started promoting parties on Queens' Hillside

Avenue, which had a few clubs. He had made a decent amount of money from selling weed and invested it in his first big party—at the Renaissance Ballroom in Queens, paying for some three hundred flyers and the rental of the club, which included a $700 bar guarantee. "That was a big number," Simmons pointed out. Kurtis Blow was the DJ that night, and the crowd consisted mostly of City College students. But the turning point in Russell's career as a promoter came in 1977, when he threw a big party at Times Square's Hotel Diplomat. More than two thousand eager B-boys and B-girls showed up to watch Grandmaster Flash spin and Kurtis Blow rap. "I had a good little run. I was doing okay in the party scene and just staying above water," Simmons recalled. "It was better than selling weed, it was safer, I felt more comfortable."

Unfortunately, Simmons got "twisted up and lost a little bit of money," as he recalled. That's when his mother loaned him money and continued supporting him for a while. When Russell's parents stopped, Danny would lend Russell money—"not because I really believed that much in him," he says, "but because he's my little brother." By then, Danny had already served a two-year prison bid for a drug charge, transferred to NYU, and kicked his heroin habit. Even at that young age, Russell was so business-minded that he once refused to give Danny back his $1,000 he had lent him because Russell wanted to reinvest it. He couldn't get the money back from the owners of a club on Hollis Avenue—"they were gonna swindle him out of his money," as Danny recalls, who came over to his parents' house to wait for Russell to come back with the money he had lent him. Instead, Russell's girlfriend's little sister showed up and told Danny that Russell was having a hard time getting his cash back.

"So I went up there and essentially got the money back for Russell," Danny recalled. He carried the money back to his parents' house in a bag and Russell showed up fifteen minutes later. But when Danny asked for his share, Russell said no. "What do you mean no?" Danny asked, furious. "I gotta reinvest this!" said Russell. So Danny asked for half. "No! You don't need it!" said Russell. "Give me two hundred dollars!" Danny pleaded, but got the same reply. "So I punched him in the face," Danny recalled. The brothers got into a huge fight: Russell kicked Danny with his boot and split his ear open, requiring him to get three stitches.

Amazingly, Danny continued lending his little brother more money after that incident, because he loved him that much. Their parents, however, finally had to cut him off, not only because he was close to dropping out of school, but because he kept losing the money that was given to him. "He went to my mother, he went to my father, he went to my grandmother—they all had given him thousands of dollars to promote these parties, and finally they just said, 'No. Go to school and get a degree.' " But Simmons had already lost interest in school.

His parents saw his party promotion as a hobby, but Simmons saw it as something that could be his career. His father "was very pissed off that he never finished college," Danny recalled. "He didn't understand it."

•   •   •

In the spring of 1983, Run-DMC got signed to a 12-inch deal with Profile Records, an independent hip-hop label based in New York, and Simmons, together with Larry Smith, produced "It's Like That" and "Sucker MCs." Simmons would spend the summer of 1983 touring with his group to support the record, while Rush Management continued to grow.

CHAPTER 3

Coming Together

S teve Ralbovsky was at his Manhattan apartment in August of 1983 when he got a phone call from Tim Devine at Warner Bros. Records in Los Angeles. Ralbovsky, a twenty-five-year-old artist manager with his own small company that oversaw the careers of clients like Tom Verlaine of the band Television, was in the middle of filling out applications to law schools, having decided to abandon his hand-to-mouth lifestyle in artist management.

Devine was calling to tell Steve about an opening at EMI Records for an entry-level artist and repertoire (A&R) person in their New York office. "Deep down inside I really didn't want to go to law school," recalled Ralbovsky. He interviewed with Gary Gersh, EMI's head of A&R, and by September was the label's new A&R rep. The decision to put off law school would affect not just his own career but, ultimately, the fate of Def Jam Records. Serendipitously, Ralbovsky would cross paths with Rick Rubin and Russell Simmons within a year and become one of the main architects of Def Jam's eventual deal with Columbia Records.

Rubin was now a junior at NYU, where his interest in hip-hop continued to grow. In October of 1983, he picked the moniker DJ Double R and started deejaying for the Beastie Boys, who had recently come back from a summer hiatus with a new member—Adam

Horovitz—and a new sound. Horovitz disbanded The Young and the Useless when he joined the Beastie Boys, and that's when the group stopped playing rock and their instruments. In place of the instruments entered Rubin with his turntables, helping transform the Beasties from a hard-core band into a trio of white rappers—or a quartet, since Rubin was essentially the fourth Beastie Boy. They even gave themselves hip-hop nicknames: Yauch became MCA, Michael Diamond was now Mike D., and Horovitz was Ad-Rock.

Rubin had also met a key person at club Negril who would help him realize his goal of producing a rap record: DJ Jazzy Jay. "He just had the best taste," Rubin recalled of Jazzy, who was his favorite DJ. "He lived the hip-hop life before there was really a hip-hop life. He was the first guy to have huge woofers in his car. There was no such thing as having a sound system in your car."

In Jazzy Jay, Rubin saw an ideal collaborator. Not only was Jazzy talented, but he had the right connections. As a member of the famous Soulsonic Force, Afrika Bambaataa's group, he had already gained worldwide acclaim. Rubin suggested to Jazzy that they try to re-create the energy of the club in a recording studio, bringing the drum machine front and center along with the DJ. While most hip-hop records at that time used live bands and real drums for beats, Rubin's goal was to incorporate the drum machine more. After listening to the collection of beats that Rubin had programmed on his drum machine, Jazzy said he would help him. Now all Rubin needed was an MC.

His favorite group was the Treacherous Three, which consisted of Kool Moe Dee, Special K, and DJ Easy Lee and had been recording since 1980. Originally signed to Enjoy Records, they became known for their much faster style of rhyming. When they joined Sugar Hill in 1981, they became the first hip-hop group to use guitars in a song, on "Body Rock." Guitars on rap records excited Rubin, but he also wanted to use scratching. He reached out to Kool Moe Dee and invited him to come to the dorm for a meeting. Sensing Rubin's enthusiasm, Kool Moe Dee obliged, despite Rubin's inexperience.

"What I saw at Negril was different than what your records sound like," he said to Kool Moe Dee. "Let's make records together that are more like what you're really like." He explained to Moe Dee his idea of making the DJ and the drum machine the centerpieces of a track. Although Kool Moe Dee liked the idea, he had a contract with Sugar Hill Records, who used their own in-house producers. So he directed Rubin to his groupmate Special K, "because he's got a brother who's really good," said Kool Moe Dee. When Rubin called, Special K was responsive. "We'll give it to T. La Rock, my brother," he said. Rubin recommended that Jazzy Jay deejay on the track.

On a weekend in December of 1983, Rubin, T. La Rock, Adam Horovitz, and his best friend Dave Skilken, all assembled at Jazzy's house in Queens. Rubin brought his 808 drum machine, where he already had the beat stored. Recording commenced once a friend of Jazzy's came over with a Southern malt-liquor beverage called the Brass Monkey, and everyone drank. (Horovitz liked it so much, he would eventually dedicate an entire song to it, "Brass Monkey," on the Beastie Boys' debut album.) The only person who never indulged in drugs or alcohol was Rubin.

"It's Yours" was recorded that day, using the $5,000 that Rubin's parents donated to mix and master the track. At first, he considered releasing the record on Ed Bahlman's 99 Records, as he had done with Hose. But he found out that a new break-dancing and graffiti film called *Beat Street* was about to start production under the auspices of Harry Belafonte, and they would be looking for music.

"You should go up there and play them 'It's Yours,' " said Special K one day to Rubin after returning from Shakedown Sound, a studio on West Thirty-seventh Street. Shakedown was owned by Arthur Baker, the man behind Afrika Bambaataa's signature electro-hip-hop sound, and one of the best mixers of his time. "He was a larger-than-life character," Steve Ralbovsky recalled of Baker. "He was a guy with a lot of charisma, a lot of smarts, a lot of coolness. Somebody that a lot of people looked up to."

Baker was also *Beat Street*'s music supervisor. Rubin had never known anyone who actually dealt with major labels and worked at a real studio, but he understood the importance of connections. Record in hand, he went up to Shakedown to play Baker "It's Yours." Baker took a listen and was impressed. "It was a really important record," he recalled, "because it was one of the first rap records that actually had the feel of a live rap performance."

Indeed, "It's Yours" consisted of a beat, the sound of a real audience, clever rhymes, and Jazzy Jay's scratching. The record, as Rubin pointed out, was "kind of the first one to use the raw sound of a drum machine." Baker said he would buy "It's Yours" for about $3,000 and release it on his own independent label, Party Time, the rap subsidiary of his dance label Streetwise, which was responsible for such records as "The Funky Soul Macosa" by the Awesome Foursome. It was small change, but enough for Rubin to continue making records, like the Beastie Boys' "Rock Hard," which he produced next—right out of his dorm room.

"Everything went on in that little room," recalled George Drakoulias, who helped Rubin with various tasks like answering the phone, taking orders, doing shipping, and getting parts, as well as calling radio stations like WBLS, Kiss FM in Philadelphia. When the Beasties had "Rock Hard" out, Drakoulias called a lot of college stations and whatever alternative-rock stations were around at the time. There was also WKTU, which "flirted with hip-hop for a minute," Drakoulias recalled.

It may not have mattered to Rubin how much he got paid for "It's Yours," but he was extremely picky about the art direction of the sleeve—at a time when few hip-hop records came with one. Baker was struck by how well Rubin "had it together" for his age and even saw him as a bit of a competitor. He was also intrigued by Rubin's categorical aversion to R&B music. "He just wasn't into it at all," said Baker. "He was a true heavy metal fan who was into rap, which I thought was interesting."

When "It's Yours" was finally released in the winter of 1984, it bore Rubin's NYU address—not Party Time's—on the sleeve.

Rubin also convinced Baker to let him put the Def Jam logo prominently on the back, which made the 12-inch look like a Def Jam release. As Rubin would soon find out, making his address public would provoke dozens of wannabe rappers from all over the country to send in their demo tapes.

Despite its cutting-edge sound, "It's Yours" didn't catch on immediately. "It's a street record, and back then, how could you market it?" Baker pointed out. Rubin, however, did recall a small but aggressive street team at Party Time that got his record into clubs. Whatever the case, "It's Yours" clearly needed help, and Rubin spoke about his dilemma to friend and Tuff City Records founder Aaron Fuchs, who told Rubin that "no one promotes rap records better" than rap manager Russell Simmons. The only problem was that he only promoted his own artists. But Rubin was intrigued. *Okay, I gotta meet this guy Russell Simmons,* he thought immediately, and started paying attention to Simmons's numerous album credits. Simmons was a coproducer of such early B-boy classics as Davy DMX's "One for the Treble," Jimmy Spicer's "The Bubble Bunch," and Orange Krush's "Action." "There weren't a lot of great rap records in those days, but any ones that were good, his name was on," Rubin recalled.

It was true: Russell Simmons had a firm hold on the fledgling hip-hop industry. He was on a first-name basis with key urban radio jocks and program directors and was about to expand his company into the lucrative world of music tours with Fresh Fest—the first all-hip-hop tour. He collaborated on the project with another promoter named Ricky Walker, who pitched Rush Management the unique idea of having hip-hop acts perform in a model of a three-ring circus, thus eliminating any downtime between sets. The tour hit the road in June of 1984 and featured Whodini, Run-DMC, and Kurtis Blow. Helping publicize the tour for Rush was a thirty-two-year-old white guy named Bill Adler, who had recently moved to New York City from Detroit and was hired by Russell as the in-house PR guy for Rush.

During their stop in L.A., Run-DMC were booked for a special show that paired them with punk bands Fear, Social Distortion, Circle Jerks, and Fishbone. The venue was the Mix Club, a new after-hours club housed in the former Stardust Ballroom—famous for some of L.A.'s most important punk shows—and managed by a young University of Miami graduate named Lyor Cohen. After being bought by a "rich Korean," as Cohen recalled, the venue stood untouched for a year until Cohen stepped in and decided to run it as a "quasi-illegal, after-hours spot." The experience that moved him to take a risk and run the club was a hip-hop show he saw one night in South Central, L.A., at the Sports Arena. "I used to drive around and there used to be these huge neon posters on the lamppost called Uncle Jamm's Army," he recalled. "I ended up going. They put in about 18,000 people—no talent whatsoever, just turntables. I was really caught up, blown away by the vibe in the room and the beat."

Cohen sensed an opportunity. The Arena was a government facility that stayed open until 11 p.m., so he convinced the DJs that performed at the Uncle Jamm's Army shows, like the Egyptian Lover and "Bobcat" Erving—and eventually the rappers, who started sprouting along with the influx of hip-hop records around 1982—to come over to the Mix Club for after-hours performances. Trying to get his way backstage at Uncle Jamm's Army to talk to the acts into coming to his club "and get paid more money" was an early example of Cohen's lifelong tenacity. He was not afraid of rubbing people the wrong way. In fact, Roger Clayton, the founder of Uncle Jamm's Army, was "really pissed off at me," as Cohen recalled. "He was looking for this white kid who started the Mix Club and was bringing talent." Clayton also ran a record shop called The DJ Booth, and Cohen would often call up there to see what groups were coming into town, so he could book them. "He figured the Mix Club was the best thing since sliced bread, but he didn't have an 'in' to get acts," recalled Roger Clayton's cousin, Dwayne Simon, who deejayed at Uncle Jamm's Army and would eventually be part of the production team L.A. Posse, responsible for LL Cool J's biggest hit, "I Need Love."

"He ran a really good club," recalled Nikki D., who performed at the Mix Club several times as an aspiring rapper and would eventually sign with Def Jam. "It was packed every week, just a hot spot to go to, and when he gave shows, it was a big deal." After a massively successful turnout for the Run-DMC performance, Cohen was confident he could pull it off again. "I actually thought I was some hot shit," he recalled, "because I made so much money." But when he booked Whodini, he couldn't come up with an act to pair them up with, and the turnout was dismal. "I sat outside, wondering where all the people were," he recalled. "It was a devastating night, a really profound feeling for me—something I try to avoid. It's like an incredible anxiety pain south of my heart and north of my stomach." Cohen failed to give the audience a big show, and he vowed to never repeat it again.

After fifteen weeks and eighty dates, Fresh Fest became one of the top-grossing tours of the summer. It was the first time that Simmons showed the music industry that he could make money, and that, most of all, he was a businessman. By the time he had returned from the tour, *Beat Street* had been on the big screen for a month, playing in a few thousand movie houses across the country. (The film's director, Stan Lathan, would fifteen years later become Russell's partner in Simmons/Lathan Productions.) *Beat Street* was a quasi-musical set in the South Bronx and was widely acclaimed as the most authentic film representation of hip-hop to date.

Maybe it was Jazzy Jay's appearance in the film, combined with the positive vibes of summer, but suddenly Rubin's "It's Yours" exploded in the streets of New York City. "I remember hearing it on car radios on the weekends," recalled Rubin's college friend George Drakoulias.

By then, Steve Ralbovsky had already been working at EMI Records for about ten months. Although he hadn't met Rubin yet, Ralbovsky knew his friend Arthur Baker, and also had a connection to Russell Simmons: their business lawyer, Paul Schindler of Grubman, Indursky, Schindler, P.C., a ten-year-old firm started by Alan

Grubman, the music industry's most powerful attorney. One day, while Ralbovsky was waiting for a meeting at Schindler's office, he noticed a young black man sitting next to him, also waiting for a meeting. A few minutes later, Schindler introduced him as Russell Simmons, the manager of Run-DMC and president of Rush Management. "He was kind of nervously holding his hat in his hands and being a little bit shy," recalls Ralbovsky. "There's a very shy and endearing side of Russell that has maintained a constancy throughout time. He's a forceful man about his beliefs, but he's just a sweet, sweet man."

Schindler was hoping that Ralbovsky would help Simmons get a production deal at EMI, which would allow Simmons to sign Run-DMC to the label. "Paul thought that this would be something that would appeal to me," recalled Ralbovsky, "which it did." He immediately began working on a presentation for his bosses at EMI. The timing was ideal, because Profile Records, which was releasing Run-DMC's 12-inches, had not yet finalized an album deal with the group.

In a matter of time Simmons would also be crossing paths with Rubin—thanks to a hip-hop sketch show called *Graffiti Rock,* which had premiered on Channel 11 in New York and in eighty-eight other markets across the country in the summer of 1984. Creator Michael Holman hosted a party at a small club on West Twenty-eighth Street in late August to celebrate the show's premiere. Kool Moe Dee and Special K were two of the hosts on *Graffiti Rock;* Rubin knew them both, so he was at the party, too. Run-DMC performed in the first episode of the show, so Simmons was also present. Jazzy Jay, who knew them both, finally made an introduction. "He looked at me with kind of shock and disbelief," recalled Rubin of Simmons's reaction upon learning that Rubin produced "It's Yours." "I can't believe you made that record and you're white! 'Cause that's the blackest hip-hop record that's ever been!" exclaimed Simmons.

The two of them connected instantly, and before long Rubin went up to the Rush Productions office on Broadway and Twenty-sixth Street. Simmons also visited Rick at Weinstein, in his "tiny-ass dorm room that was nasty," he recalled. "Everything was thrown on top of everything else." Rubin found Simmons's office equally disorganized and chaotic. "There was so much going on that it was hard for us to sit and have a conversation," he recalled. Each was convinced that the other was more disorganized, when the truth was that they both ran a messy ship.

Their fashion sense, on the other hand, couldn't have been more different. Simmons dressed "like a substitute teacher, really kind of square," Rubin recalls. Penny loafers, tweed jackets with suede elbow patches—anything *but* fashion forward—defined Russell's wardrobe in 1984. But all he was trying to do was emulate his mentor in the business, Rocky Ford—former *Billboard* writer and co-producer of "Christmas Rappin'"—and other black music executives, who all wore suits and ties. "I can remember, once we became more friendly, kind of lecturing [Russell] about how he didn't have to dress that way," Rubin recalled. "It's a record business, you can dress however you want, it's okay," he would say to Simmons. "You're good at what you do. That's what's important."

Simmons figured that if he dressed like a record executive, labels would take him more seriously and give his artists fairer deals. He was getting frustrated, watching his artists sell records, and not seeing a return. Rubin could relate: "It's Yours" had sold an astounding ninety thousand copies, but he hadn't seen a dime. Like Rubin, Simmons was working on his music virtually for free. "And that's what really attracted me to him," Rubin noted. "It was about being true." The pursuit of something genuine bonded the two young men, and they became fast friends.

"We did everything together," recalled Simmons. "We'd be at the studio every night; if it wasn't the studio, we were in Danceteria. I used to take him to Disco Fever in the South Bronx. I took him everywhere." Simmons, in turn, came to see Hose perform and started managing T. La Rock and Jazzy Jay, booking shows for them in Virginia and other cities within driving distance. Meanwhile, Rubin continued deejaying with the Beastie Boys.

•   •   •

It was actually Arthur Baker who initially tried to open doors for the
Beasties at record labels. After meeting them through Rubin, Baker
hired Adam Yauch as an assistant engineer at Shakedown. Along with
that job, Yauch also ran various errands for Baker, like "skateboarding
downtown to get drugs for me and stuff," Baker recalled, and walking his dog. In return, Yauch was given free studio time at Shakedown to work on music. They would hang out together at places like
Milk Bar, with the Beasties rolling in on their skateboards, "claiming
to have just smoked a rock of crack," recalled Baker. "They were just
fucking punk kids."

Yauch even directed a music video for Baker's wife, dance-music
singer Tina B. "I thought the guys were really talented," Baker recalled of his work with the Beasties, singling out Yauch as a particularly good kid, "a smart kid." "Yauch was sort of the quieter, leader
guy," recalled Mike Espindle, and "the funniest in terms of wit, not
in terms of acting goofy." Mike D., meanwhile, was "sort of a bullshit-
artist kind of guy," noted Espindle. "Funny and smart, just a little
more of like a salesman." Horovitz was "just a sweet kid. He was the
coolest one, I thought, in terms of just stuff he would say, and the way
he kind of looked."

Their talent was evident to Arthur Baker on the Beasties' demo—
passed on by Yauch—which contained "Rock Hard." Baker was so
impressed he decided to record a song with Yauch and his friend Jay
"Burzootie" Burnett, an NYU film student. Baker and Yauch wrote
the lyrics, Burnett composed the beats, and Yauch rapped. (That
song, "Drum Machine," would eventually become the fourth independently distributed Def Jam release, in June of 1985.)

During the summer of 1984, the Beasties were headquartered in
the West Village duplex of Adam Horovitz's generous and kind-
hearted mother, Doris, who also used her home as a kind of refuge
for city kids. Cey Adams, who was having problems with his parents
back in Queens, was staying there, along with a young girl named
Veronica Webb, the future supermodel. Adams had been approached

by Horovitz and Skilken at Danceteria about designing the Beastie Boys' logo, and the three of them became instant friends. "It was a really amazing time," recalled Adams of that summer, when Horovitz had a job scooping ice cream at New York Ice on Seventh Avenue and Greenwich, and the gang ate a lot of it for free. Because of perpetually low funds, the crew was forced to find creative ways of having a good time without spending much money. Although the Beasties were all technically on break from college, their educational status was always in a state of flux. (Yauch had been enrolled at Bard College and Horovitz at BMCC, but "it never seemed that anyone was at school," says Adams.)

After recording "Drum Machine" with Yauch, Arthur Baker tried shopping the Beastie Boys to a few labels, including CBS, where his good friend Joe McEwin worked in A&R. But McEwin ended up passing on the Beasties. "I think Joe just thought it would be way too difficult to convince the powers that be at CBS records," pointed out Steve Ralbovsky, "something which Joe's probably kicked himself for since then."

The Beasties nearly got a record deal at Manhattan Records, which was a subsidiary of EMI. Manhattan's claim to fame would be 1985's "Sun City" benefit record against apartheid, which Baker had produced. The label's priority was pushing New York artists, and since the Beastie Boys "were the ultimate New York group," as Baker points out, Manhattan seemed like the perfect home for the trio. He gave their demo to Manhattan's director of A&R, Bruce Garfield, and invited him to see the Beasties perform at a showcase downtown. "It was on a Friday night," Baker recalls. "We were gonna go out to the Hamptons afterwards, and Bruce didn't wanna wait to see them, so he ended up leaving to go to the Hamptons, and he never saw them."

But by then, Rubin had introduced the Beasties to Simmons, who "knew that they needed a label," he recalled. Simmons started sending them out to performances around the city. One memorable show took place on September 28, 1984, at the Encore Club in Jamaica,

ROBERT LUND ARCHIVES

Hot club, meeting spot, favorite destination—Danceteria was a major landmark in Simmons's and Rubin's early careers. Together and independently they liked to throw parties there—like this one from 1984.

Queens. "Come celebrate the stars of Rush Productions, as we honor Kurtis Blow, the King of Rap's Return to the Throne," the flyer proclaimed. There was a cartoon of a B-boy's head in the corner, wearing a baseball hat that said "Rushtown." The entire Rush stable performed: Whodini, Oran "Juice" Jones, Davey DMX, and R&B singer Alyson Williams.

With the release of "It's Yours," Def Jam—its logo still prominently displayed on the back of the 12-inch—was transforming from more than just a hip logo into a potentially real label. Rubin, who was now a senior at NYU with his own room at Weinstein, was receiving a constant stream of visitors. The Beastie Boys would always be stopping by after a night out and leave their graffiti tags in the elevators and hallways. Adam Horovitz, who lived closest to the dorm and was seen there the most, was put to use: he helped Rubin sort through shoe boxes full of demos that had accumulated around his room.

Because Rick's dorm address was on the back of the "It's Yours" record, every aspiring rapper in town without a record deal sent him a tape. But most of them "were horrible," Rubin recalled. Horovitz listened to each and every one and usually tossed them to the side. One tape, however, got his attention, and he played it for Rubin. "I can't say it was great," he recalled, "but it was different, and I liked it. There was something about it that just struck us as funny, and we wanted to hear it over and over again. I eventually learned that when something makes you laugh, that's a really good sign." (Comedy had always been a major influence on Rubin. He often stayed up until early morning to catch reruns of his favorite show, *Abbott and Costello.*)

The demo was LL Cool J's.

Back in 1984, LL—whose real name was James Todd Smith—was a skinny, "hyperactive, had-too-much-sugar-in-the-morning kid," recalled his first DJ and childhood friend, Jay "Cut Creator" Philpott. By the time Rubin had gotten Todd's demo tape, the fifteen-year-old had been rapping at block parties and battles for nearly four years and had given himself a moniker, which stood for Ladies Love Cool James. "He was probably one of the hardest rappers ever," Philpott recalled. "He created the hardness." LL was an observant, attentive kid who was heavily influenced by his grandparents, both of whom were voracious readers and former schoolteachers. LL's grandmother was "a lady with a lot of wisdom," according to Philpott. "Someone to really guide you. She was about five foot tall, but a really powerful lady."

Although LL could often be painfully shy around strangers, when it came to rapping and putting on a performance, he always had a big mouth. Sometimes his outspokenness got him in trouble with his peers. But Philpott, who was a football player and two years LL's senior, always had LL's back. "We lived in the same neighborhood, and he was a guy that had talent and I took him under my wing," recalled Philpott, who was also a DJ at high school and block parties, which involved getting a permit from the city to set up the barbecues and play the music. Sometimes, two DJs would play at the same party, one set up at the opposite end of the block from the other, splitting an hour of play time. "Or if the block was big enough, you'd play at the same time," recalled Philpott. "And when it takes off, whoever gets the crowd, gets the crowd."

Philpott liked to spin a lot of instrumentals popular among B-boys, like "Mardi Gras," "Love Is the Message," or "Bounce, Rock, Skate, Roll" and "Good Times." He always got the crowd—thanks to his secret weapon: LL Cool J. LL would rap over these instrumentals, often using "big words," Philpott recalled. Sometimes, the crowd couldn't even understand what he was saying, but he made sure it sounded cool. When he wasn't rapping, LL played a lot of football, studied martial arts, and even tried boxing. But he never discussed college, although "he's one of the smartest guys I know," says Philpott.

"He was the first person I ever called based on a demo tape," recalled Rubin, who invited LL to meet him at the dorm. "He was wearing these high leather boots, which were kind of where hip-hop style was in those days," Rubin recalled of LL's attire. "You'd wear your tennis shoes to get to the place, but then when it was showtime, you'd take off your tennis shoes and put on your boots." LL "was really shy," Rubin remembered.

He already knew he wanted to work with LL and played him some of the beats he had stored in his drum machine. LL really liked a few of them and wrote a rap on the spot. He continued writing "just pages of lyrics," recalled Rubin, who would examine them and tell LL which parts he thought were worth keeping and which weren't. He encouraged LL to think in terms of verses and choruses. "Growing up listening to the Beatles and to rock music, the song structure was really just a very familiar part of my vocabulary in understanding music," Rubin explains.

He may not have been the most technically skilled beatmaker—"I was never a great programmer," Rubin admits—but his ideas were possibly the most cutting-edge and progressive of any hip-hop producer at the time. "I just know what it's supposed to sound like," he says.

Within a day of their meeting, Rubin and LL recorded a song that they thought was worth putting out commercially, called "I Need a Beat." The lyrics were a perfect example of what Jay Philpott referred to as LL's use of "big words," like *syncopate, acute,* and *duel.* Adam Horovitz also wrote a verse. At first, Rubin considered releasing the song on 99 Records, just as he had done with Hose. Using Arthur Baker's imprint Party Time—which released "It's Yours"—was a "one-off thing," Rubin explained, so that wasn't an option.

Then he took the record to Simmons. "It's a hit, it's fantastic!" Russell gushed. But Rick didn't just want an opinion—he wanted Simmons to be his partner in Def Jam Records. Simmons was reluctant at first and suggested that they put out "I Need a Beat" on Profile. "Why?" Rubin questioned. "All you do is complain to me about Profile, and how they don't do anything and they don't pay the artists. Why don't we just do it ourselves?"

"I can't, I wanna do a production deal down the road, like Robert Ford," said Simmons, referring to the deal with Rush Productions that Steve Ralbovsky was trying to work out with his bosses at EMI. Simmons was convinced that he could get a better deal than Rubin, who was "making an independent company, and I already had connections and some success," Simmons recalled. But the deal with EMI would fall through. "It was just too much of we-don't-get-this, we-don't-understand-this; no, thank you," recalled Ralbovsky.

"Let's do this together," Rubin kept insisting to Simmons. "I'll make all the records, I'll do all the business, and you just be my partner." As a college student with four independent records to his name, Rubin needed Simmons's experience with major labels, tours, and management. "He thought about it a good little while," recalled Tony Rome of Simmons's decision. "It wasn't like he just jumped right in. He talked to me about it, he talked to Heidi [Smith] about it."

Finally, Russell agreed, swayed by Rick's personality, his talent as a producer, and the tracks they had already worked on together. "This is the company we're gonna sell," Simmons said to Rubin. "Why do I need to make a separate label? This is our joint label." Paul Schindler drew up an agreement between the duo that made them equal partners in Def Jam, while Rubin's parents donated $5,000 and Simmons put in another $1,000 to get it off the ground.

They didn't bother with job descriptions, a decision that would eventually create many internal problems. "Both of us were so inexperienced as far as building an organization," Rubin admitted.

The first Def Jam release as an actual label became LL Cool J's "I Need a Beat," in November of 1984. The label's logo looked slightly different from that on Rubin's Hose EP. Rubin kept the classic lettering—which has remained to this day—but he now added a drawing of a Technics turntable arm around the two letters, which he designed at his aunt Carol's Estée Lauder offices. (The drawing itself had been done by a girlfriend of Hose's lead singer, Mike Espindle.) "Reduced by Rick Rubin," the record sleeve read. "Written by J. Smith and A. Horovitz."

Because Rubin was still a student, NYU agreed to give him credit for his work with Def Jam and he ran the label out of his room, which was "packed tighter than Afrika Bambaataa's," said DMC comparing Rick to the legendary record collector and MC. "He had every beat jam that you could possibly have." His room was also a mess, littered with newspapers and take-out food wrappers, even deemed "unfit for living" by Weinstein's health authorities. But everyone wanted to be there. "Rick was cool, 'cause he knew all the cool beatmakers, and could make a beat like nobody," recalled Tony Rome. Dante Ross, who would in the future produce everyone from A Tribe Called Quest to Everlast, used to tag along with his friends the Beasties. To him, Rubin's appeal was obvious. "He was just mad fun," recalled Ross. "He knew how to play AC/DC songs. He had a checkbook and cash, and we didn't, and he'd take us to eat after Danceteria." Ross also admired Rubin's willingness to hear opinions about his work. "Rick was never shy about anything he did," recalled Ross. "He was really into getting people's feedback," said Mike Espindle.

To help answer the phone and run errands at Def Jam, Rubin recruited college friends Adam Dubin and George Drakoulias, who also received college credit for their work. Although they weren't paid, they did have one main perk. "I got fed for the first two years," said Drakoulias. From the album pressings—done by a plant called Soundworks in New Jersey—to the independent distribution, the operation was as grassroots as it got. Often, Drakoulias would take a cab out to Long Island City, Queens, where one of the distributors was located, with two boxes of records. He would drop them off, receive about $300 in cash from the distributor, "stuff it in my pants, and take the cab back," he recalled.

Rubin also continued throwing parties at Weinstein as the head of the party committee. One month, he decided it would be a good idea to throw a wet T-shirt contest. He and his friends put up flyers around campus, promoting the event: "Bodies for sale," the flyers read, next to a hand-drawn cartoon of a scantily clad coed and a price tag of $200 (the prize for the winner of the contest). "It just caused an uproar on campus," recalls Drakoulias of the series of women's group meetings and school-paper write-ups on the party. When the party finally took place, in the basement of the Weinstein dorm, NYU "kind of had enough of Rick's antics," recalls Drakoulias. Although Rubin had put up his own money for the party—just as he had for years, writing checks and then being reimbursed by the party committee—NYU refused to pay him back. "That was the end of the parties," says Drakoulias.

When he wasn't working on Rush Management–related issues, Simmons was also running over to the dorm room. "Scrawny Bone, I'm out! I gotta go meet Rick," he would call out to Tony Rome (Scrawny Bone was a nickname Rome picked up on the road). Before heading upstairs at Weinstein, Simmons would stop by the reception desk to chat with Ric Menello. "Ricmenello," he would always greet him, stringing his first and last names together. Oftentimes, Simmons would stay late at the dorm, end up sleeping over, and shower at the dorm. "One time, I went to the bathroom, and he was standing on the toilet," recalled Drakoulias. "The shower is running, but he was standing on the toilet and lathering himself." "It has to do with the steam," Simmons explained. "You get more clean with the steam."

Also dropping by the dorm was a student from Long Island's Adelphi University named Andre Brown. Around campus, he was better known as Doctor Dre, the moniker he used as part of a four-man DJ troupe called the Concept Crew, who did frequent gigs at downtown clubs and loft parties. Dre first came to Rubin's attention from the parties deejayed by the Concept Crew. When he heard a promo called "Knowledge Me" that the crew recorded for the *Super Spectrum Mix Hour,* a popular radio show hosted by Adelphi student Bill Stephney on the university's WBAU FM, he became interested in signing Doctor Dre. Rubin wanted to make "Knowledge Me" the next Def Jam release, right after "This Is It" by Jimmy Spicer, an artist that Simmons was already managing. There was just one problem. The Concept Crew needed a new name, after they learned of another group called The Concept. Adam Horovitz, however, assured Dre that he had nothing to worry about. "You're the *Original* Concept, so it doesn't matter," he said, and the name stuck.

Andre Brown and Bill Stephney weren't the only Adelphi students that Rubin would come to know. There were also brothers Hank and Keith Boxley and their friend Carl Ridenour, who all hosted a hip-hop mix show on WBAU FM. Like Doctor Dre, they were part of a mobile DJ crew; theirs was called Spectrum City, which deejayed parties, mini-concerts, and roller rinks all over Long Island. And like Dre, they had started creating their own beat-and-scratch-oriented records to fill up the three hours of their radio show (there simply weren't enough hip-hop records back then). Spectrum City mixed these tapes at a quasi-studio at 510 South Franklin Street in Hempstead, Long Island, and Ridenour—who went by the nickname Chucky D. that he would later change to Chuck D.—would sometimes rap over them. While rappers like Eddie Cheeba were "saying nothing," as he recalled, Chuck D. decided to make his raps a little more profound.

He was also promoting local parties, designing flyers (he was a graphic design major) and putting them up locally. When Hank Boxley, another Adelphi student and former grade-school classmate of

Chuck's, commented that his flyers were "weak," the two bonded. Hank came from Roosevelt, Long Island—"the capital of black Long Island," as he described it—and graduated three years ahead of another notable Roosevelt High student: Eddie Murphy. In October of 1979, Chucky D. and Hank promoted their first party, the Thursday Night Throwdown. Chuck got on the mike, while Hank—who changed his last name to the more punchy Shocklee—deejayed in the background. Spectrum City was born. Shocklee didn't recall Chuck as political per se, but he did recall him becoming "conscious," after a life-changing trip they took as kids to Hofstra University. It was a summer program called The African Experience, and the boys took dance and drum classes and learned some Swahili. "That experience stayed with us," Shocklee recalled, "and [since then] we've always been very, very Afrocentric in our beliefs."

Chuck D. and Shocklee got most of their hip-hop records through a record pool, which meant "we were getting records coming from major distribution companies, which had twelve-inch divisions at the time—or dance music," Shocklee explained. Record pools were created for DJs who weren't well-known enough to automatically get the records in the mail. The labels would usually send one of each record to the record pool, which would then be divided between the DJs.

To find more hip-hop records, Shocklee and Chuck D. usually headed to Jamaica Avenue in Queens, or to Bobby's Records on the corner of 125th Street and Frederick Douglass Boulevard in Manhattan, where they could get their hands on an assortment of other B-boy records. The only way of knowing if they were actually buying a hip-hop record—since they couldn't listen to them in the store—was by seeing "if there was any kind of 'crew' on the name of [the record], any kind of number after the artist," Shocklee recalled.

"I saw it in the rack," recalled Chuck D. of T. La Rock and Jazzy Jay's "It's Yours." "And I remember looking at the words *Def Jam,* and [thinking that] it could only be a rap record. La Rock was a very popular MC surname back then." The words Def Jam meant that this was "the ultimate record," says Chuck. "It was beyond your sonic

understanding; it was just real fantastic." Chuck also liked "the bold-
ness of the graphics" on the album cover.

Rick Rubin couldn't have known it then, but "It's Yours" was already inspiring Chuck and Hank. "That record was in heavy rotation
for us," Hank recalled of the summer and fall of 1984. They knew
they could make a record like "It's Yours," but even better, by using
samples. They wanted to sample the number one street record in
Long Island, Nassau County, and southeast Queens, which was the
JB's's "Blow Your Head." Like "Dance to the Drummer's Beat," it
was a huge B-boy record, one that when played at a club or party
would instantly summon the break-dancers to the floor. So Spectrum
City decided to use "Blow Your Head" as the foundation for their
song.

Because of outdated technology, Hank and Chuck couldn't sample a long chunk of a record. Instead, they used an old trick in hip-
hop mix tapes known as the pause tape, where one piece of a song
was recorded, the tape was paused, then another piece was recorded
to create a collage. Using the pause tape technique, they recorded
"Blow Your Head" from a turntable onto a cassette and since the
JB's's version was too fast to rap over also slowed down the original
song considerably. A beat was then added, and Chuck came in and
rapped over it. Later that day, Chuck—who was also moving furniture to support himself—played the tape to his furniture-moving
partner, William Drayton, who went by the nickname MCDJ Flavor.
When Chuck came by Spectrum to finish recording his vocals, Flav
was waiting for him in the next room. "Put a beginning and an end
to it," Chuck said to Flavor.

The result—pause-tape glitches and all—became known as "Public Enemy No. 1."

Although the recording was intended as a promo tape for WBAU,
it "caught on like gas in this area," recalled Shocklee of December
1984. "It even penetrated outside of the area, because people were
taping BAU and putting it on their mix tapes." The tape became one
of WBAU's biggest-requested records. Soon, it would make its way
into Rick Rubin's hands.

CHAPTER 4

Dorm Room
to Boardroom

By fall of 1984 Rush Management had become the hottest name in hip-hop. Run-DMC's self-titled debut went gold in November, Kurtis Blow's third LP, *Ego Trip,* was fast approaching the same figures, and *Escape* by Whodini—another Rush-managed rap trio—yielded bona fide hits like "Friends" and "Freaks Come Out at Night." Now, with the success of the Fresh Fest tour, Russell Simmons was being recognized as a businessman to be reckoned with. But he wasn't chasing the kind of flash and cash that personified his black contemporaries in the music business. He wanted mainstream America's acceptance without compromising his blackness. He would become a success by being himself: a chain-smoking, fast-talking rap manager. The *Wall Street Journal* had already dubbed Simmons the "mogul of rap" in a profile, and everyone gravitated to him. Some—like twenty-two-year-old singer Tashan—took a two-hour train ride all the way from Poughkeepsie just to be in the office and around its "incredible energy," he recalled. "Everybody knew that Russell was the man. He embodied the whole vision, the whole dream." And the dream was to take hip-hop to the masses.

Sometimes wannabe rappers would come into the Rush office with demos and attempt to audition for Heidi Smith by jumping on her desk. "Just listen to this!" they'd scream. To manage the chaos,

Russell's look changed shortly after he partnered with Rick. Gone were the penny loafers and white starched shirts; on went the fisherman's hat and sweatshirts. Here they are at the entrance to their office in 1985.

artists and staff multitasked. Cut Creator helped messenger packages, while LL Cool J sometimes answered the phones. As his company expanded, Simmons began entertaining the idea of making a film around his most successful act, Run-DMC. The timing was good, as hip-hop was already being featured on the big screen and on TV—with films like *Beat Street* and *Style Wars* and TV shows like *Graffiti Rock*.

In January of 1985, Simmons met with an Israeli producer named Menahem Golan, whose company, Cannon Films, had put out break-dancing movies like *Breakin'* and *Breakin' 2,* as well as vigilante B-movies like *Death Wish 2*. Golan wanted to make his next movie about rap music and planned on calling it *Rappin'*. Bill Adler, as well as Simmons's lawyer, Paul Schindler, attended the meeting, but another voice was in the room that afternoon, heard through the speakerphone. It was that of Lyor Cohen, the L.A. promoter and club manager that Simmons had met several months back. "I don't know how many receptionists, secretaries, and bullies he had to pass to get into this meeting, but he did," Adler recalls. "All of a sudden, he's in the meeting on a speakerphone, because he just wanted to. That was Lyor."

According to Russell's old friend Cara Lewis, Cohen came to New York to get the money that he was owed by Richard Walters,

Norby Walters's son, for a Run-DMC date at the Mix Club that was canceled at the last minute. When Cohen's deposit for the show wasn't being sent back in a timely fashion, he took it upon himself to get it back. Perhaps it was just an excuse to come to New York and try to get a job, or perhaps it really was about money. Whatever the case, Lyor Cohen's life was on a new course. "I remember sitting at my parents' table and my mother said, 'What's the worst thing that could happen? You come home,' " Cohen recalls. "And she explained to me that I should take the maximum risk of my life early. As I grow older, I would become more and more conservative."

When Cohen landed in New York, the only place for him to stay was in a tiny room at a welfare hotel, the Greystone, on Ninety-first Street and Broadway on Manhattan's Upper West Side. Tony Rome, who could usually be found at the Rush offices during the week, recalled that there wasn't exactly a welcome mat rolled out for Cohen when he arrived. "He was in New York, just calling, calling, trying to get to see Russell," recalled Rome. "But at that time, everybody thought he was like a geeky college kid: 'He's a promoter from L.A., what does he want?' But Lyor has a tenacity that I hadn't seen in anybody. He's not taking 'no' for an answer. It's not in his vocabulary." Cara Lewis recalls, "Nobody wanted to talk to him because it was about money."

As far as Cohen striking Simmons as someone who could work for Rush, Simmons says, "not really." In fact, he claims that it was Andre Harrell—Simmons's good friend and the new president of Rush Management—who gave Cohen his break. "Andre brought him to New York, and he used to help Andre, just picking up his slack. People could just do such a great job that they kinda get under your skin, and become an important part of whatever you're trying to get done." According to Cohen, however, Simmons invited him out to New York and "offered me a piece of the company," he says.

Finally, Cohen got an assignment. Run-DMC were going to London but their road manager suddenly disappeared at the last minute, leaving them at the airport with no passports. Cohen ended up going as the replacement road manager. One of the first shows they did when they got to the UK was a matinee at the Electric Ballroom. It was an unusually hot afternoon and with no air conditioning inside the venue, the crowd was getting increasingly anxious. To make matters worse, Runny Ray—a buddy from Hollis who helped tour manage the group—had forgotten all of the records, which were a key element of any show in the pre-DAT (digital audio tape) era. "The ceilings were dripping, kids were passing out, it was an ugly situation," Cohen recalled. "This is a terrible event for me. People are gonna get killed. My first job responsibility is a disaster, and what a short career." Suddenly, he got an idea: What if all the kids who brought Run-DMC records with them to be autographed were asked to pass them on stage, under the pretense that they would be autographed first. "We need to prioritize by signing those that have records," Cohen said to the audience when he got onstage. The show went on. "That was the moment that I became a very important person in Run-DMC's life," says Cohen. "They realized through action that I could really add value. And suddenly, we became a very tight unit."

A few months later, Cohen was introduced to Rick Rubin at his Weinstein dorm room. "I remember he was really tall and wearing this big black coat and had a big fur hat on," Rubin recalled. "Russell really liked him, and I just thought that he was an unusual person, his accent was heavy, and he was just a funny, odd person." Rubin enjoyed listening to Cohen's tales about the L.A. hip-hop scene. When Cohen left, someone else in the room remarked that he didn't get good vibes from him, which surprised Rubin. "I thought he was an interesting character," Rubin recalled. Cohen *was* different, but "for some reason, you didn't mind hanging out with [him]," said Rome, "because he just wanted to be down *that* bad." In February of 1985, Cohen joined the Rush Management staff. To Rubin, the hiring "made sense," because at the time the management company was "booming," while Def Jam was less busy.

Meanwhile, Simmons continued kicking around his idea for a Run-DMC movie, since his meeting with Cannon Films had not led to a deal. He soon met a young producer named George Jackson and his partner, Michael Schultz—director of *Cooley High,* one of Simmons's favorite films—who suggested that the movie shouldn't be exclusively about Run-DMC. "The movie is you guys' story, how you started this record company in the dorm," Schultz said to Simmons and Rubin one winter night, after spending the evening hanging out with them at Danceteria, and then grabbing a late dinner at the Empire Diner on Tenth Avenue and Twenty-second Street. "Run-DMC could be *part* of it," said Schultz. Rubin and Simmons agreed—as long as their artists could be in the film, because as Rubin pointed out, "Russell really cared about finding new ways to expose the music to a bigger audience."

Tentatively titled *Rap Attack,* the film would be tied into a Rush-produced radio show called *Rap Attack,* which was set to debut in the country's top twenty markets on June 1, 1985. But the producers decided to change the title to the name of the fictional label around which the film revolved: *Krush Groove.* Although the script was good, most major studios wouldn't even bother to look at this black film with a $3 million budget. However, one studio did see the vision, and Rubin and Simmons made a connection there while looking for a distributor for Def Jam. The partners had gone out to L.A. to seek major label distributors for Def Jam and stayed at the Mondrian Hotel, a popular entertainment industry lodging. (They couldn't afford single rooms so they shared a bed.)

One of their meetings was with Warner Bros. and its chief, Mo Austin. When Russell played "I Need a Beat" for the staff, "everybody was quiet in the room, except for Mo Austin," Simmons recalled, "the only one who seemed like he was paying attention." Even though Austin didn't sign a deal with Def Jam, he turned out to be "the reason we got *Krush Groove* made," Simmons explained. Warner Bros. Pictures' president, Mark Canton—who also produced Prince's *Purple Rain*—gave Schultz and Simmons the financing to do the film.

During that trip to L.A., Simmons received an interesting phone call from Madonna's manager, Freddy DeMann, who was interested in booking a rap group as the opening act on his client's Virgin Tour. Specifically, Madonna wanted the Fat Boys, and DeMann called up Simmons, thinking that he was their manager. Simmons didn't manage the Fat Boys—someone else did—but he played along. Simmons said that the Fat Boys were busy; when DeMann inquired about Run-DMC, Simmons said they were too expensive and offered De-Mann the Beastie Boys, which he'd planned on doing all along. After all, they had been on the same bill as Madonna two years earlier at CBGB's and had been acquainted with her from hanging out at downtown clubs. A deal was struck.

Meanwhile, Rubin was sitting right next to Simmons in the hotel room, shaking his head in protest. He didn't think the Beasties were ready to play arenas on a high-profile tour. "It felt like a crazy idea," he recalled. But after Simmons got off the phone with DeMann, having effectively convinced him to hire the Beasties as the opening act, he told Rubin not to worry. "It's gonna be great," he said.

Rubin and Simmons returned to New York and started preproduction for *Krush Groove* in March of 1985 at Silvercup Studios in Long Island City, Queens, and for the first time in movie history, both the producer, George Jackson, and the director, Michael Schultz, were black, as were most of the cast and crew. Rubin played himself, although his acting was "awkward," he later admitted. "I don't think it was anything I was good at." The shoot was not without its dramas. "During that time, there was a tremendous amount of animosity from the other artists towards Run-DMC, and the attention that Run-DMC was getting," recalled Tony Rome. Some artists demanded more attention. Jalil from Whodini, for example, refused to appear in the film altogether, because he thought the part he was given by the producer was too small.

Simmons's old friend Steve Ralbovsky from EMI, meanwhile, had gotten a new job at Columbia Records. Known as Big Red—for the color of its logo—Columbia had the cream of CBS's world-class roster of pop artists, including Barbra Streisand, Bruce Springsteen, and Billy Joel. Epic Records, another CBS label, was home to big sellers like Michael Jackson and Cyndi Lauper.

Ralbovsky quickly distinguished himself as a superior talent scout in Columbia's A&R department, signing bands like Jason and the Scorchers and The Outfield. "He was a young, aggressive, hip A&R

guy," remembered Jeff Jones, who had joined Columbia as a marketing director a few months earlier. Perhaps it was his youth and his keen ear for new sounds that got him called into a meeting with his immediate boss, Mickey Eichner, who was the head of A&R, and Columbia's president, Al Teller, one day in March of 1985.

Looking back, Ralbovsky still doesn't really understand why he was called in, because he knew little about the music that Eichner and Teller were about to play him. They wanted his opinion on a record by the Jonzun Crew, an electrofunk duo who had released *Lost in Space,* the first full-length album from Tommy Boy Records—a two-year-old New York label that specialized in electrofunk and was best known for Afrika Bambaataa's "Planet Rock." The Jonzun Crew was led by Boston-based writer/producer Michael Johnson, who would later be credited as discovering New Edition and producing their hit "Candy Girl."

CBS had been looking to beef up its black music roster, composed of traditional artists like Maurice White, Bill Withers, and Gladys Knight. "There was nothing streetwise or fresh, or reflective of more youthful urban hip-hop culture whatsoever [at CBS]," Ralbovsky recalled. With business going well—profits at CBS had skyrocketed from $22.2 million the year prior to $109.4 million, in large part thanks to Michael Jackson's multiplatinum *Thriller* album—the label was willing to take a chance on something edgy that could ultimately pay off. They had done just that in 1977 when they signed the punk-rock outfit The Clash and in 1962 with a twenty-year-old, unknown backup guitarist named Bob Dylan.

Teller asked Ralbovsky what he thought of the idea of doing a label deal with Tommy Boy. *Oh my God, my friend Russell!,* Ralbovsky suddenly realized. Through their mutual lawyer, Paul Schindler, he had kept track of Simmons and knew about his formation of Def Jam with Rick Rubin and his success with Run-DMC and other acts. "I got another idea for you," said Ralbovsky to Eichner and Teller. He had a feeling that Def Jam would be a better fit for CBS than Tommy Boy. Ralbovsky immediately called Simmons, and the two of them got together—along with their lawyer—to work on a presentation for CBS. (Rubin was not involved in this planning stage, because for much of that month he was on the set of *Krush Groove,* acting and overseeing the production.)

A few weeks later, Ralbovsky, Simmons, Schindler, and his partner Alan Grubman made their first presentation to CBS bosses. "Russell came in and started laying it all out for them: the different names of the groups, the different artists," recalled Ralbovsky. "And it just had a flavor."

Certainly, having two distinguished entertainment lawyers like Grubman and Schindler on their side helped seal Def Jam's credibility. But it was Simmons's speech, his articulation, his style, his charisma, Ralbovsky recalled, that truly impressed the Columbia execs. "It was just this unveiling of this subculture that was received with these big smiles and laughs, and headshaking. Like, 'Oh my God, there's this whole other world out there.' " The corporate world of CBS and the streetwise world of Def Jam Records were about to collide.

•   •   •

"I'm the king of the Paramount!" Ad-Rock stood onstage at Seattle's Paramount Theatre, screaming to an audience filled with teenage girls with frosted hair and Ray-Ban shades. They weren't the Beastie Boys' typical audience, but that was because they didn't come to see the Beastie Boys. It was April 12, 1985, and the girls had come for their idol, Madonna. This was *her* tour, the Virgin Tour, and the Beasties were just her mismatched opening act. The little girls didn't like these three sweaty, potty-mouthed, obnoxious, pimply young guys. The Beasties knew this, and in the words of Rick Rubin, who joined them as their DJ, Double R, "We made the *worst* of it."

"It was a miracle that they weren't kicked off the tour," recalled Cey Adams, who came along for the ride. "Had Madonna been the Madonna she is today, they probably wouldn't have survived." But back then, she "really took a chance," points out George Drakoulias. On most nights, the Beasties were practically booed off the stage. The press either got the Beasties' joke or it went completely over their heads. Some journalists called the act "unfortunate" or "embarrassingly amateur." Others pointed out that the Beasties made up for what

Madonna lacked in a sense of humor and irony about the entire situation, along with being musically adventurous. "Whoever thought of doing a rap over an AC/DC track should be given a medal," wrote one reporter.

At the end of each performance, Rubin would throw a few records off the turntable right into the audience. "It was like a drummer throwing drumsticks in the audience," he explained. "Just part of the rock 'n' roll thing that you would do." At one show, security took note of the record-tossing and came backstage accusing Rubin of injuring an audience member hit by a record. "I didn't throw any records!" Rubin insisted. "I need these things, I wouldn't throw them." Once again, he was able to avoid consequences for his mischief.

When the Beasties played in L.A. on April 26, they were treated like any other opening act. "The goal at that point, was [for the Beasties] to get a photo with Madonna," recalled photographer Glen E. Friedman, who served as a kind of part-time West Coast rep for Def Jam. But Madonna refused to be photographed with them. So the Beasties went outside the venue, and Friedman started snapping away various poses of them next to Madonna's face on the theater marquee. Although she refused to pose for a picture, Madonna was nonetheless "supportive" of the Beasties, recalled George Drakoulias.

The night after the show, the Beasties rented a Lincoln Continental and skidded up to Madonna's platinum-record party at forty miles

Mike D. and MCA spray Madonna with water guns during her final performance on the Virgin Tour at Madison Square Garden, on June 11, 1985.

per hour, blasting AC/DC's "Back in Black," "like it was *their* gold-record party," recalled Friedman. As a joke, he started shooting paparazzi-style pictures of the Beasties inside the club with "all these peculiar eighties celebrities." Rob Lowe, Billy Idol, Weird Al Yankovic, and David Lee Roth, all posed, even though "no one knew who the fuck [the Beasties] were," says Friedman.

Rubin got an ear infection midtour and was told by his doctor not to fly for at least a few months. "It was the beginning of the end of me being in the Beastie Boys," Rubin admitted. Doctor Dre was asked to fill in for the remaining dates. With Rubin back in New York, Def Jam released its third independent 12-inch, "The Def Jam," with Jazzy Jay doing some impressive scratching in the background, and a rambling rap/spoken-word performance courtesy of Russell Simmons, during which he gave a series of shout-outs, including "We got Ric Menello here from Weinstein!"

From June 6 until June 11, Madonna played New York City—at Radio City Music Hall for the first three nights and at Madison Square Garden for the remaining two. Rubin deejayed with the Beasties on the closing date. The experience of playing the legendary Garden was "insane," he recalled, "just too much to believe." His nerves were calmed somewhat by the anticipation of the new AC/DC album, coming out the next day. "They were really hated," George Drakoulias recalled of the audience's reaction to the Beasties. Perhaps well-deserved after statements like: "I've been around this country of ours, and I wanted to say, there's no pussy like the pussy in New York City," one of the Beasties yelled to the audience, according to Drakoulias. After Madonna finished her set, Drakoulias gave the Beasties water guns, and they ran out onstage just as Madonna was finishing her set, spraying her with water. She ran off the stage, giggling.

Steve Ralbovsky got a call the following day from a Columbia executive who had seen the show. The Beasties' antics left him wondering if this was the right band for Columbia. "Is this really what we wanna be doing?" he asked Ralbovsky, who assured him that the Beasties were harmless.

Meanwhile, Simmons was rolling out the second Fresh Fest tour, with Run-DMC, the Fat Boys, and Whodini. LL Cool J came along for a few dates, not as a performer, but as a student. For him, the Fest was an opportunity to learn from the masters—Run-DMC. From the start, LL was clearly in competition with Run, who had always been the youngest; the slim, cute guy. Whenever they got a chance, LL and Run would battle-rap each other in the Rush office. "Those little contests in the office were electrifying," recalled Bill Adler. "They were kind of chasing each other in the Rush office, snapping away." "He was a sponge," says Tony Rome of LL. "He would sit there and watch the show and study you like a book. Run onstage is very braggadocio; LL just formulated his show from some of what he saw. He didn't steal anything, but he got ideas and he just improved upon those ideas."

Appropriation of styles was common at Rush and Def Jam. Run himself, having started out as DJ Run, "the son of Kurtis Blow," had been influenced by Blow, who had in turn picked up performance techniques from disco and funk stars like Rick James and Larry Blackmon of Cameo—as their opening act in the early eighties.

When it came to working in the studio, LL got his lessons from Rick Rubin. Because they were both perfectionists, LL and Rubin were ideal collaborators. After the Virgin Tour wrapped, Rubin continued producing tracks out of his old dorm room, now with the addition of a new Korg drum machine. Adam Dubin came over a few times, just as Rick was finishing work on a new song by LL Cool J, "Rock the Bells." "All right, get out, I gotta work on this and make it better," Rubin said after a few minutes. Dubin was amazed by his old roommate's level of focus. "That was probably the most I saw him concentrate."

•   •   •

On May 15, 1985, Rubin fulfilled his parents' wish, as well as his own, when he graduated from New York University with a bachelor of fine arts degree in film and video—although he barely made it. At the last minute, Rubin realized that he was eight credits short of his degree. Ric Menello remembered once getting independent-study credits for writing a screenplay and suggested to Rubin that they ask the administration to give him retroactive independent-study credits for starting his own record company out of a dorm room. The two of them wrote a "very eloquent" letter to media relations, and their plea worked.

The Beasties, meanwhile, were doing spot dates around the Northeast post–Virgin Tour, and appeared at the fifth annual New Music Seminar on a panel called "Young People's Perspectives" with Rubin. They already acted like "minicelebrities," recalled Mike Espindle. "They were pretty used to being in a cool situation with a lot of cool people around." They arrived with Rubin, acting like their usual obnoxious selves and insulting the audience. Their parting words reportedly were "We don't have to play for free anymore in front of a bunch of faggots." Sean Carasov, who'd moved to New York City from England after road-managing the Clash, was in the audience and thought the Beasties were "a bunch of dicks." But within a few months he would be wreaking havoc around the city with the Beastie crew, which included photographer Sunny Bak—who had a studio on Broadway and Twenty-eighth Street, where the Beasties often hung out. "We would start at the studio and have sushi parties," Bak recalled of a typical night out. "Then we would zip over first to Palladium and drink, and then go over to the Milk Bar." But most often, they'd end up at Danceteria.

The Beasties were friends with downtown "it boy" and sometime actor Haouie Montaug, who was Danceteria's main gatekeeper and hosted a cabaret there every Sunday called No Entiendes ("you don't understand"). Everyone from downtown locals to celebrities like David Byrne and Madonna—who did her first showcase at No Entiendes back in 1982, landing a deal with Sire Records soon after—would put on random performances at the cabaret. The Beasties' shows were decidedly less polished, but they were hilarious. Their most famous skit was called "Three Bad Jewish Brothers," during which they dressed up in Hasidic clothes and performed renditions of Run-DMC songs. With a friend deejaying in the background, Cey Adams would lay down the basic part of the rap, and the Beasties would do the Jewish phrases, like "We are three Jewish brothers / We rock the house and we turn it out / Oy!"

Mike D. needed help organizing spot dates on the weekends, so they hired Sean Carasov, who quickly understood that he was part of the Beasties' in-joke. To outsiders, they appeared "horrendous," as he recalled, but the joke was that they completely exaggerated their real-life personae. Adam Yauch, for example, was actually the super of the building where he lived, which his parents owned. Mike D.'s mother was an art collector who lived on the Upper East Side and had raised Mike as a smart, cultured guy. He was also the group's "business guy," recalled Scott Koenig, a former assistant at Def Jam, "always looking over Rick's and Russell's shoulders and asking, 'What are you guys doing?' "

While they waited for CBS to draft a contract for Def Jam, Rick and Russell took a meeting with an Elektra Records executive who had recently signed Grandmaster Flash and the Furious Five to Elektra and was interested in hearing what Rubin and Simmons had to tell him about their artists. The deal didn't happen, but at least the partners got a memorable lunch meeting. "Me and Rick always remember this," Simmons recalled. "We were having a discussion, and [the executive's] wife fell in her salad; fell and banged her head on the table." She was clearly doped up. Her husband just glanced over at her and continued talking to Rubin and Simmons as though nothing had really happened. "We had never seen that kind of decadence," says Simmons.

On August 3, 1985, he and Rubin went out to L.A. again, this time for the taping of Run-DMC on *American Bandstand*. While in town, they met with Glen Friedman and brought him the very first black Def Jam jacket. To Friedman, the differences between Simmons and Rubin were immediate. "Russell was more of a businessman, Rick was more of an artist," he says. Def Jam was still negotiating a deal with CBS, but Simmons and Rubin had a feeling everything was going to come together. They told Friedman, "Pretty soon, we're going to do something major."

·   ·   ·

In early September of 1985, the NYU administration finally forced Rubin to vacate his beloved Weinstein Hall, where he had stayed long enough to see students move in for the new school year. (Rubin was able to "blackmail" the school's administration, as George Drakoulias recalled, into letting him stay for free all summer in exchange for his unrefunded party expenses from the infamous wet T-shirt contest.) Now twenty-one years old, Rubin scrambled to find a new apartment, and the timing couldn't have been worse. "I was really busy with so much stuff," he recalls, "there just wasn't time to think about things like finding a place to live." Luckily, Rubin found a small loft only blocks away, at 594 Broadway, between Houston and Prince. It would become an almost exact replica of his former digs.

Rush Management was also moving to a new space—a 600-square-foot former dance studio at 40 East Nineteenth Street. Simmons and Lyor Cohen shared an apartment space next door to the office—a rather unconventional, but convenient, arrangement. Where once dancers took classes in front of wraparound mirrors, now sat six Rush and Def Jam staffers behind desks that all faced each other (Heidi Smith's desk had two phones). "It was an exercise in sensory bombardment," she recalled of the never-ending chaos in the space. Artists, friends, and business associates of Rush and Def Jam turned the office into a kind of "drop-in zone," recalled Smith. The Beastie Boys came in and skateboarded circles around the desks. Some of the artists even slept in the office. The reception area was monitored by Jimmy Spicer, a Def Jam artist himself, who spent more time on the phone chatting with girls than answering calls.

The other drop-in zone was Rubin's new home in SoHo. His apartment, located in a commercial loft building, had been converted from a wide hallway that was cut in half and came with a laundry list of quirks. After one in the morning, the water in the building would be turned off, and a strong chemical smell seeped out from the photo studio next door. Occasionally, a rat would be seen scurrying across the floor. Still, Rubin loved his "little cave," and amid its clutter of paperwork, porn magazines, and records—much like in his old dorm room—he usually held all of his meetings. Rubin usually sat in his "magnificent, big chair" that had no legs but was supremely comfortable, recalled Ric Menello. Back at East Nineteenth Street, the running joke was that Rubin seldom left his apartment and spent most of the day watching pornography and eating Chinese food.

In September of 1985, Def Jam finally closed its $2 million multi-album deal with CBS, a budget that included recording, marketing, and overhead at Def Jam. "At the time, people might have thought, 'You're giving these two street guys how much money?' But if you could do that in hindsight, you'd multiply it by ten and do that deal today," says Steve Ralbovsky, who did not get a bonus check, despite his key participation in the early stages of the deal. In the end, the combined enthusiasm and personalities of Simmons and Rubin, as well as their insider status—thanks to their relationship with Paul Schindler and their support from Al Teller—helped seal the deal between the stodgy suits at CBS and the young, rebellious company. "I was taken with their passion for the music, their belief that this was going to be, without question, a mainstream music genre that had a very long future in front of it," says Teller. It also didn't hurt that Simmons was Run-DMC's manager. "Russell's an incredibly smart, clever businessperson, but what gave him carte blanche to do what he did was the fact that he managed the number one rap group," said Arthur Baker.

Simmons and Rubin were about to become part of the intricate structure of a major record label, which consisted of ten major departments that all made sure records were sold: A&R (Artist and Repertoire), which was staffed with talent scouts who found and nurtured new talent; Sales, which made sure the record got into stores; Marketing, which included advertising, publicity, art, promotional videos, in-store displays, and promotional merchandise; Promotion, which made sure the records got played on the radio; Product Management, staffed with people who kept all the other departments on time and on track (Sales, Marketing, Promotion, etc.); Artist Development; Production; Finance; Business/Legal; and International. To assure Rick and Russell that Def Jam wouldn't get lost in the corporate hierarchy, Teller said he would attend every meeting with them in every department "to help them get acclimated and to get the CBS people acclimated to them," he recalls.

Apart from signing new artists, majors also signed independent labels to multi-album deals—also called label deals—the most basic deals between an independent and a major, under which the signed label (in this case, Def Jam) had to deliver a certain amount of artists to the big label (CBS). CBS had been doing custom deals with boutique labels for decades. In 1969, the Isley Brothers got one with Epic Records for their T-Neck label; Barry White signed a custom label deal with CBS Records in 1980 for his label Unlimited Gold.

But Def Jam's was touted as one of the most lucrative of all custom deals between an indie and a major. "I put in place a deal structure that gave them the room to do what they had to do," says Teller, "and provide them with the appropriate level of resources." Def Jam had almost complete autonomy: they would work out of their own space, with their own staff, and be fully operational—from finding talent, to recording budgets, to starting promotion of records in the clubs and on the street level. From there, Columbia would take over and handle national promotion and marketing. Def Jam was paid an advance to cover their rent, payroll, phone, and other overhead costs, in addition to covering a recording budget for each album.

On the downside, CBS had final approval of each artist that Def Jam signed and owned all of Def Jam's masters. Def Jam's fourteen royalty points did not mean a whole lot, because if they released a hit album along with two or three stiffs, they could possibly not see *any* royalties: CBS would recoup the stiffs' deficit from the hit album's royalties. "It was a bullshit deal," Simmons recalled. "You're bound to have one flop that will eat up all your profit." But Simmons knew, as well as everyone else in the business, that it was the only kind of deal that a tiny hip-hop label could get from a giant like CBS. "It was the greatest opportunity in the whole world," Simmons acknowledged. Besides, the deal could be renegotiated in two years.

CBS and Def Jam also had to determine the number of albums that Def Jam could deliver each year under the contract. CBS decided that in the first year of its deal, Def Jam would release a maximum of four LPs by four different artists; the second year called for two LPs, but that number could be renegotiated. For 12-inch singles, Def Jam was not given any limit. Steve Ralbovsky's job was to approve all the groups that would come out through the deal, while Jeff Jones was the product manager for every Def Jam project. More than anything, Def Jam was like an A&R source for Columbia.

Ralbovsky picked LL Cool J, the Beastie Boys, Oran "Juice" Jones, and Davey DMX as the first four LP releases. Under their un-limited 12-inch release agreement, Rubin—also a lover of go-go music—signed a new go-go band called The Junkyard Band. "Each one of these projects had a certain definable look and style to it," Ralbovsky said. "It wasn't just about the beats and the songs." One project that Ralbovsky passed on was Rubin's college band, Hose. "The decision didn't make Rick happy at the time," Ralbovsky re-called. "We just didn't think it was something that we could really be successful with, compared with all the other great things that they were coming up with."

But Rubin was happy that once the artists were approved he con-trolled the art. "The goal was for [the music] to be as cutting-edge and radical as it could be, but we weren't elitist about it," he said. "We didn't want people not to be able to have it. We would focus on making music, [CBS would] focus on selling it and getting it into stores, exposing and advertising it." And CBS was as good as it got when it came to selling records. The Harvard University of the record business, as many industry people referred to it, CBS had the best distribution mechanism of all the major labels and was the first record company to build distribution branches. And distribution, as Fredric Dannen wrote in his definitive music industry book, *Hit Men,* "is no small matter." Along with radio play, distribution was the best way in the eighties to launch an artist. "The most effective national advertising is worthless if you cannot get shelf space for your product in stores across the country," wrote Dannen. By being able to get records into many stores quickly, CBS had helped turn artists like Pink Floyd, Barbra Streisand, Neil Diamond, and Bruce Springsteen into 5-million-plus sellers.

Unfortunately, Columbia and CBS had no experience selling hip-hop. Their marketing department had never written a plan to launch a hip-hop record, their promotions department had never helped get a hip-hop record on the playlist at a radio station, and their art department had never designed a hip-hop album cover. Everything would have to be made up along the way. Prior to Def Jam's arrival, CBS had dealt in the most traditional kind of black music and was the pinnacle of corporate America. Even the building that housed the label at 51 West Fifty-second Street—or Black Rock as it was dubbed for its charcoal-gray granite exterior—looked ultracorporate and even "ominous," as Walter Yetnikoff, the president of CBS, recalled. Inside, "every detail down to the last pushpin conformed to code," said Yetnikoff. In other words, experimentation was allowed only to a degree, and unruly behavior was not tolerated. (Ozzy Osbourne, a CBS artist, was famously banned from Black Rock in 1982 for biting off the head of a dove during a company meeting. CBS's huge overhead survived on hit records.) "It was important to have records that sold millions of copies, because there was a big machine to support," Jeff Jones pointed out. "So the idea of being an entrepreneurial, cutting-edge label, willing to take lots of chances and lots of risks—there were no major labels that were doing that at that time."

Luckily, the marketing and A&R departments at Columbia were

staffed with a lot of "young, aggressive, fun" men and women, as Jones recalled. In addition to Steve Ralbovsky and Joe McEwin in A&R was another forward-thinking staffer named Karen Duran, who worked in Core Marketing, which served as the liaison between CBS-distributed labels, like Def Jam, and the corporation. Unlike the Black Music division—which was staffed with mostly white, middle-aged men and conservative black professionals, "making syrupy R&B," recalled Duran—Core Marketing and the A&R departments consisted of young people "who could talk the talk" of the hip-hop scene. This was significant, because most urban, black professionals in the industry in the mid-eighties turned their noses up at hip-hop, preferring R&B in the vein of Luther Vandross instead and hanging out at R&B clubs like Liviticus. But that kind of attitude only made the hip-hop community stronger, giving them "a kind of us-against-them feeling." "Back then, everybody [in hip-hop] rooted for every-body," recalls Lyor Cohen.

To celebrate their new deal, Def Jam threw a "White Castle Party" on the roof of Danceteria, with invitations designed in the shape of pink Valentine's Day cards addressed from Def Jam to CBS. To get enough hamburgers to feed all of the guests, George Drakou-lias was sent out to a White Castle on Queens Boulevard, where he ordered a thousand each of hamburgers and cheeseburgers. (He man-aged to stuff most of the hamburger-filled boxes inside of a cab—and tied the rest to the roof.)

"As I'm walking around the very crowded rooftop, I heard so many comments being said among CBS people: 'What is this?' 'Who are these guys?' 'Is this music?'," recalls Al Teller. "And occa-sionally I would hear a comment directed at me, saying basically that I was out of my mind. I sort of laughed to myself." At some point during the party, a 16mm print of the Beasties' first video, "She's on It," was screened from the roof onto the building across the street.

In true form, the Beasties decided to throw burgers from the roof at approaching partygoers, and eventually the party turned into one giant food fight. "[CBS chairman] Walter Yetnikoff got hit in the head with a cheeseburger," Drakoulias recalled. "And I remember just being horrified, because it got really out of control." But neither Simmons nor Rubin seemed to care. "Rick definitely was an instigator," said Drakoulias. "He encouraged that kind of behavior."

Meanwhile, LL Cool J was walking around "with the biggest boom box you've ever seen in your life," recalled Ralbvosky. LL kept playing his new single, "Rock the Bells." It was

GLEN E. FRIEDMAN

LL Cool J was a natural star, who was in constant competition with not only himself but fellow rappers like Run of Run-DMC.

Glen Friedman who had recommended that Def Jam put the track out as a single and also use the group Trouble Funk's version on the B-side. The idea was inspired by punk records, which "always gave you an alternative version of the song on the B-side," he explained, unlike hip-hop records, which only put instrumentals on the B-side.

CBS quickly got to work preparing to ship the first batch of Def Jam 12-inch releases: the first of these were "She's on It" backed with "Slow and Low" by the Beastie Boys, and LL Cool J's "I Can't Live Without My Radio," the latter to be included on LL's debut album, *Radio*. Apart from a few tracks he did while still at the dorm, Rubin recorded most of *Radio* at Chung King studios in Chinatown. As much as he loved the space, he didn't really want the industry and the fans to know that he recorded there. The studio was actually called Secret Society, but Rubin called it Chung King on the *Radio* album.

"It was such a dump, it was like an embarrassing place to record," he said. "So we made up this fictional place."

When he wasn't at his apartment, Rubin was at the studio, working on future classics. He had a full plate. The first priority was Run-DMC's *Raising Hell* album, which he was hired to produce after Larry Smith, their usual producer, became busy working with the group Cameo. Rubin understood Run-DMC's style and philosophy so well by then that he was a natural choice for their next producer. *Raising Hell* would be the group's sophomore release on Profile.

A shared office space at East Nineteenth Street between Def Jam and Rush proved both beneficial and problematic for the upstart record label. Rubin thought it was a good thing. "There was a synergy, where anything that was going on in hip-hop was coming out of our office, one way or another," he explained. The Def Jam staff, however—which was essentially made up of two people: George Drakoulias and freshly appointed promotions director Bill Stephney—was often sharing duties with Rush, which could be overwhelming.

When Stephney, who had known Rubin since Bill's days as a DJ at Adelphi's WBAU, was first offered the job as promotions manager at Def Jam in early spring of 1985, he initially refused. The salary was low, and there was no real office. The whole situation seemed marginally stable. This all became particularly obvious when Stephney came for his job interview with Rubin and Simmons at 1133 Broadway, commuting in from Long Island, only to find that neither of his prospective employers had shown up. This happened more than once. With four years of radio experience, Stephney was considering getting a job with a major station and becoming a "suit guy" with benefits. Accepting a low-paying job at Def Jam sounded risky. But at the end of the day, considering he was only twenty-two years old with no family, Stephney decided to take the risk. If there was ever a time to take that chance, it was now.

One of his first tasks at Def Jam was to help Columbia promote the early singles, such as LL's "Rock the Bells." Because there was no proper urban-promotions department at Columbia, Def Jam's releases were "kind of ghettoized" in the dance department for a short time, according to George Drakoulias, who also helped Stephney in promotions. Def Jam was given a budget to hire indie promoters to take the music into the radio stations and clubs, which was Bill Stephney's job to coordinate. "Our job at Def Jam was to get about thirty percent of those one hundred or so black-music-format radio stations to show significant interest in airplay of our music," explained Stephney. "Columbia's role was to cross [the record] over to the white pop side."

But Stephney's duties quickly became blurry. "I want you to go on the road with Whodini, and then I want you to go on the road with Captain Rock [Dr. Jekyll and Mr. Hyde's former DJ]," Lyor Cohen announced to Stephney one day. Because these Rush-managed artists were not on Def Jam, Stephney was confused. "I just want to figure something out here," Stephney said to Rubin. "Who am I working for? Because Lyor wants me to go out on the road." Rubin was furious. "You work for Def Jam!" he screamed. "You don't work for them! You've got records to promote!" The artists themselves were often unsure whose directions they were supposed to be following: Rubin's, Cohen's, or Simmons's.

But it was hard to get organized when there were no rules. "It was all jazz," Stephney recalled, "improvisation." As long as Rubin could make his music on his own terms, not much else concerned him. "I don't think he cared if the building fell down," said Adam Dubin. "To guard the artistic integrity of the record—that was important."

On October 23, Warner Bros. held a premiere party for *Krush Groove* at Studio 54. It may have been planned as a vehicle for Run-DMC, but the film also provided invaluable exposure to Def Jam's fledgling artists. LL Cool J, who was putting the finishing touches on his debut album, *Radio,* had one of the most memorable moments in the movie, doing a "live" rap of "I Can't Live Without My Radio." The Beastie Boys, though reduced to a thirty-second cameo, also stood out as the white talent-show contestants at Disco Fever, the premier hip-hop club in the Bronx. (Mike D. was actually wearing the original maroon Def Jam jacket in the scene, even though the film is about the fictional Krush Groove record label.) Their single "She's on It" was on the Warner Bros.–released *Krush Groove* soundtrack.

The film grossed $11 million at the box office—triple its budget. Despite being in the company of gory movies like *Nightmare on Elm Street 2, Commando,* and *Death Wish 3, Krush Groove* experienced all the movie-house violence. In the first two weeks of the film's release, three separate theaters in New York reported mêlées, one even resulting in a seventeen-year-old boy being thrown through a window. No one could understand why this fun rap musical had set off such sparks. "Kids are so excited to see their heroes, and it's not playing at enough theaters," Andre Harrell tried to explain. Harrell, along with the Reverend Al Sharpton, organized a publicity event outside the RKO-Warner Theatre on Broadway to appeal to teenagers (and promote the film) on November 6. One of the theater owners where a mêlée occurred even confirmed that the incident "had nothing to do with any reaction to the film." Still, *Krush Groove*'s "controversial" reputation would follow it around screenings nationwide—casting a shadow over Def Jam. Indeed, the next three years would result in an unfortunate pattern of violence and mayhem at both the label's and Rush Productions' live events.

In early November of 1985, Adam Yauch, Mike D., and Jam Master Jay all stopped by to do an interview on Doctor Dre's *Spectrum Mix Show* on Adelphi's WBAU FM. During the show, Dre played them the tape that Chuck D. and Hank Shocklee had made back in December of 1984, "Public Enemy No. 1." Jam Master Jay loved it and said he would bring it to Rick and Russell.

Dre claimed that even before he played the tape for the Beasties and Jam Master Jay, he had introduced Rubin and Simmons, back in the spring of 1985, to Chuck D.'s music. He remembered the day he was hanging out with them in Rubin's dorm room, when he popped a tape of another Chuck D. track, "Check Out the Radio/Lies," into the stereo. "This is just a bunch of noise! That's garbage, man!" Sim-

A defiant-looking Rick Rubin (*center,* arms folded) and LL Cool J celebrate their success, surrounded by the corporate heads. To LL Cool J's immediate left is Al Teller, president of Columbia. On the far right is Steve Ralbovsky, and next to him is Ruben Rodriguez, the VP of Black Music.

mons exclaimed, according to Dre. "And he took the tape out and threw it out the window," Dre recalled. "Rick wasn't sure he liked it either."

LL Cool J's *Radio* album was on the release schedule for December of 1985, and as with the previous Def Jam releases, Rubin played a key role in its cover artwork. It was his idea to put a giant boom box on the cover. "Every single point, when it came to these groups, he was clear," recalled Jeff Jones. "So you just trusted that these guys must know what they're doing." Indeed, Rubin now had a better handle on how the music business worked, and how to make money. When it came to understanding the lucrative world of song publishing, Rubin "was no fool," as Adam Dubin recalled, and decided to give sole writing credit to himself and LL Cool J on LL's "I Need a Beat," completely removing Adam Horovitz's cowriter credit from the album.

With hundreds of CBS staff working out in the field—from Miami to Philadelphia, to San Francisco and Dallas—it was important to get everyone excited about the new Def Jam venture. "Part of your job was to first and foremost get your own company motivated and incentivized about working any particular project," says Jeff Jones. On November 11, 1985, Columbia's marketing department completed a video presentation to introduce Def Jam to the rest of the company. The presentation—a snapshot of Def Jam in 1985—was pulled together at the last minute. "Everything was on the fly," Jones recalled.

Before the new year even started, the Beastie Boys were already getting themselves in trouble with the suits at CBS. Columbia, having done just one press conference with LL Cool J, who was rather shy, had no idea what they were in store for when the Beasties decided to hold a press conference at Black Rock. "I couldn't believe how crazy [the Beasties] were," recalled Karen Duran of an infamous press conference at Black Rock. "I stepped out of the room for a minute to make sure the food was okay, and they stole the cameras. No one could point the finger at them, but they all knew the Beasties took them." Another staffer described it as "an ugly incident" that cost the group access to the Black Rock building. Like Ozzy Osbourne, who bit off a dove's head during a label meeting in 1982, the Beasties were the only CBS act in 1985 to be banned from the building. The extra publicity didn't exactly hurt the group. Rush Productions immediately sent out a press release, glorifying the trio's naughty exploits. Lyor Cohen also recalled booking the Beasties for a Sweet 16 party for the chairman of EMI Records, Charles Koppelman. "He ended up having to throw them out of the party, because they were putting things in their knapsacks," says Cohen.

Rubin and Simmons had no doubt that the Beasties and LL were future stars. "Russell's greatest strength was he believed in [hip-hop] as a commercial venture, much more than I did," says Rick. "He believed in it as something that the world was gonna listen to." Columbia knew the music and images were cutting-edge, but commercially, Def Jam was an experiment.

Thankfully, Columbia's marketing staff and upper management like Al Teller "were true, intoxicated believers in what we did," recalls Lyor Cohen. For former staffers like Karen Duran, the experience of launching Def Jam was profound. "There is nothing that I've experienced in my life since that has been as exciting as the birth of Def Jam," she says. "Because we knew nothing, we expected nothing, and we got *everything.*"

CHAPTER 5

(Dysfunctional) Family

Whenever he got a chance, Rick Rubin liked to stop by one of his favorite record stores in Greenwich Village, It's Only Rock 'n' Roll, which carried rock memorabilia and New York's largest collection of bootlegs. Rubin showed up there in November of 1985 with Adam Yauch, asking the store clerk if he'd heard of an extreme heavy-metal group called Slayer and their new album, *Hell Awaits.*

"I thought their stuff was incredible," recalled Rubin, who had seen Slayer perform a few months before at the New Music Seminar and owned both of their previous EPs: *Live Undead* and *Haunting the Chapel.* Slayer was based in L.A. and signed to a small West Coast label called Metal Blade, which spawned the resurgence of heavy metal in America by putting out its "Metal Massacre" compilations of L.A.-area bands like Metallica and Ratt. Slayer was the most extreme of the metal bands in L.A. Unlike many L.A. rockers who wore makeup and attracted a mostly female following, Slayer fit much better in the East Coast metal scene, which was "very punk-oriented, very street-oriented," recalled Slayer's lead singer, Tom Araya.

"Yeah, Slayer's awesome," said the clerk at the store, a twenty-one-year-old named Scott Koenig. "I'm gonna go see them in Brooklyn next Friday at Lamour's." Rubin invited himself along.

Slayer was touring to promote *Hell Awaits,* their first full-length album, and Lamour's, the famous Bay Ridge, Brooklyn, nightclub, was considered one of the premier showcases of the metal bands of that time.

After the show, Rubin decided to go backstage and meet the band, and tell them how much he wanted to sign them to his new label, Def Jam. The group said they had never heard of it or Rubin, but he gave them his number anyway.

The group's contract with Metal Blade Records was pretty iron-clad, and knowing how much Rubin wanted Slayer on Def Jam, Simmons helped secure the band. "It was something [Rick] wanted to do," Simmons said, explaining his support. "I trusted him." "This really means a lot to Rick," he urged Tom Araya and guitarist Kerry King, the group's leaders. Once Araya and King realized that they would be the only metal band on Def Jam, they got excited. "That was my selling point to the other guys: they're gonna fucking treat us like kings," recalled Araya. Slayer signed, and Simmons "really saved the day," says Rubin.

The group had already written most of the songs that would end up on their Def Jam debut, *Reign in Blood,* and when Rubin got together with them at Hit Studios in L.A., where he spent five weeks with the group in December and January, he "really liked what he heard," says Tom Araya. "He took our sound and kind of fine-tuned it: that Slayer sound that we could never capture in the studio. We kinda realized, 'Oh my God, this guy, he's got the touch of gold.' "

When Rubin returned to New York to mix *Reign in Blood,* Slayer came with him and met Russell and Lyor for the first time. Araya found Simmons "very, very likable. I got the impression that whatever Rubin was into, he was into."

Meanwhile, LL Cool J's *Radio* had hit stores and became a hit with both consumers and critics. No one had ever heard anything like it: a record where there was hardly any music; "it was all hard beats and rhyming," as Jeff Jones explained. To support the music, Rubin also ensured great marketing, including giant, six-foot-tall street snipes that were put up around New York City. The album was also positioned well in stores, and there was "a huge press campaign," as Jones recalled.

On February 4, Rubin flew to London with Simmons and the Beasties to do some press around Def Jam's UK launch and meet with the CBS staff out there. The Beasties made an instant impression as "a trio of young and slightly mad white rappers," as one reporter called them. The British press seemed excited about the "dynamic, crucial, exciting, relentless" new record label called Def Jam. A party was held to celebrate the launch, and stars like Boy George and Mick Jones turned out. A new artist named Doug E. Fresh, who had recently had a hit with his single "The Show," also performed. With him onstage was a guy with an eye patch, covered in gold chains and rings. His name was Slick Rick.

A British citizen, Slick Rick had actually been living in New York since the age of twelve with his mother. He was cocky onstage, but that was partly a defense mechanism. When he was a kid, Rick was often teased by other schoolkids for his physical quirks. "I was real small for my age, plus I was blind in one eye," he recalled. Slick Rick was also teased because of his British accent, which he worked hard on losing. He found his confidence in rap, while enrolled in the drawing program at Manhattan's La Guardia High School of Music and Art. Another aspiring rapper, who went by the moniker Dana Dane, also went to the school, and the two of them formed a small group called Kangol Krew. They didn't use turntables, but made beat sounds by banging on desks and dressed in blazers and Kangol hats. "That's the next Def Jam artist," Rubin said of Slick Rick that night in London to Simmons. "That's who we *have* to sign, whatever it takes."

On March 9, back in the States, Rubin drove to Philadelphia to record the "Walk This Way" collaboration between Run-DMC and Aerosmith, a concept that Rubin had masterminded. "[Aerosmith] were touring at the time, and it was a big deal, because Joe Perry was back in the band," recalled Adam Dubin, who was also a huge fan of

Aerosmith. "It was really a culmination of what [Rick] had been thinking about for three or four years: bringing together rap and rock." Inspired by his rock-rap collaboration, Rubin went back to New York City to continue work on the Beasties' debut album—on which he would take the idea of mixing rap with rock even further—while finishing mixes for Slayer's album.

To capitalize on the buzz surrounding Def Jam in New York City, Simmons and Cohen booked a special night at the Apollo on March 23, called "Def Jam at the Apollo." They decided to pair up Def Jam and Rush acts with pop and rock acts; for example, LL Cool J performed on the same night with The Jets, and Kurtis Blow with Trouble Funk.

In June, Simmons and Rubin spent a chunk of their $600,000 advance from Columbia to buy a four-story building at 298 Elizabeth Street, which was located at the top end of the street, right around the corner from the busy East Houston, parallel to the Bowery, and a short distance from Washington Square, in the middle of what was considered "crack central." Rubin's main attraction to the space was its convenient location. "Rick got tired of people coming up to his house, talking about music," recalled Doctor Dre, who was with him the day the new office space was purchased and remembered the space being "a piece of shit." But Rubin thought it was a great idea, especially since it was so close to his apartment. He also liked the building's basement, where he was determined to set up a recording studio. "We'll never go to Chung King again," he declared.

Rubin and Simmons found a contractor to start renovating the space, which needed a lot of work. A former machine shop, it had a gate that would lift through a pull chain through which trucks could enter. Rubin's plan was to stay at his dingy Broadway loft for a few months, then move into Elizabeth Street with Simmons, who was sometimes hard to get hold of. Rick found it "hard getting stuff done, because I always felt like we didn't spend enough time together," he recalled. "I suggested that if we lived in the same place, we'd be able to get everything done and know what each other is doing." But that plan would never come to fruition. By the time construction at Elizabeth Street was completed, some fourteen months later (Rubin blamed the delay on his lack of "experience with construction"), Simmons already had his own place.

●   ●   ●

Steve Ralbovsky was in the middle of a phone call one March afternoon when Jeff Jones came over to his desk and left a note that Ralbovsky has kept to this day. It read: *LL's gone gold*. He immediately picked up the phone and called the one person who would be most proud. "Your grandson's record just went gold!" Steve told LL's grandmother Ellen Griffith. Everyone from the artists to the staff at both Def Jam and CBS was thrilled, because earning a gold record was always a group effort, and a big deal even for veteran executives. "That is the most gratifying experience to break a new artist," says Al Teller. "But when you do it in a brand-new genre, it's even more gratifying, because it validates the belief that this was a sensible thing to do, and you put the bet on the right people."

"LL just had that charm, that charisma that people gravitated towards—women, men," pointed out Brian Latture, a childhood friend of LL's who would later become his comanager. "LL became a rap icon very fast." His appeal was nationwide, and he was soon declared America's "hottest rap star" by *Time* magazine. When Rubin and Simmons came out to L.A. in the spring of '86, they were shocked by LL's popularity there. They rented a Porsche and hung out with Glen Friedman in L.A. on Westwood Boulevard, which was a popular spot to go cruising. "We would just sit on top of the car and park it on the side of the street," Friedman recalled. "Cars are cruising by at like one mile per hour, and every single car is playing either Run-DMC or LL. Rick and Russell just couldn't believe it!" L.A. radio, like KDAY, played nearly every single track of *Radio*.

Unfortunately, the Beastie Boys' second single, "Hold It Now, Hit It," wasn't getting as much of a reaction from radio and retail. But Rubin wasn't worried: he knew he had something special up his sleeve and continued working on the Beasties' debut album at Chung

King studios, where he now had carte blanche. It was a bizarre place. A couch that continually smelled like cat urine was in a room that was dubbed "the cat piss lounge." The walls were covered with graffiti, and the owners didn't care. Because Chung King was right near the busy and crowded Canal Street in Chinatown, "the whole vibe was just grimy," recalled Tashan, who also recorded there. "It felt rock 'n' roll," said Rubin. "It was like stepping back in time, something in a film noir." He loved that the studio was in his neighborhood and was inexpensive and "had a really free vibe," he said. It also had the best sound of any studio he could find. "No one could sound the way Chung King's shit sounded," recalled Nikki D., who signed with Def Jam in the late eighties. "It might stink, you might see a mouse, but you wouldn't go nowhere else in the city and get that sound at the time."

"It was all fun, it wasn't serious work," says Rubin of his sessions with the Beasties. But others, like Scott Koenig, saw a different picture. The Beasties were "dead serious" when it was time to work on the music, says Koenig. Rubin wasn't a "twelve-hour-sits-behind-the-console" kind of producer, according to Ralbovsky, so the Beasties "had a very strong point of view about what they wanted to be. I'm sure they feel like they invented their own thing." Few people knew, for example, that the Beasties produced "Hold It Now, Hit It" by themselves. "They didn't have the credit they deserved early on for being creative," says Simmons. He also claims that the Beasties produced "Fight for Your Right (to Party)" all by themselves. "That's not true," Rubin counters. "I don't even think they liked that one. 'Hold It Now, Hit It' they had a lot to do with, 'Paul Revere' they had a lot to do with." Ad-Rock complained to reporters that Rubin was always credited with every aspect of the production. "*We* come up with most of the ideas," he said.

"Rick's involvement basically consists of being present, and then listening and going, 'Maybe you should do this and that.' But you can tell he's worked on something, because you can hear it!" says Slayer's Tom Araya of the special Rick Rubin "touch."

At the control board with Rubin was Chung King's in-house en-

SUNNY BAK

Tooling around at Chung King studios: Ad-Rock at the beat machine, Rick Rubin directing, and Steve Ett (sitting) engineering. Contrary to popular belief, the Beasties were hands-
on when it came to recording their tracks. "They didn't have the credit they deserved early
on for being creative," says Russell Simmons.

gineer Steve Ettinger—or Steve Ett, as he was usually called. He was
a tall, shaggy-haired white guy who, like Rubin, appreciated both
rock and rap. "He was a huge, huge piece of all these productions,"
said Doctor Dre. "Steve Ett was in there doing a lot of it with
[Rubin], for sure," concurred Ralbovsky. "He's the undercredited
guy on that record."

If the album ultimately was Rubin's vision, there were plenty of
contributions. "Slow and Low" was inspired by a popular dance song
out at the time called "The White Horse," which had a sound effect
of a car accelerating and then crashing, which Rubin used in the
song. "Slow Ride" re-created the horns from War's "Low Rider,"
and "No Sleep 'Til Brooklyn" was inspired by the title of Motor-
head's 1981 hit album, *No Sleep 'Til Hammersmith*. The track
"Girls"—inspired by the Isley Brothers' hit "Shout"—was written by
Ad-Rock and Rubin on a train ride from D.C. to New York. "It was
kind of a reductionist take on that breed of music," says Rubin.

"It all kind of came together," says Ralbovsky of the sessions. "It
was a true collaboration that could probably never be again or
couldn't be revisited a second time." There were reports in publica-

tions like the *Village Voice* about the Beasties using drugs while in the studio, but Ralbovsky couldn't recall seeing the Beasties "in any kind of state that I thought they were completely out of it. They would party the way city street kids would party."

When Rubin wasn't in the studio, he was at the front desk of his old dorm, Weinstein, working on a film script with Ric Menello. Ever since *Krush Groove,* Rick and Russell had wanted to make a film on their own terms and market it themselves. "In the same way that our records didn't sound like anything else on a major label, it felt like our movies shouldn't have anything to do with the normal system either," says Rubin. Nearly every day after working at Chung King, Rubin would take a cab to Weinstein, where Menello was still working as the head clerk, and write early into the morning. By the end of March 1986, they had a script. "It came out very funny," Menello recalled. "A sort of latter-day blaxploitation flick." Originally titled *Who Killed Runny Ray?* the film was about Run-DMC's roadie and lifelong friend (Runny Ray) getting shot over a money disagreement, and how his friends (Run-DMC) go on a hunt to find the killer. Rubin cast himself as the killer, named Vic. "But it needed to be directed in the right style, otherwise it would look silly," says Menello. Rubin was convinced he was the man for the job.

Meanwhile, the Beasties were perfecting their live act, with such performances as the "East Village Map" party with go-go dancers on-stage and tossing beer into the audience. Their set was so compelling that one reporter even compared them to the Sex Pistols. The Beasties would take this act on the road with them two months later, as the opening act on Run-DMC's Raising Hell Tour in June of '86. The Beasties weren't getting any tour support from Def Jam and were hardly being paid, since Simmons treated their stint on the tour as "a promotional thing," recalled Sean Carasov, who was hired as their road manager.

The first couple of weeks on tour were "like hell," Carasov recalled. A few times, Rush Management forgot to book the Beasties a hotel, leaving the group to look for lodging in the middle of the night. "There was a lot of bitching [from the Beasties] about how disorganized they were at Def Jam," recalled Carasov. Thankfully, the Beasties' audience experience during Raising Hell was much better than on their tour with Madonna. "The Beasties would go out and do their thing, and the people gave them respect," said Carasov. Despite their short sets—they performed three songs: "Slow and Low," "Hold It Now, Hit It," and "Time to Get Ill"—the Beasties were building a quick audience. They were a new phenomenon: white rappers who had street credibility because they were down with Run-DMC and LL Cool J. To calm their nerves before a performance, the Beasties would ask everyone to leave their dressing room and engage in a kind of secret pre-gig ritual. "It wasn't clear what exactly took place," recalled Carasov. "When you went into the dressing room afterwards, the deli platter would be all over the wall."

By the second week of the Raising Hell Tour, the Beasties—who originally had to be split up among Whodini's, Run-DMC's, and LL Cool J's buses—convinced Def Jam to give them their own bus, which became a convenient place for hookups with "the girls, the girls, the girls," recalled Ricky Powell. He came along as the tour photographer, and he and the Beasties' close friend Dave Skilken were called "trim coordinators." Each night, they were given a stack of after-show stickers to give to certain members of the audience during the show. Sometimes the girls were trouble, and stories about underaged girls and police visits were not uncommon during the Raising Hell Tour. In Birmingham, Alabama, one crew member got a scare and everyone had to pack up and get into Georgia. "Everything was going down so quickly," Carasov recalled, "that some people got left behind." Among them was Lyor Cohen, who was finishing a lengthy settlement—collecting performance fees from a promoter—and had to find his own transportation. Simmons, meanwhile, was so panicked that he left all of his luggage in the hotel and jumped on the bus.

Halfway through the tour, the Beasties fired Doctor Dre as their DJ, because they thought he was "lazy," said Carasov. They had to

SEAN CARASOV

Beauty and the Beasties. Backstage during the Raising Hell Tour with the dethroned Miss America '84, Vanessa Williams, who stopped by to check out the biggest hip-hop tour of the year. Moments later, the auditorium would break out in a gang fight, and the show would be stopped.

find a quick replacement for Dre, and Jam Master Jay recommended his buddy Hurricane, who was a quasi security guy for Run-DMC's show and was part of Run-DMC's "tough-guy image," as Carasov recalled. "They'd have two of their guys standing on the side of the stage, dressed in black T-shirts, black Lee's, black fedora hats, gold chains, and swigging forties, looking tough, arms folded." The Beasties had some initial concerns about Hurricane deejaying during their set, having had some negative experiences with replacement DJs in the past. However, they gave Hurricane a chance and "he pretty much aced it overnight," recalled Carasov. "He fit in right away. And he was pulling double duty as the [security] guy on the side of the stage [during Run-DMC's set]. Family."

Periodically, the Beasties would call Rubin from the road to check on the progress of their album. "What's taking so long? When's our album going to be done?" asked Mike D., the most business-minded of the trio. "I would love it to be done," replied Rubin, who also had his hands full with other projects. "But the reality of the creative process, it just takes however long it takes for it to be great." Because *Licensed to Ill* was written over such a long stretch of time—some songs were recorded two or three months apart—each track was unique. "I think if we'd have written the songs in two months, it wouldn't sound like it does," said Rubin. "It really is an episodic journey. That was the life of the project. I've always really followed the art." LL Cool J's *Radio* album, by contrast, took only about two months to record. "That's just the way that one evolved," Rubin points out.

The Beasties, however, weren't thrilled with the copy of Rubin's remixed version of "Fight for Your Right" they got in the mail at one of their Raising Hell Tour stops. Rubin had replaced the original drums with "these big rock drums," recalled Adam Yauch, and the guitars "with a real Top Forty cheesy rock sound." But Rubin knew he had a hit on his hands and was determined to make Columbia take it seriously. When he met with Al Teller in late July, after the Beasties had come back from the Raising Hell Tour, Rubin explained that *Licensed to Ill* was just as good as Run-DMC's *Raising Hell,* and like Run-DMC, the Beastie Boys were an important group, a different group, because they had "an even more suburban flavor," he said. Teller, for his part, recognized the challenge of marketing a group like the Beasties. "That was even more complicated," he says. "Why don't we take something that's already hard [rap] and raise the degree of difficulty?"

As in any label deal, there was an inherent power struggle. "The larger label realizes if the smaller label gets too powerful, what good is the larger label," explains Bill Stephney, "other than being a bank?" The tension often boiled over during meetings at Black Rock, sometimes resulting in shouting matches. During one Def Jam meeting, the only way that Al Teller could make his point was by jumping on the table and yelling at Rubin or Simmons. Simmons would jump up on the table with him, yelling back, "You're not giving our records promotion and you're not supporting our records and this is bullshit!"

Turning bright red, Al Teller yelled back, "You listen to me! We're doing the best we can! I'm tired of getting calls from you every single day about us not promoting your records, when we're there for you at every single point and are behind you!" Bill Stephney was often present at these meetings, which also included Senior VP Bob Sher-wood and Black Music head Ruben Rodriguez. "Russell and Rick knew Columbia's job—to sell the most amount of records in the shortest amount of time with the least amount of resources—better than the guys in the corporate suits did," says Stephney, "because the suits had limitations: they weren't from the youth culture. They couldn't compete with Rick and Russell, who were really out there, in the mix." But those who worked for Columbia, like Rodriguez, believed that Columbia was on Def Jam's side, and that they were clearly doing their best. "We all worked as one," said Rodriguez.

Still, Columbia staffers had obligations to the parent company, first and foremost. "There were times when you had to walk the line be-tween doing what you thought was best for the label, and doing what you thought was best for Def Jam," recalled Jeff Jones. "They were young upstarts trying to break the rules. And Columbia Records is trying to hold on to the rules."

Sometimes to avoid complaints from Simmons, Columbia's de-partment heads actually withheld information from him or said that certain records were a priority when they really weren't. "Then you see Russell at a club, and he asks you how many stations [were adding a Def Jam artist to their playlists], and you run down a list of four, five stations," recalled Karen Duran, who worked in Core Marketing for Columbia. "That's not a lot of stations for a Top 5 priority," Sim-mons would say. "Top 5? Where'd you get that? You're not even on the priority list," Duran would reply, confused. The miscommunica-tion inadvertently "started a war, and then you'd have Lyor screaming on the phone, and Russell coming into the office next day," Duran recalled. "There were a lot of things you couldn't share. You'd avoid Russell or try not to discuss."

Another source of tension was international distribution of Def Jam product. It seemed that outside of the United States, CBS did not take care to make Def Jam visible. In Canada, for example, their sin-gles were packaged in generic cases that made them look more like "mouldy wood paneling than hot disks," one reporter wrote. Mike

D. was so upset when he saw the packaging during a trip to Toronto that he smashed one of his own records in a store and was thrown out. During a trip to London, Rubin met with the president of CBS UK. "We look at CBS records in New York as an albatross," he said to Rubin. "And we have nothing against you, but because you're part of them, we're just not interested." Rubin was completely "horrified" by what he heard. When a British publication would call CBS UK for press photos of the Beasties, the publicity department would send them pictures of LL Cool J instead. "They didn't even know which artist was which," Rubin recalled. "It was just a disaster."

When he came back to New York, Rubin immediately sought an ally in Al Teller and suggested that they find a different distributor overseas. "Let the artists have a chance," Rubin pleaded. But his proposal was rejected. "We would rather see the projects go away than let someone else have success with them," Teller said, according to Rick. "That's corporate policy. It would make us look bad." The international distribution infuriated Rubin and became a source of tension between him and Simmons, "because Russell didn't care so much," recalled Rick. "He was like, 'Let's just leave it at CBS.' It wasn't that big of a deal to him, and I'm not sure why. But it drove me *insane*."

Rubin was about to make an even more infuriating discovery. Apparently, Mickey Eichner had come to Steve Ralbovsky one day and said, simply, that Columbia would not be putting out the Slayer record *Reign in Blood,* which was already being set up for April '86 release. "It was on the highest level," recalled Rubin of the music, the promos, and the artwork. To Rick, it was "the album of their lives [and] of that genre." Somehow an advance copy of *Reign in Blood* got to *Spin* magazine, where it received a positive review, but which quoted some of the lyrics from "Angel of Death," which described concentration camp torture, from the point of view of the Nazi. "My shareholders are all Jewish!" Walter Yetnikoff exclaimed when he read the lyrics written by Slayer guitarist Jeff Hanneman.

CBS's decision not to put out the record was swift and firm. "I thought there should have been more conversation about it," recalled

Ralbovsky. "I think that Rick took, rightfully so, a lot of exception to being told that his record wasn't coming out." Rubin claimed that CBS—which had initially felt that Slayer could be as big of a seller as marquee acts Ozzy Osbourne and Judas Priest—got "cold feet" after a lawsuit charging Osbourne with contributing to the suicide death of a teenager in July of 1986 (it was later dismissed). "It wouldn't surprise me that it started a rift in Columbia and Def Jam," says Tom Araya.

Ralbovsky delivered the message to Rubin about the halt of the *Reign in Blood* release, but he also called a few of his A&R friends, one of whom was Gary Gersh, his old boss from EMI. Gersh worked at Geffen Records and passed the Slayer info to John Kalodner, Geffen's director of A&R. Kalodner was always looking for new studio whizzes and reached out to Rubin, because "he knew David Geffen would put [Slayer] out," recalled Scott Koenig. With his new distributor, Rubin was able to avoid a massive delay in the original release date. Amazingly, neither Araya nor the other members of Slayer had any idea that their project had gone to a new distributor. In many ways, Rubin did them a favor, saving the group the headache of worrying about a new distributor for their album. "Rubin took it upon himself not to fuck us over, and the deal that he had with the band," says Araya. Not until the actual date of release of their album did Slayer learn about their new distributor.

With Slayer crossed off the Def Jam/Columbia roster, Rubin needed to quickly sign another group to fulfill his multialbum deal with CBS. Despite Doctor Dre's memories of Rubin showing disinterest toward Chuck D.'s early material, Rick claims that he wanted Chuck from the moment he heard his voice. To that end, he enlisted the help of Bill Stephney, who had known Chuck D. for years and had been promoted to Def Jam's general manager. Rubin, only half-jokingly, would threaten to fire Bill if he didn't convince his friend Chuck D. to sign with Def Jam. "This is crazy! We have all this success, we're doing so well," Stephney would say to Rubin. "You want Chuck that bad? I'm telling you, he put out a record called 'Check

Out the Radio,' and no one checked it out!" Stephney didn't think it was worth that much effort. But Rubin was adamant.

Although Russell thought Chuck's demo was "great" when he first heard it through DMC, "following Chuck around to make a record after first meeting was not, for me, that important," said Simmons. "But it was Rick's favorite thing." Like Stephney before he took his job at Def Jam, Chuck wanted to be in radio. He was twenty-six, working for a photo service, and had the same reluctance about the stability of a music-based career as Bill Stepheny had once had. Stephney met with Chuck and assured him that he, personally, would oversee their project, which convinced him and his partner, Hank Shocklee, to sign with Def Jam. "All right. As long as you're overseeing everything, Bill, it's cool," they said. They also asked him to produce their records.

But Chuck knew that he couldn't be the only face of Public Enemy. He and Hank wanted to create "a company within a company." In a word, a collective of performers outside of the conventional band structure, who would be conscious of their image and how to market it to their audience. The first supporting member that was added was Flavor Flav, who was essentially the hype man. Their DJ would be another college friend, named Terminator X. Next, they added Professor Griff, a long-standing member of Nation of Islam whom Chuck had known since fourth grade. Griff would become a kind of liaison between the group and the media. They dubbed him "minister of information." Through Griff's ties to the Nation of Islam, Chuck decided to add three men to serve as the group's onstage security force; he wanted them to be dressed in outfits that were part Black Panther, part soldier, and dubbed them the S1W's—short for Security of the First World.

When it came time to sign their Def Jam contract in June of 1986, Public Enemy got "one of the worst record deals that you could possibly have," according to Shocklee, who as the group's cofounder and producer also got points. "We understood the whole scenario as Def Jam was an experiment by CBS," said Chuck D. "It's not a case where Russell and Rick ripped us off, and we got a fucked-up contract because of them. It was the climate."

The royalty, which was in the neighborhood of five points—which meant 5 percent of the retail price of each recording—had to be split between the group and their producers. (In other words, if a cassette typically cost $10, the group received fifty cents per copy, minus 20 percent for a packaging charge, leaving them with forty cents for each copy sold.) As with all of their artists, Def Jam retained half of the group's publishing. But Chuck and Hank knew that, once they proved themselves, they could try to fight for their publishing, so "it wasn't like we were blind when we were going in," said Chuck. "We knew exactly what the parameters were." But Public Enemy made up for low points and publishing with complete autonomy, according to Chuck, from Simmons and Rubin, who agreed that once Chuck and Hank signed, they would pretty much be left alone. "I don't think it would've worked if it was a hovering situation," says Chuck.

Steve Ralbovsky came by the Def Jam office to meet Public Enemy for the first time during the signing, an occasion that was commemorated with a group photo. Chuck gave Ralbovsky some music. "The production was unbelievable, just blistering stuff," he recalled of the tape. "I thought they were amazing," Arthur Baker recalled, "I couldn't believe [Def Jam] had done it again." Noticeably absent from the group shot, however, was Russell Simmons. He was on the opposite coast—in L.A.—for the annual Black Radio Exclusive (BRE) convention, which he never missed. "He was always out there, pushing his music, and believing in what he was doing," recalled Ruben Rodriguez, Columbia's president of promotions. Ever on the lookout for fresh talent, Simmons parked himself in the middle of his hotel's lobby and started listening to people's demos.

A long line quickly formed, and two local producers/DJs/promoters came over and popped in their tape. They fast-forwarded through a few songs, then Simmons told them to stop at one called "Popcorn." He thought it was so good that by the end of their meeting, the duo—Darryl Pierce and Dwayne Simon, who had always

Public Enemy's Chuck D., center, flanked by the S1W's, DJ Terminator X (*second from left*) and Professor Griff (*third from left*) near Def Jam's office at 298 Elizabeth Street.

dreamed of "one day getting on that burgundy Def Jam label," Pierce recalled—were invited to New York. The artist they had been grooming for stardom—a high school kid named Breeze, who rapped on "Popcorn"—was also invited to New York by Simmons. The idea was that Breeze would be Simmons's newest protégé and that Pierce and Simon should come to New York and record a few demos.

Heidi Smith booked a flight for Pierce and Simon two days after the BRE convention. At LAX airport, another fledgling L.A. rapper and friend came to congratulate them and see them off—Ice-T. But when Pierce and Simon arrived at the East Nineteenth Street office of Rush, they were greeted with puzzled expressions from the staff. Apparently, no one had been told that they were coming.

After the confusion was cleared up, the guys were put in the Collingwood, a dumpy hotel across from the Empire State Building. The experience was nothing short of culture shock. "Coming from California, it's clean there, and New York was dirty to me; it was very aggressive," Pierce recalled. Within a few days, they were at Chung King working on songs. "It was everyone's dream: to work at Chung King, where Run-DMC worked," as Pierce recalled. "And to work with the engineer Steve Ett! Oh my God!" Inspired, they recorded

Flavor Flav, the clown prince of hip-hop and self-proclaimed "world's greatest hype man," provided much-needed comic relief for hip-hop's most serious group.

nearly sixty songs with Breeze, but Russell would ultimately pass on each one.

The following month, Pierce and Simon had to return to L.A., and back to the grind. It didn't seem possible then, but within a few short months, they would be back in New York and become two of hip-hop's hottest producers.

•   •   •

Yo! Bum Rush the Show, Public Enemy's debut, was made on a rock-bottom budget of $12,000 in July and August of 1986. "Our ideology was take less, make more out of it," recalled Chuck D. "Miuzi Weighs a Ton" was actually written back in March of 1985, when Chuck was still at WBAU. Shocklee, who admired Marley Marl's work on "The Bridge," decided to take a similar approach to production, but with a twist. "Instead of the music being on the chorus, I wanted the music on the verses," he says. To achieve that effect, he added a high-pitched noise. "I wanted to create a sense of urgency, a sense of importance, a sense of immediacy," he said, "something that was almost apocalyptic, if you will. I'm very much into those kinds of sounds: anything that feels disturbing, final." The production matched the lyrical content and imagery perfectly.

Although many years later, Public Enemy would become known for its militant black image, the evolution of the group was an incredibly multicultural collaboration—a perfect example of Def Jam's united colors. "All the people that were a part of the Public Enemy experience, they weren't all African American. They were all different kinds of people. It was more of a human-spirit thing that everybody felt." Chuck and producer Eric Sadler were responsible for the mechanicals, and Steve Ett was the engineer. "Rick felt like we can retain the Def Jam sound by retaining Steve Ett," Shocklee explained. "Steve had developed that sound. It's hard to say what it is, but you know it when you hear it. It almost feels like a heavy-metal hip-hop record."

The famous Public Enemy logo was designed completely by hand by Chuck D., using an X-Acto knife, paper, and markers. He started with the stenciled letters, which he said were inspired by a gangster movie on TV that used the same style of letters in its opening credits. Chuck added a Run–DMC–style crossbar to the letters but felt it needed something more. "Being a graphics major, I knew that the best logos were the ones that were able not to have letters, and then still speak out an image," said Chuck. He was sitting at his worktable one day, trying to enhance the Public Enemy logo he already had, surrounded by copy-machine printouts, logos, and magazines. He saw a logo that he had made for a group that never actually existed, Funky Frank and the Street Force, during his Spectrum City party days. "So I just took my X-Acto knife, cut it out, and pasted it next to the Public Enemy stenciled letters and the crossbar," he recalled. "And voilà! It just fit like a message of God or something. It was that eerie."

Chuck took the logo and put it over a photograph of E-Love, LL Cool J's good friend and prop man during the *Radio* era, from an edition of *Right On!* magazine. "So I cut E-Love out at the waist, etched in the silhouette, and then put a cross over it, and then—boom—there it was," recalled Chuck. Inside the silhouette, Chuck was able to "use the great invention of Wite-Out," he recalled. "To make the inner circle. I was a brilliant cut-and-paste person in college."

Just like Rubin, who was always involved in creating the imagery for his artists and for Def Jam, Chuck understood the power of design and presentation. That helped the two of them truly click. "It was a hand-in-hand thing," said Chuck of their collaboration. Chuck also shared Rick's "disdain for eighties' R&B." And so, Rubin let Public Enemy work on their art, separate from Def Jam, and separate from the intense energy of New York City. "I was the un–New York guy," said Chuck. "I came into New York City to do my job, and I left. I never hung out with Russell or Rick. To me, it was totally business."

The Beastie Boys, on the other hand—perhaps because of their age, perhaps because of their personal relationship with Rubin— would get almost the opposite treatment. Rubin would become so involved in their art and marketing that eventually he would be called their "Svengali."

Public Enemy's arrival may have been the first crack in LL Cool J's relationship with Rubin. "I think [LL] got intimidated by other acts," said his former comanager Brian Latture. "Somebody had to do the work for the other artists, and it was the same people who were doing the work for him. He was very self-centered. Anybody on Def Jam, he felt that he was responsible for their success. Almost like he gave birth to the label and he's part of the reason why they're there." LL also was a little suspicious of Lyor Cohen, who was still new at the company and was helping Simmons manage his artists' careers.

LL may have been concerned, like many young artists, "that there's a lot of money going around, but they're not getting their fair share," as Latture pointed out. In other words, with so many artists being managed by the same company, favoritism was inevitable.

•   •   •

On July 15, 1986, Run-DMC's *Raising Hell,* distributed by Profile Records, went platinum—a hip-hop first—but there was little time for celebration: Def Jam and Rush were moving into their new offices at 298 Elizabeth Street. Although everyone was happy to be out of the dance loft, it would take a long time to settle into the new space.

The remodeling sometimes defied practicality and logistics. The entrance to the building, at Rubin's insistence, was done in glass brick. Not the smartest decision, considering the office was right behind CBGB's and one block from the Bowery. "It was literally a crack resort," recalled Heidi Smith of the neighborhood. "The streets would sparkle from all the broken glass from cars, from which crackheads were trying to steal radios." As soon as the glass door was installed, it would get broken by somebody. "Rick, don't you think we should get rid of the glass door?" Smith asked. "No. I like a glass door," he responded. "Here we are in the middle of nowhere, with an abandoned church across the street that is quickly becoming alternative housing. What if [the door] breaks?" she would ask Rick. "We'd fix it," he would say. Immediately past the "broken glass door" were double doors that opened into the office, which made it possible for people on the street to see the action inside the office.

Behind the postmodern metal desk at the front sat an attractive eighteen-year-old receptionist, Simone Reyes, "with various young men around, all trying to play upon [her] good graces," recalled Stephney. The first floor also served as the office for Rush Management, which had an open-floor plan, with the exception of the two back offices for Simmons and Cohen. There was an old woman on the second floor who refused to vacate the building. She could not legally be removed, even though some believed that she was just a squatter. "She didn't care how loud the music was, she wouldn't leave," Menello recalled. The remaining section of the second floor, unoccupied by the old lady—and no more than 150 square feet—became Def Jam's office. "So the only thing that separated the two entities was a staircase," pointed out Brian Latture. "It was like a sweatshop back then."

The staff at Def Jam was small, but it was dynamic and colorful. "The company always was this great mix," said Lisa Cortes, who joined Rush in 1986 as Cohen's assistant. "Downtown meets uptown meets socialite meets gangster." That everyone was in the open made it difficult to conduct business. One can only imagine trying to talk to an accountant or a lawyer about a contractual point when people are yelling for an artist to hurry up and get on the tour bus outside, among other things.

The third floor became Rick's apartment—"a big, beautiful loft," recalled Ric Menello—and the fourth floor housed the Def Pictures offices. Within a year, Def Pictures would move to Spring Street, and Rubin would take over the fourth floor as well. The basement, which was really a garage, was to house a recording studio.

Heidi Smith had to deal with the constant string of office-related crises, like broken air-conditioning, false fire alarms, the lights going out and no one being able to find the light switch. To escape the drama, she would often hide out in the modern coed bathroom on the ground floor. It felt good to "just close the stall and put your head on the cold metal door," she recalled. Sometimes, people would stick a phone under her stall and say, "It's for you."

Two years earlier, Rubin had hoped that he and Simmons would be able to share the upstairs apartment, allowing for more frequent interaction and thus a smoother-running business. But by then, Simmons had moved to a penthouse on La Guardia Place, which became his main office. Bill Stephney soon took over Simmons's underused Elizabeth Street office, where Cohen could often be found, hanging out on the couch, asking Stephney all sorts of questions about life and music. "Very inquisitive guy, very confident about his talents," Stephney recalled. "The vibrancy of his mind was amazing." Although the entire Def Jam and Rush staff were overworked, the hours were especially tough on Stephney, who had a two-hour-long commute from Long Island and usually did not get home until three or four in the morning. Simmons and Rubin eventually loaned him some money to get an apartment down the block from the offices.

With Rubin never up before noon, and Simmons hardly in the office, it was hard to "catch these guys," said Stephney, "so you had to hang out with them in their element." Rubin's element was, of course, the studio, and Simmons practically lived in nightclubs. After work, he and Stephney—sometimes joined by Def Jam's then promo man Gary Harris—made the rounds to different clubs like Save the

Robots, the Milk Bar, Palladium, and MK's. Stephney would bring a stack of 12-inches for the DJs, while Simmons brought his natural charm. He was the king of hip-hop's integration into the downtown scene, a man-about-town, the life of the party—a Stoli and OJ in one hand, and cigarette in the other. Stephney remembered those nights as "sociological studies" more than just clubbing: they came to see how people reacted to certain types of music. "Russell changed," Tony Rome recalled. "He was always business, and the life of the party, but now the conversations at the parties changed. Every night out was a networking session."

Most often, Simmons would be at Danceteria, where one's social status was measured more by how many free drinks you were served than how easily you got into the club. Simmons always drank for free, but he tipped generously, sometimes even sliding a vial of coke across the bar. "Russell never really hung out at the hip-hop spots like Rooftop, Union Square, or Latin Quarter," recalled Faith Newman, who was an intern at the time at Columbia Records and a future Def Jam employee. "He was the downtown, arty guy. Always with a fisherman hat on, smoking cigarettes, just happy to be out. Always his own person, style-wise." Simmons took great pleasure in meeting new people. "He had a huge appetite and desire and interest in other people," says Cohen, who often joined Simmons on his after-work club outings.

Like many young, hip New Yorkers, Simmons favored Danceteria because of its large, open-floor plan. The second floor of the club was essentially a giant dance floor, with a lot of the action taking place in the DJ booth. Often, Afrika Bambaataa could be found spinning there. "The best was in the summer," recalled Julie Lanke, a former bartender. "When they'd open up the roof and put a barbecue up there. It was so unsafe to think about it nowadays. We'd set up a makeshift bar up there and big tubs of ice and giant vats of potato salad, and people were cooking hamburgers and hot dogs."

After Danceteria closed for the night, patrons filed across the street to the illegal after-hours club Berlin. Sometimes, the fire department and police dropped by for a raid, and people "would pull their dime bags and their drugs out of their pockets and throw them on the ground," recalled Lanke, "because no one wanted to get caught with their drugs. Bartenders would grab the cash drawers and go out the back door."

Back in early 1986, there was never a shortage of after-hours spots in New York City to get high in, and Simmons never hesitated to indulge. He could often be found at Bentley's on the West Side, a high-styled urban after-hours club "where the black and brown yellow-power-tie wannabes, Jheri-curl mishaps, and big hair all came together," as one former patron described it. Simmons liked putting a little bit of cocaine into a cigarette and smoking it that way. "I remember the smell of burning cocaine in the cigarette: a sort of sickly sweet smell," recalled producer Arthur Baker, a fellow night owl and drug aficionado, who would often run into Simmons at Bentley's. Since his work with the Beasties and Rick Rubin in the early eighties, Baker had continued becoming an in-demand producer, working with Diana Ross on her track "Swept Away," among other credits. Invariably, Simmons's and Baker's discussions would turn to music. "That beat's too *nervous,* man," Simmons would criticize a particular song that Baker had produced. "He was always trying to tell me about beats," Baker recalled. Seeing Simmons getting high so often, Baker wondered how anything ever got done at Def Jam. But by then, Simmons had major help in Lyor Cohen.

It was Cohen who figured out how to maximize profits at Rush and Def Jam through clever marketing ideas and endorsement deals. By July of 1986, Adidas had offered Rush a $5 million deal to have Run-DMC push their products, something that Cohen had actively been pursuing since December of 1985, when "My Adidas" first started to hit. When Run asked a sellout crowd of twenty thousand hip-hoppers at Philly's Spectrum on June 21 to show him their Adidas, Cohen filmed the event and sent it to Adidas, along with reports of what had happened at Run-DMC's in-store appearance at an Adidas outlet in Baltimore on June 27, when thirteen thousand kids showed up and the entire mall had to be shut down.

Cohen also cut a deal to produce T-shirts for Run-DMC, and all

Rush artists, with Winterland, the largest national retailer of rock merchandising and memorabilia, and a division of CBS since 1985. Getting the deal was "a defining moment," recalled Tony Rome, "because [Cohen] brought in additional funding. Lyor was just a deal-maker, natural at it." Def Jam would continue to use Winterland for all of its future tour merchandising. (By September of 1987, Cohen would negotiate a national TV campaign for Run-DMC endorsing Adidas, the first for rap stars, created by Young & Rubicam.)

In addition to his other responsibilities, Cohen also had to do most of the damage control while his groups were on the road. One famous example was in Long Beach, California, on August 17, when a near riot ended the entire show. Apparently, L.A.'s two rival gangs—the Crips and the Bloods—had arranged for a fight to take place inside the venue. The performers, of course, had no idea. As small pockets of fighting started to break out while LL Cool J was onstage, it was announced that unless people calmed down, the rest of the show would be played with the lights on.

But the situation only escalated, and the houselights went on just as Run-DMC started their set. Jam Master Jay, as usual, came out to tune up his turntable—he always started their show by scratching "Run, Run, Run"—with an enormous rope chain around his neck. "Jay's chain was so big, Stevie Wonder could have saw that chain, from the mezzanine seat at Madison Square Garden," recalled Tony Rome. "Every time he would cut the record, the chain would start swinging, and the lights hit it, and it would just be gleaming." Suddenly, the crowd got even more excited, and a flood of people began moving toward the stage. Apparently, the gangbangers got incredibly excited by Jay's giant gold chain. "Stop, stop, stop," the promoter, Roger Clayton of Uncle Jamm's Army fame, suddenly screamed out to Jay. "Get off the stage! They're coming for your chain, man!"

Jay ran off the stage, followed by the rest of the artists and crew, keeping themselves in a secure space backstage. Meanwhile, the Beastie Boys and Sean Carasov had already fled the building during Whodini's set. They had a feeling something terrible was going to happen. "Let's get the fuck out of here," Sean Carasov said to Adam Horovitz. The two of them had invited a few friends to the show and were going to get them to drive them back. "We escaped right before the police locked the building down," Carasov recalled. "The security of the venue had lost control of things." The concertgoers started to storm the building.

But for the Beasties, the wild night didn't end there. Five minutes after pulling out of the venue, the rim on their getaway car suddenly broke. Miraculously, an auto parts store was open about one hundred yards away, and as the guys waited in the car for someone to get the part, another car full of gangbangers pulled up. "We probably would have been dead that night" if the Beasties weren't in the car, said Carasov. The gangbangers didn't at first believe that it was really the Beasties. They told them to prove it. So the guys rapped their way out of the situation. As Carasov pointed out, "They rapped for their lives."

CHAPTER 6

Invincible

Coming off the unexpected success of LL Cool J's gold-selling album, *Radio,* Columbia and Def Jam went to work in late August of 1986 setting up the Beastie Boys' *Licensed to Ill,* which they wanted to hit stores by Christmas. (The album was planned as an early September release, but had to be pushed back because of a Bruce Springsteen boxed set that was being released that month, which was an obvious priority for CBS.) The first single would be "It's the New Style," with "Paul Revere" on the B-side, to be released in late September and followed by "Fight for Your Right (to Party)" in November. Columbia's sales solicitation sheet positioned the Beasties and their debut as a musical event: "PRESENTING THE DEBUT ALBUM FROM THE ONE, THE ONLY, THE BEASTIE BOYS—*LICENSED TO ILL!* THIS IS THE ALBUM THAT THE WORLD HAS BEEN WAITING FOR. THE WORLD OF RAP! THE WORLD OF ROCK! LITTLE GIRLS WILL LOVE THE BEASTIE BOYS!"

Although written by Jeff Jones, Columbia's product manager, the solicitation sounded as if it had come right out of the mind of Rick Rubin, who made sure he was involved in every step of the setup. Columbia might not have gotten as excited about the project if Rubin hadn't been there, constantly cheerleading for his group. In preparing the cover art, Rubin's ideas were exact—"down to that [turntable] tone arm," recalled Jones. "He knew what color it was gonna be, where it was gonna be positioned on the label." Jones then had the challenging task of getting Rubin's demands approved by Columbia's department heads. "Rick wants a gatefold with a four-color inner sleeve," Jones would tell his boss, and get an immediate and categorical no. The excuse was always the same: it would cost too much. But Rubin was relentless. "You *gotta* do this," he would say to Jones. "We *need* that photograph inside the inner sleeve." Just like in his NYU days, when he would try to convince his friends to participate in pranks, Rubin knew how to get a person to say yes. "He was a spoiled kid, so he behaved like a spoiled adult," said ex-roommate Adam Dubin. "He does what he wants."

Ultimately, Rubin did get a deluxe four-color interpac, and the *Licensed to Ill* cover would become one of the most original and daring that year. For some CBS executives, it was a little too daring.

One afternoon, Al Teller got a call from "a very agitated" Larry Tisch, the chairman of CBS, Inc. "Al, do you have an artist . . . something called the Beastie Boys?" asked Tisch. "Yeah, it's an artist that we're very excited about, on Def Jam," Teller replied. "Well, apparently, their cover has an American Airlines plane crashing into a mountain, and we got a call from the airline complaining bitterly that this is a terrible image," said Tisch. "They must change the album cover."

Teller explained to Tisch that, in fact, it didn't say American Airlines anywhere on the cover. "Secondly, Larry, you must understand," Teller continued, "that if we were to tell an artist that they couldn't do a cover because it possibly offended an advertiser on the CBS television network, our whole credibility with the artist community would be put in doubt. So there's no way in the world we're gonna change this thing. We're just not going to do it."

Tisch called him crazy and hung up the phone. "I was really not expecting a call from the CEO of CBS, Inc., twisting my arm to get the artist to change the album cover," Teller recalled. "I thought it was a good-looking cover."

In many ways, the album set itself up. Thanks to their stint on the high-profile Virgin and Raising Hell tours, the Beasties had created a buzz "before we solicited for this record," pointed out Jones. "It wasn't like you were starting from ground zero." Furthermore, their association with Run-DMC, who produced two of the tracks on the album ("Posse in Effect" and "Paul Revere"), also lent their project instant credibility. Simmons was fond of telling the press that the Beasties were "Run's favorite group." Having Rick—who was becoming one of the hottest producers in the industry after the huge crossover success of "Walk This Way"—attached to the project also helped.

All of this almost guaranteed that the album would do well at retail, and it did. The LP was released in early November and immediately started "tearing up"—industry-speak for doing well—retail (the CD and cassette versions were scheduled for release on January 4, 1987). The two years it took to make *Licensed to Ill* paid off. The album sounded nearly flawless. Had there been a rap category at the Grammy Awards in 1987 (there would not be one until the following year), the Beasties would most likely have taken the trophy for Best Album. Big beats tangled with rock guitars, Latin percussion, jazzy horns, and obsure samples. The lyrics were sharp and witty. Radio, however, was much slower to follow. Programmers considered the lyrical content too offensive, with its frequent references to sex, alcohol, drugs, and violence.

Columbia had tried to clean up the album as best as they could. At the last minute, they pulled a song called "The Scenario," which was originally a flip side to "Hold It Now, Hit It" and used the same beat as Schooly D's "PSK." They singled out one lyric that made the song unacceptable: "Shot homeboy in the motherfucking face." (Ironically, the same week that Columbia decided to take "Scenario" off the Beasties' album, the company ran a big ad in *Billboard* magazine proclaiming themselves "the most daring label," thanks to artists like Hooters and the Outfield.)

Another track that didn't make it on *Licensed to Ill* was the Beasties' hip-hop rendition of the Beatles' classic "I'm Down." This time, the problem was not in the lyrics, but in the licensing rights, the gatekeeper of which was none other than fellow CBS artist Michael Jackson, who had recently purchased the entire Beatles catalog. Jackson deemed the Beasties' version a downgrade of the "I'm Down" copyright's value and denied them permission to use the song. Although it wasn't the Beasties' greatest work, nothing about their version mocked the original. Several people tried to change his mind, including CBS honcho Walter Yetnikoff and his friend/producer Quincy Jones, who was also pals with Russell Simmons, but the Gloved One wouldn't budge. The Beasties were not happy about this and didn't mince words when it came to their thoughts on Jackson. "If I ever meet Wacko Jacko, I'm gonna punch his head in," said Mike D. to a reporter in January. (Four months later, a tape of the song would somehow end up in the hands of DJs at L.A.'s KROQ FM station, who played it for a month until Jackson's lawyer sent them a cease-and-desist order.)

Rubin took it upon himself to make sure the Beasties' wild image got across to their audience. When it came to promoting the group, Rubin took on the persona of a pro-wrestling manager, à la Lou Albano. "The future! Of America! Is . . . Thebeastieboys!" he would scream during radio and TV interviews. He created an out-there TV commercial to present the Beasties as future icons of American culture—modern music's "founding fathers." Shot right after the Beasties returned from the Raising Hell Tour—which finished its extremely successful run on September 13 at London's Hammerstein Odeon—the commercial aired during late-night shows and on MTV and became a big hit. To the tune of "Yankee Doodle," "George Washington" signed the Constitution in front of the American flag, then passed the pen to "Abraham Lincoln" (Lyor Cohen was originally cast as Lincoln, but couldn't make the shoot). Suddenly, as the music changes to "Fight for Your Right (to Party)," the Beasties jump into the frame. Ad-Rock grabs the pen out of Lincoln's hand, haphazardly adds his signature to the Constitution, and accidentally spills the ink all over the document, and the Beasties run off. The final shot is of Mount Rushmore, onto which the Beasties' faces are cheaply superimposed, and Ric Menello slowly narrating, "Beastie Boys: American rock 'n' roll."

JANETTE BECKMAN

Def Jam's R&B king, Oran "Juice" Jones, with his mentor, Russell Simmons, in the fall of 1986. Simmons's fondness for R&B and Rubin's love of rock would soon divide the company.

Simmons had his own pet projects, his R&B acts: Oran "Juice" Jones, Alyson Williams, and Tashan. "I think B-boys are gonna love Juice," he said about his favorite, Oran, who was riding the success of "The Rain" single.

On October 2, Juice embarked on his five-week tour as a headliner (Anita Baker was one of his opening acts). Alyson Williams, another Def Jam artist, was sent out as Juice's tour manager. But the tour would not be without its own drama— a great example of the Def Jam family dysfunction.

When Juice arrived at Elizabeth Street to board the bus, he realized that he had left his jewelry at home. So a Def Jam in-house messenger was sent up to Harlem to pick up the jewels; however, he never brought them back. Supposedly, he got mugged on the way back, but Heidi Smith had different suspicions. The messenger finally called her back, screaming into the phone, "I have to call you right back, I'm being chased!" Then minutes later, he called again, saying, "They got the jewelry." Smith didn't believe him. "You should never come back," she said, "or I'll call the police."

•   •   •

"HE'S THE KING OF RAP, THERE IS NONE HIGHER. CBS EXECS ALL CALL HIM SIRE." The words ran across the *Village Voice*'s November 4, 1986, cover like a telegram to the music industry. Russell Simmons would have been flattered—if the story had been about him. No, the "the king of rap," according to the *Voice,* was really Rick Rubin. Even though Simmons had been declared rap's "mogul" just two years earlier by *The Wall Street Journal,* it seemed that the industry was starting to look at Rubin as the preeminent hip-hop producer, if not the spokesperson for the entire hip-hop scene. (Or as one reporter sarcastically described it, the *Voice* profile "credited him with everything but freeing the slaves.")

There was no question that Rick was a young, maverick producer, busy with different projects: *Licensed to Ill* was about to be released, Slayer's *Reign in Blood* was ready to hit stores in December, and he was starting work on The Cult's new album. He had just added Public Enemy and Slick Rick to the roster and had already produced two gold rap albums and dozens of singles. After the incredible success of *Raising Hell,* Rubin was such a hot property in the music industry that Mick Jagger—now recording solo for CBS records—asked him to produce his second album, *Primitive Cool.* "I don't think our schedules are going to work out," Rubin said nonchalantly. "I don't even own a Stones record." (The album would become one of the biggest stiffs of 1987.) Despite his status, however, Rubin was not "the sole force behind Def Jam," as Ric Menello points out, and that false assumption certainly irked a few people in the Def Jam family.

"If anybody's the King of Rap, it's Run-DMC," wrote Run in a letter to the *Voice* the following week. "And if it's not us, it's my brother Russell Simmons, who's charted twenty-one singles this year. Rick Rubin is not just a very close friend of mine, he's a great multi-talent deserving of acclaim. But it fucks me up that anybody thinks that he made my album. When I write my lyrics, I write the music and the final mix at the same time, and that's the motherfucking truth!"

"I felt bad," Rubin recalled of the reaction of his colleagues to the article. "It did kind of hurt my feelings, 'cause I felt like we were all on the same team. And if anything good happened to any of us, it furthered our cause. It's not like I had my own publicist working for me."

But others remember it differently. "Rick and Lyor would both hire publicists to hype themselves up back then, and deny it to no end," remembered Scott Koenig. Cohen denies it. "I was the anonymous one," he says. "There were a lot of secrets back then, a lot of jockeying for position between Lyor and Rick," says Koenig. "I think it was because [Lyor] had Russell's ear." Indeed, it was Cohen, not Rubin, who constantly pushed Simmons's pet projects, his R&B acts. "I remember Lyor being really aggressive with the radio promotions department on some of these R&B records," Jeff Jones recalled.

The week of the *Village Voice* article, production for *Tougher Than Leather* started. Rubin, Simmons, and Run-DMC were so hot that a few movie studios started calling the office offering to buy the movie sight unseen. But the partners were not interested. They wanted to produce the film themselves, finance it for $500,000 of their own money (half of it was contributed by Run-DMC), and *then* find a distributor—but there would be a price for that kind of ambition. With that in mind, Rubin and Simmons formed Def Pictures, a production company that they temporarily ran out of the fourth floor at 298 Elizabeth Street.

"The idea of making a movie, having no experience as a director and working all with nonactors, was a real questionable choice that we made," said Rubin, whose only experience as a director consisted of a few student films. On the eve of the first shot, the crew list was still being revised (the "third electric/driver" was a young guy named Andy Hilfiger; his brother Tommy was developing a fledgling fashion line). Just before shooting was scheduled to begin, some of the crew had to be replaced at the last minute. They'd threatened to quit if they didn't get raises, and when they didn't—because the budget wouldn't allow for it—they walked away. Directing a film, as Rubin discovered, was an entirely different animal from producing a record. "Definitely we were in over our heads," he admitted. "I was opposed to [the film]," Cohen recalls. "I believe in commodity economics: do what you do best."

Rick was not the best director. As a record producer, he was used to getting up at noon, showing up at the studio in the evening, and working with a small staff of three or four people. But as a film director, he had to be on set early in the morning, ready to manage a crew of at least thirty. Because of the modest budget, Simmons and Rubin decided to hire inexperienced crew and actors, which Rubin thought would be fine. "We don't need actors! We're gonna get *killers* to play killers," he would say jokingly of the mostly amateur cast. On a typical day, the crew showed up at six in the morning, with Rick missing in action. A production assistant was sent over to Rubin's apartment on Broadway. "The door's locked, he's not answering," the PA radioed back to Vincent Giordano, the film's producer. "Break the fucking door down and drag him out to the set!" Giordano screamed back. Eventually, Rubin opened the door and the PA told him that they needed to set up the first shot. "Call Menello," Rubin said, as he slammed the door shut.

Ric Menello, who lived in Brooklyn and still worked his night-shift job at Weinstein, would get woken up just as he was going to sleep and asked about the first shot. "How the fuck am I supposed to know?" Menello would scream back. "Tell Rick he's an asshole!" But he would relent and give the director of photography some instructions. As soon as Rick showed up on set, however, around 9 a.m., "he would tell them to change everything," recalled Adam Dubin, who was the film's assistant production manager. "They were losing time like crazy."

The production quality and acting were mediocre. Rubin, who "liked the idea of acting," as Menello recalled, played a bad-guy record executive named Vic. Simmons played himself, but poorly. The actors improvised most of the dialogue—which "probably hurt the story," Rubin admitted—and what started out as a funny script ended up weak on film.

By the second week of the shoot, Rubin was exhausted. "Waking up at six a.m., and going out into the cold, and showing up on the set with fifty people, saying, 'What do we do?' and having no idea what anyone's supposed to do. My creative clock doesn't operate at six a.m.,

JANETTE BECKMAN

Rick Rubin channels his homicidal gangster character, Vic, from his film *Tougher Than Leather.* The ambitious project was a financial risk for Def Jam that did not pay off.

unless it's still from the night before," Rubin recalled. "It was brutal." Instead of treating directing like a full-time job, he approached it more like an extra-credit school project. "Rick, in his pursuit to make all the money and have all the creative control, did not get as good of a project as we wanted," says Lyor, "and put us in financial risk."

There was also the issue of the music. Profile Records, which was already feuding with Simmons over his attempts to get Run-DMC off the label, gave him the ultimate dis: they refused to license any of Run-DMC's songs in the film.

On top of everything, Rubin and Menello were developing an MTV show for the Beasties, a kind of punk rock *Abbott and Costello.* Rubin and Menello had already written a teleplay for an episode called "The Beastie Boys Get Stupid."

While Rubin was trying to hold it together on the set of *Tougher Than Leather,* LL Cool J was looking for a producer for his next album. However, even if he weren't busy with the film, Rubin still wouldn't have worked with LL. In fact, their relationship had experienced such a dive over the past several months that LL, who was originally supposed to be in the film, was taken off the project. "There was stuff going on in LL's world that made me uncomfortable," recalled Rubin, who felt that the "pure, naïve energy" of their early collaborations would never be repeated. Furthermore, LL Cool J's father, Jimmy Nuña, came seemingly out of nowhere to manage his son. That was a shock to anyone who knew LL's history: ten years earlier, Nuña (formerly known as James Smith) had almost shot LL's mother to death.

LL's mother, who up to that point was helping her son manage his finances, had reached out to her ex-husband, in hopes that he would exert some control over LL's spending. But what LL was looking for was not a manager but a father. "It doesn't matter how rotten or how much of a lowlife a child's father is, a kid wants to point to a man and say, 'That's my daddy,' " LL wrote in his autobiography.

LL was also facing a legal issue. A man named Larry Humphrey from Virginia was threatening a lawsuit against LL and Def Jam, claiming that he was the *real* LL Cool J, whose stage name was stolen by LL and put on *Radio*. "It's totally ridiculous," Simmons told a reporter. "He might as well be suing Bruce Springsteen. He'd probably get further." Still, the lawsuit was holding up work on LL's next album (Rubin may also have held off work with LL because he wanted to protect himself against a possible cross-claim suit from CBS), and LL was getting anxious to get back in the studio. "I want you to work with these new producers that I have," Simmons finally said to LL. The producers were Dwayne Simon and Darryl Pierce, the two guys he had met in L.A. over the summer and invited out to New York with their rapper, Breeze. "I want you to call LL, and set up studio time with him," Simmons instructed Simon and Pierce a few days later.

"It was very uncomfortable," recalled Simon of their first meeting with LL at Chung King. "This guy's a star. We're nothing." *Wow, he's a businessman,* thought Simon when LL walked in with a briefcase—even though it turned out to be filled with just pages of lyrics. After the meeting, the producers decided to follow LL and check out what kind of car he drove. But he was already gone. So they walked to the subway to catch the train back to Brooklyn, and when they got to the platform, they saw a familiar face on the opposite side, waiting for the uptown train. It was LL Cool J. "LL was still catching the train," Pierce marveled. From that moment on, the three of them became more comfortable with each other.

For two weeks, the producers worked with LL, feeling out their process, drinking beer and smoking a lot of weed, recalled Pierce. "It got us in a comfort zone," he says. Before they knew it, the guys had produced four tracks. Then they started calling LL by his real name, Todd, which only those who knew him well did. "He knew how to record vocals and all that stuff," Darryl recalls. "We learned a lot from him." They continued writing, until they had about sixteen tracks.

When they weren't working, the producers and LL would talk, and the producers learned that Rick and Russell weren't that "pleased with LL," recalled Simon. "I guess LL had an abrasive, cocky attitude. And all he really wanted was a little respect." The level of success that Run-DMC was enjoying at the time just wasn't happening fast enough for him. Walking from Elizabeth Street down to Chung King one day, he complained to Dwayne, "I just gotta get this Adidas off my back!" Adidas represented Run-DMC, and he wanted to have his own trademark, to stand on his own. "You know what, let's do this! Let's take the Adidas off your back," replied Dwayne. "And you put a Nike on your back, and let's go!" From that moment on, Nike became LL's signature brand.

"The team worked well together," says Dwayne, so when he suggested to LL that they record another ballad for his new album, LL was open. "Man, you have ballads on your first record that were the bomb!" insisted Dwayne. "Dangerous" was one of the ballads on *Radio* that they thought "was kinda fly." So LL began writing a ballad called "Sincerely Yours," which was a kind of a love letter to his girlfriend at the time. "Hot to death," Dwayne recalls. But they decided to pass on it, and LL wrote another one, called "I Need Love," as "all the creative minds came together."

Together with that track, they all realized that there was enough material for an album. But they were nervous—this was the very first album they had produced, Dwayne points out. "Yo, I don't know if Russell's gonna use these songs on your album," they said to LL. "I'm using *all* of this on my album," he reassured them. "This is *my* album. I'm done. I don't wanna work with any other producers."

The Beastie Boys, meanwhile, were on their way to becoming stars as "Fight for Your Right (to Party)" was starting to explode on the radio, breaking in Orlando and the Southeast, and moving up toward New York City. MTV immediately started demanding a video. The Beasties would see Rick on the *Tougher Than Leather* set almost every day (they played themselves in the film), and wanted to know when they were going to make a video. Rubin's hands were full with the film, so he directed them to Ric Menello, who in turn recommended Adam Dubin, who had already directed a short film.

The Beasties didn't object, and Rubin insisted that the shoot take place during the upcoming Thanksgiving weekend. "You have to get it to happen," he told Dubin, who somehow managed to pull together one of the landmark videos of the 1980s in two hectic days—with a tiny budget of $20,000. He went to Mike D.'s apartment with Ric Menello, and all of them came up with a treatment of the video, which they knew would have to involve some kind of party and a lot of gags. They cast as many of their own friends as they could find who were in town for the holiday.

Dubin begged the Beasties' friend, the photographer Sunny Bak, to rent her studio for the shoot for $300. "Next thing you know, they're knocking pictures off the walls, knocking the door down," she recalled.

"It was one of those things that happen really fast," said Dubin of the shoot. "You film, and you don't know if you're getting something funny." He and Menello modeled the video after the party scene in *Breakfast at Tiffany's*. "I practically had to move because of that video," Bak recalled, "'cause there was so much whipped cream in the carpet in the bathroom that it smelled sour after that."

Tougher Than Leather wrapped on December 9, and Simmons was ready to hear the songs Dwayne and Darryl had been working on

The video that launched the "Beastie revolution" in 1987 came together last-minute during a hectic Thanksgiving Day weekend, on a budget of $20,000. Adam Dubin created the storyboard for the video. The images below ended up on screen.

with LL. They played him "I'm Bad." Simmons loved it. They played him "I Need Love." He hated it and called the song "homo, New Edition bullshit," as Darryl recalls. (These days, Simmons claims that he thought the song was "a smash" when he first heard it.) "You gotta make more *songs*," Russell told them.

He wasn't the only one who thought that "I Need Love" was terrible. Bill Stephney didn't like it; neither did Rick Rubin. "They were stuck on the *Radio* album," recalls Dwayne. "But this was a sophomore album. You have to grow, you don't stay in the ninth grade forever. Nobody dug that record, except the people that made it." Dwayne, Darryl, and LL knew they had a hit, and they refused to let anyone change their minds.

Perhaps their biggest supporter was Jam Master Jay. "He was instrumental in our lives, and not just musically," says Darryl. "Jay was there for us when we were down. He showed us a lot about New York," says Dwayne. Jay even taught them how to drive in New York in his brand-new Lincoln Continental. He often stopped by their house in Brooklyn after a studio session downtown. He showed up there one early morning and handed them a bag full of groceries. "I'm hungry, man. Here. Cook," he said. Since the guys lived right across the bridge from the studio, Jay figured he would just eat at their house, instead of driving all the way back to his house in Queens.

Darryl and Dwayne knew that they had talent but lacked a clear image. One evening, while driving up the West Side Highway with Jam Master Jay in his Lincoln, they had an epiphany. "We were frustrated, we were mad, we didn't have any money, we were getting no respect," Darryl recalled. Suddenly, Jam Master Jay exclaimed, "Y'all don't have an identity! Here in New York, we have crews. You guys got a crew, but don't nobody know who you are." He pointed out their unique look: baseball hats and jerseys. "You guys should call yourselves like the L.A. Crew! Or the L.A. Posse."

"And a light went off," Dwayne recalled of the moment. "We're L.A. Posse now!" Suddenly, the guys got the "new energy" that they so desperately needed.

• • •

Success on a massive scale happened quickly for the Beastie Boys. If in October of 1986 they were still "struggling to pay their rents," as old friend and producer Sam Sever recalled, then right after "Fight for Your Right (to Party)" was added as a "Hip Clip" to MTV in late November, the Beasties became stars overnight. Sales of the album began to skyrocket, too. "We're doing ten thousand a week, twenty thousand, thirty thousand, fifty thousand," recalls Jeff Jones. "All of a sudden, your whole record company is like, 'We *get* this.' It worked on an urban level and it worked on a suburban level." Sever recalls their performance at the 1987 MTV New Year's Eve Ball. "It's like one minute I'm hanging with them and dudes can't even buy a beer, and the next minute they hanging out with Bon Jovi."

With their album doing well, the Beasties wanted a big-budget video for their next single, "No Sleep 'Til Brooklyn"—in those days, that meant around $60,000—and they got it. Ric Menello was picked to direct. Rubin, as usual, offered some suggestions: he wanted Slayer's Kerry King, who plays the guitar solo in the song, to appear forty feet tall next to the Beasties. Adam Dubin, who was producing the video, explained that a shot like that would be too expensive. Instead, they thought it would be fun to have a real monkey play the solo. But it was too expensive to hire a trainer. Finally, they decided to just have someone wear a gorilla suit. There was some talk of David Lee Roth possibly wearing the suit, but ultimately, Dubin ended up as the guitar-playing gorilla, who gets pushed out of the way by the real Kerry King.

When the shoot was done, the Beasties visited Rubin at Electric Lady studios, where he was working on the Cult's album, to talk to him about their MTV show. They told him they wanted to be more than just performers in the project, but to have a real financial stake in it. But the discussion was short: Rick dismissed them and refused to give up a piece of anything. "The Beasties wanted to invest in their future success and were turned down flat," recalled Adam Dubin, who was in the studio that day. The group came out of the studio "absolutely flushed" after their meeting. "He was young and they were young," reflects Simmons. "He was trying to protect them, in some way. If I was older, I would have stopped him from being so controlling. Would I have been right to say 'Go do whatever the fuck you want' to the Beastie Boys? I don't know."

On that sour note, the Beasties departed two days later for their first national tour as headliners: the Licensed to Ill Tour. (Murphy's Law and Fishbone were the supporting acts on most dates.) It was a critical moment in their relationship with Rubin and Def Jam, because during the eight months they stayed on the road, communication between them and Rubin practically ceased; the friendship and business relationship would never be the same.

The Beasties wanted the biggest, most outrageous live show in rap, and to that end they enlisted production designer Eric Moskowitz, who told them he could create whatever they wanted. "A twenty-one-foot penis that comes out of a box!" Mike D. exclaimed, somewhat jokingly. To their delight, Moskowitz pulled off their request—along with giant cans of Budweiser and dancing girls in cages. In effect, the Beasties would end up with the most expensive stage show of any of the Def Jam and Rush artists. "They came up a little after everyone else and had a chance to outdo what everybody else did," points out Tony Rome, who had recently been hired as LL Cool J's road manager. "Everybody was constantly trying to outdo one another, but it was all in-house. So you had healthy in-house competition."

The Beasties arrived in L.A. on January 23 and were booked on the *Joan Rivers Show* and *American Bandstand*. They stayed at the Sunset Marquis—the preferred accommodations for rock stars and Hollywood types—but through a booking error ended up at the $800-a-night villas—the most posh accommodations at the hotel.

Split up among four villas, the Beasties would "go from room to room without using the front door," recalls Scott Koenig, who stayed with them for the first night. "They went through windows and side doors." They called room service incessantly with ridiculous requests. "Could you get me a glass of water?" one would ask. "Do you have a jockstrap?" another chimed in. On their second night, they borrowed the hotel's Rolls-Royce—charging it to the TV shows, of course—dressed up in suits and went to fast-food drive-ins, ordering burgers from the sunroof of the car.

By the end of the night, "it looked like a tornado has passed through" the rooms, Sean Carasov recalls. The next morning the Beasties "got dragged down" to *American Bandstand* for a full day of activities. "Everyone was looking really bad," recalled Carasov of the group's hungover state. The Beasties made it a point not to censor themselves, though. They insulted the makeup woman, who unbeknownst to them was also Dick Clark's wife, and stole a cordless microphone. (Later on, they sent flowers to Mrs. Clark, with a note of apology.)

The *Joan Rivers Show* went better, because she, like Yauch, was from Brooklyn. Nonetheless, they sat on her desk and backstage gave her husband a book on female orgasms. (Rivers must have enjoyed herself, too, because she thought the boys were "adorable," as she wrote to them in a personal thank-you note two weeks later. "Please come back and throw more ice cubes. Love and Kisses.") Toward the end of the day, the gang couldn't wait to get back to the luxurious villas. But when they got to the Marquis later that evening, the found that the hotel had packed all of their things and moved them into the balcony rooms surrounding the swimming pool. "We were so upset that we had been downgraded," says Sean, "that Yauch actually threw his balcony furniture into the pool."

•　　　　•　　　　•

Public Enemy's *Yo! Bum Rush the Show* album was finally on the calendar for March of 1987, and to create the artwork for the cover, Hank and Chuck met with photographer Glen E. Friedman and graphic-designer/graffiti-artist Eric "Haze" Lieber. They wanted the artwork to be as urgent as the sound of the group. Friedman shot the famous photo of the group, gathered around a large map spread out on a table, using a low-budget camera requested by Rick Rubin, who wanted the cover to look "grainy." "I knew that shooting PE's first album cover was gonna be like shooting the Clash's first album cover," says Glen. "To me, this was the first overtly political hip-hop group."

Haze was then enlisted to art-direct the cover. He sized and cropped the photo and typeset the lettering of the group's logo—all by hand—with the line "the government is responsible" running across the bottom of the cover. He finished the work, but had to show it to Simmons and Rubin separately. They were so involved in their own projects—Rubin with hard rock and Simmons with R&B—that they hardly came together to discuss the projects they had signed together.

As *Licensed to Ill* continued climbing the charts, the potential for some kind of endorsement deal seemed unlimited. Adam Yauch, an avid skater, suggested creating a Beastie Boys skateboard. Lyor liked the idea and hired Haze to design a sample board to present during The Action Sports Trade Show which coincided with the Beasties' stay in L.A. on January 24. Haze was flown in to pitch the skateboard idea—along with friend and Def Jam messenger Dante Ross, who was also a skater and was familiar with the scene.

"Dante was sort of the mouthpiece, and I was the creative director," Haze recalls. They ended up getting strong interest from a well-known skateboarding company called Vision. When they got back to New York, Haze immediately began designing a prototype board. After about three different sampling processes, Vision, Rush, and the Beasties all agreed on a design. Vision was ready to offer Cohen a standard—but in his opinion, small—$15,000 advance. So he kept playing hardball, pushing for $20,000, and the negotiations dragged on.

But Lyor did help the Beasties set up meetings with a few film studios in L.A. to discuss a film project. Fox Studios and Scott Rudin Productions were the most interested in doing a film with the Beastie Boys, and a negative pickup deal was struck (this meant that an independently-produced and investor-financed project enters an acquisition agreement with a distributor for release of the picture). To be called *Scared Stupid,* the movie would show the Beasties' adventures in a haunted house—"a stupid-ass, *Nerds* kind of movie," recalled Simmons. "But it actually suited the Beasties." In true Beastie style, Yauch said to *People* magazine, "We're pretty confident that it really will be the greatest film anybody has ever made in the history of the entire world."

As *Licensed to Ill* began to explode—by early February, it climbed to No. 2 on the *Billboard* pop charts, right behind Bon Jovi's *Slippery When Wet,* and landed at No. 1 within three weeks—the Beasties' audience began to change from downtowners to suburban teens and some as young as twelve years old. This was amazing, given their "X-rated stage show." In Jacksonville, Florida, the Beasties' show got slapped with an X rating, which appeared on all of the posters and advertising, resulting in lower than normal attendance. "Someone got the idea that the penis actually was in full working order and would ejaculate all over the audience," recalls Sean Carasov. Those kinds of rumors contributed to the group ultimately getting banned at several venues.

In Corpus Christi, Texas, their show inspired a religious protest and in Louisville, Kentucky, the Beasties actually got arrested for obscenity. "We knew it was coming, 'cause I remember the lawyer being there," Carasov recalled. "The Rush damage-control team had to be ready to go into action at a moment's notice." Despite all the problems, there was never any discussion of making the show more tame—except for the beer-throwing being toned down a bit.

The onstage debauchery was a reflection of the action behind the scenes. When the crew stopped in Seattle, they booked themselves at the Edgewater Inn, a hotel that famously surfaced in *Hammer of the Gods,* the Led Zeppelin biography that became the Beasties' bible on the road. The Edgewater sat right on the bay, so lodgers were able to rent fishing poles and fish right out of their windows. By the time the Beasties arrived, the hotel was well past its prime. "The bay had been overfished and heavily polluted, so nobody was catching shit," Carasov recalled. But that didn't stop the Beasties. While on the phone, conducting business one afternoon, Carasov saw a piece of furniture floating by in the bay. Evidently, after attempting to catch fish out of their windows, the Beasties got either bored or frustrated and started throwing out furniture.

A few weeks later, the Beasties were invited to host MTV's "Spring Break in Daytona" special. MTV organized a contest in which the winner would be "kidnapped" and flown to Daytona for an all-access pass to a Beasties concert. The contest was rigged, however, because MTV didn't want the Beastie Boys to kidnap a girl; the Licensed to Ill Tour had had some problems with underage girls, and they didn't want to take any chances.

Now at the height of their popularity, the Beasties got MTV to rent them a private plane. "We had never seen such luxury," recalled Carasov. The entire gang, including Rick Rubin, Cey Adams, and Ricky Powell, was picked up in New York and flown to Pittsburgh on March 11, 1987. The Beasties then were piled into a minivan, wearing stocking masks, and driven to "kidnap" the winner of the contest from a local McDonald's. The winner was thrown into the van with the Beastie crew—while his brother, who had set up the whole fiasco, tried reassuring him that everything was going to be fine—and driven down to Daytona, where spring break was already in full effect.

"It was good old drunken revelry," Carasov recalled. "But the kid ended up being a dud." As part of the contest, the winner received a shirt that read "The Drunken Hero." But everyone ended up calling him "the drunken zero." The Beastie Boys weren't exactly having the best time themselves. "They were miserable and hating it," says Sean, even though MCA had the pleasure of judging the "Best Female Body Contest." They left early because of bad weather, and the "puking-drunk kids" who had overrun their tent.

The day of the MTV special, the Beasties were served with a lawsuit from Budweiser, who claimed their logo was being illegally used in the group's live show. Eventually, the Bud cans were replaced by

SUNNY BAK

The Beastie Boys perform during their infamous Licensed To Ill Tour in the spring of 1987. When they designed the stage production—with its giant inflatable phallus that emerged mid-show, along with a dancing girl in a cage and beer can props—no one at Def Jam predicted that such a large majority of their audience would be preteen girls, who came chaperoned by their parents.

replicas of Jolt, a new energy soft drink. The Beasties became inadvertent endorsers of another beverage company, Heublein, Inc., which distributed Brass Monkey, the full-strength, premixed cocktail to which the Beasties dedicated their "Brass Monkey" single, which hit No. 1 on the *Billboard* charts in April. As a result of this tribute, sales of Brass Monkey had more than doubled, and the consumers' traditional age expanded to include younger drinkers. Mike D. also started a bit of a trend with his Volkswagen hood-ornament chain. By April of '87, there were reports that hood ornaments were disappearing from foreign cars at wholesale rates; so much so that dealers started leaving the ornaments off cars until delivery.

The Licensed to Ill Tour returned to the Northeast on April 7, and Public Enemy, who were promoting their own album, *Yo! Bum Rush the Show,* were sent out to open for the Beasties on their dates in Passaic, New Jersey. Sean Carasov recalled that there was "really no camaraderie [between Public Enemy and the Beastie Boys], except for Flavor Flav, who partook in scoping out girls, drinking, and shit. PE were super-uptight and serious and kind of militant. We used to laugh at them because they had the S1W's that used to stand on the side of the stage with the fake Uzis."

Back home, Rick Rubin had been thinking about reorganizing Def Jam's new publishing company, Def Songs. He was well aware of the lucrative business of music publishing, especially now that the Beastie Boys were selling millions of records, but he didn't have enough staff to register each song. As a result, the rights to most of Def Jam's songs were still floating somewhere. "There were a lot of things done wrong," says Simmons. "But we had the *intention* to do it." So Rubin, at the recommendation of a mutual acquaintance, reached out to a recent NYU graduate and Columbia Records intern named Faith Newman.

Newman had almost accepted another job at Rush Management in March, and the day before her orientation there, she came back from class and found a note on her fridge that read, "Rick Rubin called." She thought that her roommate was playing a joke, but decided to call the number anyway. To her surprise, Rubin picked up the phone. "I've heard all these great things about you from Russell and people at Columbia," he said. "We want to expand Def Jam. Would you like to work for us?"

"I almost dropped the phone," Newman recalls. "Def Jam was the ultimate at that point." She immediately accepted the offer. "When can you come in to talk about this?" asked Rubin. "Today!" she said. Half an hour later, she was at Rubin's apartment on Broadway. He told her about the situation at Def Songs and the absence of a system for registering the acts' songs. "We don't really know what's involved," Rubin said. "We know you're smart and can talk to people and figure it out." They also talked about some of the new hip-hop records coming out. "I'm really kind of over that right now," he said of hip-hop. Rubin offered her a job at a starting salary of $18,000.

Newman was so pleased about the job that she didn't even tell her friends, for fear of jinxing the opportunity. On a Monday night at Nell's, a few weeks before she started her job, Newman had no doubt that she was part of the Def Jam family. Nell's was a white-hot downtown Manhattan nightclub that was the 1980s answer to Studio 54. It was where Simmons could most often be found. As Newman made her way to the entrance, where a huge crowd had formed, Simmons suddenly popped up behind her and said to the doorperson, future superpromoter Jessica Rosenblum, "Jessica, this is Faith. She works for me now, so make sure you always let her in."

As soon she started her new job, Newman became acquainted with one of the biggest administrative problems at Def Jam: None of the songs that Def Jam had recorded were registered with either the American Society of Composers, Authors and Publishers (ASCAP) or Broadcast Music Inc. (BMI)—the two largest performing-rights organizations. Working closely with the lawyers, Newman figured out how to register each song and even organized "a class trip" to ASCAP for the artists, so they could do all their paperwork. (Flavor Flav insisted on typing the lyrics himself. "Flav, just dictate it to me, and I'll type it out," Newman said. "Nah, G, I can do it," he said, typing with one finger.)

Registering a song was actually as simple as filling out a membership packet and paying $10 annually. It guaranteed that for each song, publisher and writer received a performance royalty for every calendar quarter. Def Jam had mostly overlooked registration for three years.

Because the staff still didn't have computers, all of Def Jam's records were masses of paper files. Newman also organized the entire filing system and created a tape library, which was kept at Chung King. She did all of this work out of a tiny office that she shared with Bill Stephney's assistant, Lindsey Williams. Next to them worked Stephney, George Sommers in administration, and Dave Klein, who handled promotions. "Nobody had real job titles," Newman recalled. "You had to make your own way, and that's how you survived and thrived." They worked without air-conditioning, despite the summer heat. When they took breaks to go outside, they were greeted with "the friendly neighborhood crackheads lighting up every day" across the street, Newman recalled. For lunch, she said, "The only place to eat in the entire neighborhood was NoHo Star."

Without enough desks to accommodate the entire staff, Dawn

Womack, the accountant, sat with the papers on her lap. There was no guarantee that if you left your desk for a few minutes, someone wouldn't be sitting in your place. The office was in such disarray that new visitors were often shocked. "People would come from all over the world, excited about Def Jam," Newman recalled. "And then, when they would come upstairs, they would be like, 'Oh.' "

Def Jam and Rush also received a constant stream of wannabe rappers. That was before Def Jam had installed a security door and Simone Reyes had to buzz in each visitor. One guy managed to get past reception, screaming about how Def Jam hadn't listened to his demo, until the police came and escorted him out. "It was the first time I ever saw someone put into a straitjacket," Newman recalled. "That was how fervent people were about Def Jam." Another kid wanted to be signed so badly, he would show up at the office nearly every day and leave Bill Stephney threatening notes to listen to his demo. Sometimes wannabe rappers would camp outside the office for an entire day with their demos.

Considering the type of neighborhood the office was in, it was remarkable how little attention was paid to security. One late night, a dead body was found in a barrel on the corner of Elizabeth Street and East Houston. The police came by to ask Heidi Smith if anyone at Def Jam had heard anything. Smith was hardly fazed. Back then, the scariest thing that could happen, she says, was if "the record would take a dive."

Fortunately, the hits kept coming. In May, LL's new single, "I'm Bad," hit the streets, with the album slated to hit stores in mid-June. The following week, before Def Jam even got a chance to ship it as a 12-inch, "I Need Love" got snatched up by radio.

To discuss the cover for *Bigger and Deffer*—art directed by Eric Haze—LL came over with E-Love to Haze's studio in TriBeCa to discuss some concepts and suggested that they do some graffiti-type lettering. But Haze insisted that instead of "break-beat-album-type artwork," they needed some "hard shit." He did not have a chance to listen to the whole album, but he went ahead and applied his concept.

A few weeks later, LL came by to look over the print proofs, rolling up to Elizabeth Street in his new red Audi 5000. Haze got in and listened to a copy of the album. Then he showed LL the cover. Shot by Glen E. Friedman, the photo had LL posing at night in front of a building (the light cast an eerie greenish tone, making the photo look more "street"), standing on top of his red Audi, leaning against a railing and looking confidently into the camera. He was wearing a black leather suit with a red Kangol and red Nikes. Haze used the same font for LL's name as the one used by Kool cigarettes, and in the bottom-right corner, he positioned the title of the album: *BAD* (for *Bigger and Deffer*).

"Yo! That shit looks like gettin' paid!" LL exclaimed with delight. It was, as Haze puts it, "the ultimate B-boy compliment."

Rick Rubin, who usually made it a point to be involved in his artists' artwork, was in L.A., focusing on his latest project: the soundtrack to *Less Than Zero*. He recorded a few new songs for it including: "In-A-Gadda-Da-Vida" with Slayer. Rubin also worked with Glen Danzig—a former member of the legendary punk group the Misfits, whom he met in L.A. through Glen Friedman—on the track "You and Me (Less Than Zero)." Glen Danzig had perhaps one of the most powerful, pure, yet underrated voices in rock—the kind of vocalist who could sing hard-core as well as he could probably sing opera. While working on the soundtrack, Rick seemed to have found his new musical soul mate in Glen and knew that he wanted him on Def Jam. Rick would spend most of the summer of 1987 working on Danzig's debut album.

Rubin also recorded a song called "Going Back to Cali" with LL Cool J, their first collaboration since *Radio* two years earlier. It would also be their last project together. Simmons also contributed to the soundtrack with his R&B artists. "I put a Juice record on there, which I still love," he says. "And the Black Flames record. Rick didn't think those records were good. I thought I made two good records, but no one played them." If *Less Than Zero* marked the final separation, genre-wise, between Rick and Russell, it also marked a major separation as business partners. "He was in L.A. making a bunch of rock 'n' roll records that had nothing to do with Def Jam," says Russell. "And I was making a bunch of R&B records."

Still, Simmons did sign a new rapper to a five-album deal with Def Jam on May 17: Nikki D. Once Simmons had finally gotten around to listening to her demo handed to him by Darryl Pierce and Dwayne Simon of L.A. Posse, he decided right away that he wanted her on the label.

Nikki D. had come to New York in October of 1986 with one dream: to become the first female rapper signed to Def Jam. Nikki—whose real name was Nichelle Strong (the *D* in her moniker didn't mean anything; she'd simply picked it because of rappers like Chuck D., and Schooly D.)—had been invited to New York by Dwayne and Darryl to record a demo after they'd heard the seventeen-year-old rap over the phone for them back in L.A. Arriving on a Greyhound bus with her best friend, Nikki took the subway out to Brooklyn, where the two producers lived. "Back then, it was like, 'You going to Brooklyn? Aight, good luck,'" she recalled. "We come out of the train station at Clinton and Washington: crackheads everywhere, drug dealers is everywhere, fiends is everywhere."

The girls stayed with L.A. Posse for about a week and eventually had to put all of their things in storage at Penn Station. But Nikki was more determined than ever to get to Simmons. "We'll just go find the clubs where Run-DMC is, and where Run-DMC is, there's gotta be Russell," the girls reasoned. Unable to get real jobs without a permanent address and after their luggage got stolen from Penn Station storage, the girls were homeless, sleeping in the World Trade Center, and even outside for a few nights. "The odd thing about that whole situation was, it wasn't scary," recalls Nikki. The scary part, she says, was not knowing when the big break would happen.

But when Dwayne and Darryl invited her to come to Chung King, because they had some spare time during the sessions with LL to work on her demo, Nikki jumped at the opportunity. In four hours, she recorded two songs.

MC Breeze—the rapper that Dwayne and Darryl had brought with them to New York—was also waiting for his big break. "How come this isn't my song?" he would ask each time he heard something new from the producers. "Sometimes I thought that Russell signed Breeze *not* to release Breeze," says Dwayne. "To keep the lanes open for LL," Darryl explains. Indeed, although "Popcorn" had been in prerelease through Columbia, and Breeze had actually received an advance, the 12-inch never came out.

By then, Nikki had moved to Queensbridge, crashing with MC Shan and his crew, whom she had met earlier during her nights of club-hunting for Simmons, and got a job in a video store that was constantly getting robbed. She kept in touch with L.A. Posse, hanging out at their house in Brooklyn on the weekends. One night, she and the guys returned home after a night out, and there was a message on the answering machine. "Yo, L.A. Posse, what's up, what's up! It's Russell! It's Russell! Yo, the tape, the tape of the bitch you gave me. The bitch is dope! I wanna sign her!" Nikki D., the "bitch" that Simmons was ranting about, was listening to the message in stunned silence. Then another message followed. It was Russell again. "Yeah, what the fuck? Why no one fucking call me back yet? Oh, yeah, by the way, the bitch's name! She says her name fucking ten times in a song. Bitch name . . . Nikki D.! I wanna sign that bitch!"

Simmons was at Nell's that night, hanging out with his best friend, Andre Harrell, who was now working at MCA Records. The Beastie Boys were also there, back in town from their Licensed to Ill Tour. "She's dope, she's def," Russell started telling everyone, when Nikki came down there with L.A. Posse. "Spit something, Nikki D.!" She did, and everyone was impressed. Being homeless, broke, and hungry finally had its payback. "I went from high school on a wild-ass mission, a goose chase if you may, a needle-in-the-haystack," she says. "And it worked."

In mid-May the Beasties were back on the road, this time on the European leg of the Together Forever Tour, coheadlining with Run-DMC. Adidas, which by then had a line of Run-DMC gear and shoes, sent out the head of their entertainment division, Angelo "Jumpers" Anastacio, to join them on the road full-time. Anastacio presented Run-DMC and their crew with giant, shell-toe Adidas gold sneakers on rope chains. DJ Hurricane turned his into a ring, which would come in handy during a fistfight on one of their European dates.

"For the most part, Europe was thoroughly unenjoyable for everyone," recalls Sean Carasov. At the Paris show, someone ran out of the audience and onto the stage, and one of the Run-DMC crew "cracked" him. "And bedlam broke out," recalled Carasov. The crowd rushed the stage, someone set off a tear-gas grenade, and everyone had to run down to the dressing rooms and lock the doors. Keith Haring, who was in town, was also in the dressing rooms with them, as was Ad-Rock's father, and they stayed there for two hours. The crowd had evidently turned over their tour bus and set it afire.

But for sheer insanity, nothing topped the performance in the blue-collar hometown of the Beatles, Liverpool, England, on May 30. The show was at an old, double-decker theater, and the security was so minimal that anyone could come in with alcohol. When the Beasties got onstage, the lights were so bright that they couldn't see the crowd. By the second song, the audience started pushing against the barricades and the security. Suddenly, the crowd started spitting at the stage. Apparently, it was a sign of respect in parts of England. "People were throwing chairs off the balcony on the people below," Carasov recalled. "I think it was a soccer thing." By the third song, cans started flying out of the audience and onto the stage. Then bottles. "Adam stood on the stage with my baseball bat, taking swings at cans coming onto the stage," recalled Sean, "and batting them back into the audience."

"We got out the back of the building, got on the bus, and we didn't even go back to our hotel," recalls Sean. "We hightailed it to London. We just wanted to get the fuck out of there." So they sped out of Liverpool back to London, on a four-hour drive. But when they got to London, the adventure wasn't over. In the middle of the night, the cops came to arrest Ad-Rock because a girl in the audience said that one of the cans he'd thrown had hit her in the head.

"He was just kinda in shock," remembers Sean. Horovitz was forced to go back to Liverpool, where he was put in a local jail. Carasov stayed in the UK with Adam, while everyone else flew back to the States. (Adam would have to return for the trial on November 12, and eventually the charge was dismissed.)

The endless touring was starting to affect the Beasties's morale and soon they would have no choice but to step away from the group—and Def Jam.

Part Two

Growing
Pains

1988–93

CHAPTER 7

Together Forever?

O n June 15, 1987, LL Cool J's sophomore album, *Bigger and Def-fer,* hit stores. Nine months earlier, LL had promised L.A. Posse that he was going to use only the tracks they worked on together. He stuck to his word. "Those twelve demos became an album that sold three million records," Darryl Pierce said. "He hasn't sold that many records since."

With the release of the second single, "I Need Love," which be-came a "giant, crossover single" for Columbia, Jeff Jones recalled, LL was finally becoming the star of his dreams. The single would become the first hip-hop record to hit number one on *Billboard*'s R&B charts.

Right before he had to hit the road for The Def Jam Tour '87 on June 17, LL shot a video for "I'm Bad." Because LL had never had a video from *Radio,* this was the first time that the world was truly get-ting exposed to the charisma, the sex appeal, and magnetism of LL Cool J. The video was a perfect capsule of LL in 1987: Nike track suit and sneakers, Kangol hat, a single gold rope chain, muscular physique, and pure energy. LL practically jumped off the screen.

By then, the Beastie Boys and Run-DMC were back from the Eu-ropean leg of the Together Forever Tour and were about to take off on its American leg. It was Cohen's ambitious idea to have two tours run-ning out of Rush at the same time. The strategy was essentially to squash any competition, like the Salt-N-Pepa and Heavy D. tours.

"There was nowhere for them to go," says Tony Rome. "We had the country on lock. You couldn't get a building, you couldn't promote around us, because [one tour is on] one end of the country, and the other's on the other end of the country, but we cross-collateralized the promotion."

"Don't let him turn into another Kurtis Blow," Simmons warned Rome, who was sent out on the tour as LL's road manager. "Kurt was Russell's first artist, so he felt like, if it wasn't for him, none of this would be in existence," recalled Rome. "Kurtis let the money change him." (Rubin's dislike of Blow during that time—he once called him a "lying thief" during an interview—put a strain on his relationship with Simmons, who defended his first artist.)

Joining LL on the road were Public Enemy, Whodini, Stetsasonic, Eric B. & Rakim, and Doug E. Fresh. Everyone gathered at Elizabeth Street on the first day and piled into one bus that took them to Virginia, where the individual buses were waiting. The groups caravanned in the order of the lineup. LL's bus would come into town first, and it had "a halo over it," recalls L.A. Posse's Dwayne Simon, who rode on Whodini's bus and was the group's stage manager during the tour. "[LL's crew] could do nothing on that bus. They had to be quiet, they couldn't drink beer, smoke cigarettes," Simmons recalled.

Darryl Pierce, who rode on LL's bus and joined the tour as Whodini's DJ, used to run over to Whodini's bus and ask for a cigarette or a beer. Whodini's bus, which followed LL's, was "a young man's dream," says Darryl. "Condoms on the floors, girls' panties hanging out the windows, weed smoke," recalls Dwayne. "It was the craziest bus!" No one was a more prolific prankster than Whodini's DJ, Drew Carter. He liked to call the airport or hotel where the group was staying and ask to page various individuals. "Will you please page Mr. Cox," he would ask. "Mike Cox, please come to the baggage area." Or: "Mr. Meyoff, Mr. Meyoff, you have a call. Mr. Jack Meyoff, please pick up the security phone."

Eric B. and Rakim's bus, which followed Whodini's, had "bullet holes in the back of it," says Dwayne jokingly. "They was raw, they was from the hood." Public Enemy's bus had an even more serious vibe than LL's. One day, LL and Dwayne got left behind in Baltimore and had to ride to the next venue with Public Enemy. "When we got to the venue, I *ran* to my bus," recalls Dwayne. "It was just too much. S1W's practicing and kicking karate, and Farrakhan blasting."

The last bus carried the opening group, Stetsasonic. "Stetsa's bus broke down every hundred miles," says Dwayne. A homesick eighteen-year-old Prince Paul, Stetsasonic's DJ, was on that bus, usually writing in his diary. But the tour was an adventure. "Everyone was young, running around, and there really was no mother hen there," recalled Paul. "At times, it was like a big frat party." And like real frat boys, some of the guys on the tour got in trouble. "A very popular DJ" from one of the groups, recalls Paul, "almost got hemmed up on a rape charge." When a girl came backstage and asked for some passes to the show, the DJ told her that she would have to "do everybody in this room," recalls Paul, who was in the room. The girl agreed. A few hours later, the door burst open, and the cops ran in with the girl. "Are these the guys?" The cops pointed at Paul and his friends. The girl said it was someone else. "They finally caught homeboy, and he was against the wall, crying," Paul remembers.

When the Together Forever and Def Jam '87 tours crossed paths in Atlanta in July, LL suddenly got stage fright before his set. "Rome, I don't wanna go onstage, I don't wanna go onstage," he kept saying to Tony Rome. LL's nervousness was compounded because his crew weren't able to bring his entire set with them to Atlanta. "I don't have my set! What am I gonna do?" LL kept saying. The crew couldn't bring his entire set—a giant radio, two turntables, and a kind of rap castlelike structure—with them to Atlanta. "You gotta go back to what you first did, go out there and act like you don't have nothing, and you just trying to get on," Rome told him. That's exactly what LL did that night, delivering one of his best performances. "I have to take you both to dinner! It was just so incredible!" Lyor gushed to Rome after the show.

•   •   •

After his "working vacation" in L.A.—recording the *Less Than Zero* soundtrack and Danzig's album—Rick finally came back to New

York in August of 1987. To cap off the soundtrack, Rick asked for a track from Public Enemy. At first, Hank and Chuck submitted "Don't Believe the Hype," but Rick thought it didn't fit. So they recorded a new song, "Bring the Noise," which Rick loved.

"It was the most unusual soundtrack I've ever worked on," recalled Peter Fletcher, who was Columbia's West Coast product manager. Columbia planned a big single and video for the Bangles' cover of "Hazy Shade of Winter," shot in downtown L.A., as well as a good-size print campaign and radio buys. As with most of the records he produced, Rubin was specific about his ideas for soundtrack cover art.

He didn't like the advertising campaign for the film and didn't want any reference to *Less Than Zero* on the soundtrack's front cover. Rubin convinced the studio, Twentieth Century Fox, not to use the image that appeared on all the posters and press—of the film's star, Andrew McCarthy, standing poolside—for the soundtrack. Fox agreed to make an initial run of the soundtrack with a different photo of McCarthy, with no type. The only mention of the movie was on a big sticker with the title that was put on the front cover.

Def Jam shot another video for the soundtrack; this one was for LL Cool J's "Going Back to Cali," which Ric Menello directed. The look of the video was so stylish—Menello overexposed the black-and-white film to create a kind of hot, balmy effect—that Columbia used stills from it for a reprint of the 12-inch single. Unfortunately, one of the girls dancing in the video turned out to be a minor and had inadvertently flashed her underwear in one shot. MTV refused to air the video until Columbia put a moving box over the girl's body.

Rubin didn't come back from L.A. alone: he brought his new girl-friend, former porn star Melissa Melendez, whom he met at a party in L.A. through her porn-star roommate Lois Ayers, who had been hired for *Tougher Than Leather*. A dark-haired Latina, Melendez started in porn in 1984 and retired in 1987 after fifty films, because Rubin "wouldn't have it," recalled Adam Dubin. Her porn career was a constant source of amusement for Rick's friends, who got a kick out of being able to hang out with her and then rent one of her videos.

"She was really ballsy, just didn't care what anyone thought about her. A real rock chic, too," recalls Faith Newman. Unlike Rubin, Melendez liked to go out. Sometimes Rick would send Melissa out with Scott Koenig and his friends. They would hang out at 428 Lafayette Street nightclub, which belonged to Rick's friend John Sidell, who was married to actress Rosanna Arquette. At some point, the Beastie Boys decided they didn't like Melendez and thought she was "bad news," according to Scott Koenig, because she was taking Rubin's attention away from their group.

Even though he lived at 298 Elizabeth Street, Rubin was hardly seen at the office. He did, nonetheless, show some concern about the state of affairs at Def Jam when he promoted Faith Newman to director of A&R as well as the business manager. "There was no business foundation to the company," Newman recalled. There were no formal contracts with producers, writers, session musicians, because most deals were done on a handshake.

One of the reasons for the office disorganization was the hectic touring schedules for all of Def Jam's and Rush's acts. The market was strong, and in October, Def Jam's R&B stars—Chuck Stanley, Tashan, Alyson Williams, and Oran "Juice" Jones—were sent out on the road for the Soul Songs Tour. Since the music was driven more by radio than the streets, Columbia and Def Jam wanted to make sure that there would be strong tie-ins at local radio stations.

Tougher Than Leather had finally been edited, a process that seemed to drag on forever. One of the editors was fired early on because of his lack of experience; he, in turn, "borrowed" some of the footage and refused to give it back until he was given more money. "It stayed in postproduction for a very long time, because it kept being edited," points out Ric Menello. "So the film lost a certain coherency as a result."

According to Simmons, Def Jam wasted a lot of money on the film. "It was a three-hundred-thousand-dollar movie; cost a million dollars," he pointed out. Finding a distributor turned out to be a "hell of a time," says Russell. "They didn't want to buy the movie— hell, no. There was no way to make it better or worse for them." By the time the film was finally sold to New Line for $750,000, Rubin could care less about its outcome and "really abandoned [it]," said Adam Dubin.

But Rick was proud of the *Less Than Zero* soundtrack, which was released in late December and declared "one of the most influential records" of the year. "*Less Than Zero* was Rick Rubin, all of those different kinds of records," points out Russell. While the film all but disappeared from theaters, the soundtrack stayed on the charts. But it didn't reach platinum, as Rubin had hoped, perhaps overshadowed by another huge soundtrack that year for *Dirty Dancing*. Rubin pointed the finger at Columbia and felt that another project had fallen by the wayside in the corporate system.

But there were platinum records. In fact, two of CBS's three topselling 1987 releases came from Def Jam: the Beastie Boys' four-times platinum *Licensed to Ill* and LL Cool J's *Bigger and Deffer*. This kind of profitable year would not be repeated again at Def Jam Records until ten years later. Ultimately, neither Rick nor Russell was able to bring any significant success to Def Jam with their respective "pet" genres: Rick with heavy metal and Russell with R&B. Perhaps it was because Rick and Russell really did need each other's genuine support to be able to push their product.

•   •   •

Def Jam celebrated its banner year, 1987, by throwing its first Christmas party, complete with cases of Olde English malt liquor and White Castle burgers. "The vibe was old-school, no bling-bling," recalled Lindsey Williams, former promotions assistant. Def Jam's Christmas parties would become legendary. "[It was] the right mix of people, the right DJ, just the magnitude of it," recalled Tracey Waples, a former Def Jam A&R and current VP of marketing. Not just all-access—with hip-hop celebrities of every kind rubbing shoulders in the huge ballroom—they were all-*excess,* as liquor flowed freely at the all-night open bar. Over the next few years, the Christmas parties would be held at locations like South Street Seaport, Bryant Park, and Bridgewater's downtown. The holiday party would become Def Jam's all-out event, complete with unique invitations, like one stuffed into a pillbox ("for stress relief" read the container), or shaped like a 7-inch record the following year. Even in the cold of winter, people were willing to wait in a line that often stretched around the corner of the building to get into the party. "It was a good feeling being able to cut that line," Waples reminisced. For the staff, the parties were an opportunity to put aside any differences within the company and bond.

Over at the Black Rock building, CBS Records was having a celebration of its own. After more than a year of negotiations, the record label had been purchased by the Japanese technologies giant Sony for a whopping $2 billion in January of 1988. The sale was the biggest industry news of the year. "I think people were excited about the possibility of being owned by Sony," recalled Jeff Jones, who had been the product manager for Def Jam's releases for three years. "Sony was a cutting-edge, smart company." Since Sony was acquiring 100 percent of CBS Records' assets, including all personnel, there would be some streamlining. Al Teller, the president of Columbia Records and the man who had green-lighted the Def Jam/Columbia venture, was rumored to be leaving.

In the wake of the sale, Def Jam was forced to reexamine its own structure. Although the records were selling—8 million within two years—the company didn't feel unified, organized, or motivated. The basement studio that Rubin had sunk so much money into was still unfinished, moldy and perpetually flooded because of bursting pipes. After a while, expensive studio equipment that was stored there started to disappear, but Rubin didn't seem to care. He had become distant—from the company and hip-hop in general. By January of 1988, he had signed two more hard-core acts to Def Jam: Danzig and Masters of Reality, as well as raunchy comedian Andrew "Dice" Clay. He still lived at 298 Elizabeth, but he was hardly seen by the staff.

Russell Simmons was in another world, filled with R&B music, downtown nightlife, and pretty women. He even had his own letterhead—"Russell Rush Associates"—as if promoting himself separately from Def Jam and the management company. Now thirty years old, Simmons was becoming more sophisticated; he had dumped his Queens girlfriend and was now dating actress/model Marita Stavrou. Like Rubin, Simmons worked almost exclusively out of his home, at 111 Barrow Street, a building filled with sprawling lofts and enormous twelve-foot ceilings, on the corner of Greenwich Street.

When he wasn't holding meetings directly in his apartment, Simmons communicated with the staff mostly via speakerphone. Like a true bachelor, he had decorated his apartment sparsely. Apart from the typically eighties lacquer bedroom set, there was not much except dozens of gold and platinum records adorning his walls. Mac, Simmons's assistant and driver, was the only other permanent "accessory" in the apartment, where he slept in a loft bed. He was a necessity because Simmons still hadn't learned to drive.

"I got the feeling that he didn't want to be bothered with the minutiae [of the company]," recalled Faith Newman. One day, during one of her frequent meetings at his house, Newman opened Simmons's freezer to get ice cubes and noticed several strange red packages. "What's this?" she asked. "Dust," Russell replied matter-of-factly. "Dust" was angel dust, the narcotic he had been smoking for years and continued to indulge in occasionally. Also known as phencyclidine (PCP), it was originally developed as an anesthetic and was known to produce a feeling of being "stuck" or "lost in the sauce." Although he wasn't advertising it to the staff, Simmons didn't seem to mind if some of them knew about his habits.

Simmons's drug use was not purely recreational; it was also a form of stress relief. Besides his splintering business relationship with Rubin, he was also concerned about the slowing momentum of Run-DMC's career. The lawsuit with Profile Records to get the group over to Def Jam was holding up Run-DMC's latest album, *Tougher Than Leather.* The suit had been dragging on for almost two years, and some put the blame on Lyor Cohen's tough bargaining style. Sometimes, his negotiations would stretch on for so long that deals—like the one the Beastie Boys had almost had with the skateboarding company Vision—fell apart.

Run-DMC's lawsuit with Profile became a terrible strain on all involved, but especially on Run. Usually lovable and entertaining, he became depressed and even talked about suicide. "He thought somebody put a spell on him," recalled Bill Adler. Simmons and Cohen were "trying to keep him from killing himself," said Adler.

It was also unclear when LL Cool J's next album would be coming out. Ever since he'd returned from the Def Jam tour in September of 1987, LL had been in the studio with L.A. Posse's Darryl Pierce, working on what would become *Walking With a Panther.* Dwayne Simon, the other half of L.A. Posse, chose not to take part in the production because of contractual issues. For LL, 1988 would be a year of decadence. Distracted by his new wealth, LL spent recklessly. During a stop on the Def Jam '87 tour in Maryland, he purchased a BMW on a whim, adding it to a growing collection of cars that included a Porsche and an Audi. "I had one for every occasion," he recalled. He had a $15,000 ring that spelled out his name across four fingers in diamonds.

LL's career seemed to be misguided by his manager/father, Jimmy Nuña, whom LL "let just run rampant," recalled Dwayne Simon, "spend[ing] his money in the way that he wanted to spend it." LL knew that his father was a troublemaker—"he liked to smoke weed, get into fights, and curse people out," as LL himself recalled in his biography. The trouble Nuña liked to cause affected his son directly. "He wanted his father, so you couldn't tell LL anything," said Faith Newman. "He had to figure it out on his own."

In contrast to LL—who was professional and "always a dream to deal with," as Newman recalled—Nuña constantly got into conflicts with people and burned bridges. Once, during a meeting, Nuña threw some change at her, called her "honey," and asked her to get him a soda. "I don't do that around here," she retorted, and threw the change back at him.

"LL stopped trusting us and having confidence in us," Cohen recalled. "He completely submitted to his father during that period. [Nuña] was extraordinarily mean-spirited, calculating, disrespectful and not particularly bright or savvy. It was all about pushing that button of LL's, that insecure button."

Rubin and Simmons hardly took meetings together anymore, making many company decisions without one another's consent. The lackadaisical approach to business at Def Jam, and the absence of a strict division between the label and Rush Management, a problem that dated back to 1985, affected the staff's morale. Bill Stephney thought that Def Jam was "in a state of total disarray, complete with a 'fuck it' attitude toward management, administration, signing, spending, hiring, artists, and teamwork," as he wrote in a letter to his bosses on January 30. Stephney felt that neither Rick nor Russell was interested in being a leader at Def Jam, being too preoccupied with making money, producing records, and promoting themselves. "Al Teller doesn't make records," Stephney pointed out, "he runs a record company. It is a full-time job!" Furthermore, the office in which the staff worked, 298 Elizabeth Street, was an "unacceptable" and "atrocious" work space, wrote Stephney.

"Anybody could come in at any time and see anybody," recalled Tonya Pendleton, who worked in Def Jam's national radio promotions. "Artists would come off tour, pull their bus up to [the office], roll in and roll out." There were not enough desks for the staff, no weekly meetings, no benefits or incentives. With the absence of any real management, hiring decisions were made haphazardly; no real job descriptions were given. "People are being hired because they were cool, not because they are capable," wrote Stephney.

The sharp division of genres at Def Jam was further complicating things and creating a distance between Simmons and Rubin. "We can no longer operate as two labels with the same bank account: Def Records, the rap/hard rock side run by Rick, and Jam Records, the quasi-R&B side, which is Russell's baby," wrote Stephney in his memo. A good example of this genre division was the 12-inch release of Public Enemy's "Bring the Noise" and the Black Flames' "Are You My Woman?" from the *Less Than Zero* soundtrack in January of 1988. "Russell's project [the Black Flames] was on the A-side and Rick's project was on the B-side," as Chuck D. pointed out. "And [rap] DJs rushed immediately on this 'Bring the Noise' shit."

It was no surprise that while Rubin was busy working with rock and Simmons was preoccupied with R&B, hip-hop artists that had been signed over the past year were forced to sit on the shelf. There was Nikki D., who had been signed since May of 1987, but still hadn't started recording her album. Original Concept, Doctor Dre's group, still hadn't delivered an album, a full two years after their well-received "Knowledge Me" single. Rubin explained that the single was "spectacular," but that none of the material they had recorded later was as good. There was also Slick Rick and his debut album, which was nowhere near being finished.

Then there was Def Jam's "always-tight money situation," as Stephney wrote, a result of millions of dollars being spent indiscriminately, "just people charging up a lot of stuff," Faith Newman recalled. Tashan, for example, spent $100,000 to make an album that sold only fifteen thousand copies. That album, *Chasing a Dream*, released in September of 1986, did not make the kind of impact Russell had hoped for. "I loved Tashan," Ralbovsky recalled. Unfortunately, there was only a small market for that type of soul singer in the late '80s. Artists were given money with no guarantee that it would ever be recouped, which made Def Jam look like "a fine welfare system," as Stephney called it. The label was spending too much money on too many projects—a movie, a building, and a recording studio—all at once. "They looked like they were the biggest label in the world, and they were broke, the way they spent," said Scott Koenig.

There were also question marks hanging over the Beastie Boys' new album. The group had made the third-largest-selling LP of 1987, but Def Jam had no idea whether there was going to be a follow-up. Ever since their return from the Together Forever Tour in September of 1987, the Beasties had been pursuing outside projects. Mike D. started a group called Big Fat Love, lived with Sean Carasov on Barrow Street, around the corner from Simmons, and generally "sat around, got very drunk, did a lot of mushrooms, and went out constantly," Carasov recalled. Adam Yauch started a group called Brooklyn and did gigs at small clubs around New York. Adam Horovitz put music aside for a while and moved to L.A. to shoot his first big-screen starring role as a troubled teenager, who gets mixed up in a gang, for a film called *Lost Angels.*

"They were just on some Hollywood shit," recalled Dante Ross, who drifted away from the group at that point. Faith Newman thought the guys became jerks—"and they would admit it, too," she said. "They acted like privileged, bratty, entitled guys. They really believed their own hype." Finally, Simmons ordered the group to get in the studio and start working on a *Licensed to Ill* follow-up. But the Beasties resented being forced to make music; they wanted to record on their own terms. In fact, the Beasties had already been working on some new material, producing it themselves, but with no intention of playing it for Simmons or Rubin. Publicly, they did not display any ill will toward Def Jam, telling reporters that they hoped to have a new single out by the summer and an album by Christmas of 1988. They said they were "excited" about their new album, which would be similar to *Licensed to Ill,* but "on another level," they said.

Then Rubin—who was already estranged from the group—got word that the Beasties had been looking at offers from other labels, under the table. He was so shocked that he retaliated by telling the *New Music Express* that he wasn't sure "if they'll ever make another record." Def Jam also faced renegotiations of their multialbum deal with Columbia, but Simmons and Rubin couldn't seem to agree on the type of deal Def Jam should have.

Rubin wanted to take a small advance for the sake of independence and make most of the money on the back-end profits. Simmons wanted to get the biggest advance possible from CBS, forgoing royalties, by getting a pressing and distribution (P&D) deal, which meant that Def Jam would be given more autonomy and control of its life, while getting the highest profit margin. Essentially, CBS would operate solely as a manufacturer and distributor for Def Jam, buying its records wholesale and having Def Jam pay a distribution fee of about 20 percent to cover CBS's overhead, operations, and profit. Def Jam would be putting the remaining balance directly in its pockets. They would also have complete control of their marketing and promotion. Those kinds of deals, however, were rare between an independent label and a major distributor like CBS. Furthermore, Def Jam didn't have a big enough staff to do its own marketing and promotion. There was also the possibility of a joint-venture deal, which was similar to their current multialbum deal, but instead of Def Jam getting a royalty, they would become equal partners with CBS. The two companies would now be putting all the retail income into a joint account, then taking all the expenses of operations out of the account and splitting the remaining income, usually fifty-fifty.

It was becoming clear that if Def Jam was to survive into the next decade, it couldn't do it on record sales alone. There would have to be a major shift in management and structure to keep this record label from combusting.

•   •   •

Amazingly, none of the information about Def Jam's internal problems ever got to the fans and general public. Based on all the positive and prolific press on Simmons and Rubin in major magazines and newspapers—in large part, to the credit of Bill Adler's exhaustive spin-work—you'd never know that there was any trouble at Def Jam. There was Simmons in the industry trade magazine *Hits,* talking excitedly about the upcoming Beastie Boys record and making the disastrous *Tougher Than Leather* sound like a blockbuster. "I love this film," he gushed to *Hits.* "It's as fun as *RoboCop.*"

Furthermore, Def Jam was being challenged by a new crop of hip-hop labels that had also signed distribution deals with majors: Cold Chillin' Records, home to Big Daddy Kane, Biz Markie, and Roxanne Shante, had a deal with Warner Bros.; First Priority of MC Lyte fame had inked a deal with Atlantic; and Jive, whose roster included Whodini, had signed with RCA. The "Def Jam sound" that had so dominated hip-hop in the eighties was starting to become drowned out by newer, fresher productions. As black radio continued to roadblock rap—mix shows, regulated to the weekend after midnight, were still the primary slot to get rap records played—Def Jam had to compete that much harder within the hip-hop marketplace.

Simmons needed a "heavy" to keep Def Jam and Rush competitive and the staff on their toes. Lyor Cohen, twenty-eight, became that heavy—"somebody able to say no, somebody to yell, to take the heat," as Faith Newman points out. Walking around the office with a cigar in his mouth and a Run-DMC Godfather hat on, Cohen "was always the most entertaining," recalled Bill Stephney. Whenever the records were selling well, shows were selling out, or there was good publicity, Cohen would shout things like "We are winning by the largest possible margin!" while breaking into his own version of the Wop. "We are about to hit today, baby pop!" he liked to shout. Or, "It is time for us to get money!"

If Simmons was more of a visionary manager, Cohen was becoming known as the top direct rap manager, the best at taking care of details (or at least overseeing the details, as some have claimed that he relied heavily on myriads of assistants, such as Dante Ross and Big D.). "Even when he's having fun, he's probably still thinking of ways of making money," Sean Carasov pointed out. Cohen was so driven and almost machinelike that he seemed to have no interests outside the office. Once, Cey Adams discovered a collection of jazz and blues records at Lyor's house and was shocked. "You listen to music?" Cey asked. "Since when?"

A tough negotiator, Cohen would sometimes stay behind after shows to finish a settlement with promoters. During the Together Forever Tour, Cohen took his negotiating skills to another level. Some even claim that he went into settlements with a gun, but according to Tony Rome, "He's the most nongun person ever. Lyor's gun was his mouth."

Because the "normal, high blue-chip promoters," as Cohen puts it, didn't like working with hip-hop shows, he had to settle for shadier characters. "A lot of them put their pistols or machine guns on their desks to intimidate us," he recalls. "I wasn't so scared about the ones with the pistols. I remember there was one guy in the South that put his leg up and there was a huge knife stuck in his boot, right on his ankle—he scared me."

Going over each expense with a fine-tooth comb—sometimes for up to four hours—Cohen made sure that every penny was accounted for. "You had to be on top of your game to deal with Lyor," says Rome. Often, Cohen found mistakes in the numbers. "I don't even need you guys!" he would yell at the accountants. "I'll do this myself!" He was one of the first rap managers to front-load deals, which meant asking show promoters for payment up front. Cohen, however, "made promoters put themselves at risk," explains Rome. "After a while, I wouldn't let the artists enter the facility or allow the promoter to open the door until we had sorted out our business," says Cohen. "It gave us maximum leverage."

Cohen had hip-hop touring down to a fine art. "We never missed one performance," he says. "We never had a huge entourage, we were only five people—no security guards. We sold 360 degrees [of the arena]. We were always out of the building before the lights came on. We were so nimble and so crew-thin, we got on planes, trains, cars, limos. I would act as crazy and as psychotic as possible, slam and be gone, but ultimately we were back for the show. We were never going to put money above the kids who paid to see the show."

Remarkably, Cohen made time for a personal life and on April Fools' Day, 1988, he married a twenty-two-year-old model named E. K. Smith in a "true hip-hop wedding," guest Lisa Cortes recalled. Cohen picked Sosua in the Dominican Republic as the location, because this was where Holocaust survivors were first accepted. Eric Sermon—whose group, EPMD, had recently signed with Run's encouragement to Rush Management after the success of their independently distributed single "It's My Thing"—was sporting a white yarmulke at the ceremony, while Run had on a fuchsia one.

Noticeably absent, though, Rick Rubin, who didn't attend because he "hates weddings and funerals," as he put it. (He would also miss Simmons's 1998 wedding to Kimora Lee.) Cohen's wedding made it clear that Rubin had already separated himself from the family. "I felt like my role in working with the artists was changing," Rubin said. "Before, my role was more inclusive and I could really see my vision through. Once Lyor was involved, it just felt like that was less the case. I'm not really sure why."

Two weeks later, Al Teller was fired from his post as the president of Columbia Records. Rumors had been swirling about Teller's potential departure ever since the sale of CBS. Thirty-eight-year-old artist manager Tommy Mottola, whose company, Champion Entertainment, managed pop stars like John Mellencamp, Carly Simon, and Hall and Oates, was hired as the new head of CBS's domestic division on April 25, 1988. Mottola's history with CBS was well known: he was the protégé of Walter Yetnikoff, the most powerful man at the company, and the two shared an attorney, Alan Grubman. Yetnikoff had even tried to get Mottola a label deal at one point, but that fell through. But Mottola had never worked at a record label. Def Jam's fate was now in his hands.

The week of Teller's departure, Rush held a concert at the Apollo to raise money for Jesse Jackson's second presidential campaign. It was Bill Adler's idea to use a political event to market Def Jam and Rush artists, such as LL Cool J, Eric B. & Rakim, Public Enemy, Jazzy Jeff & the Fresh Prince, Stetsasonic, Whistle, and EPMD, who all performed during the fund-raiser. In charge of the planning was attractive thirty-five-year-old Carmen Ashhurst, who had recently come to New York from Grenada, where she'd worked for a nonprofit film fund.

"So, Bill, did you stick her yet?" Simmons was on speakerphone, as usual, asking Bill Adler a not-so-tactful personal question about Carmen Ashhurst, who was in the room. It was a conference call between them and Lyor Cohen, and Ashhurst's first introduction to Simmons. Having spent much of her career in a feminist environment, she was stunned, but decided to overlook Simmons's remark because she liked that Def Jam and Rush were a black-owned company and that "everybody was following this black person's vision."

In May, Cohen—impressed with Ashhurst's work on the Jackson

event—hired her as Adler's liaison during another Rush event: the Run's House Tour, with Run-DMC, Public Enemy, Jazzy Jeff and the Fresh Prince, Stetsasonic, and JJ Fad. The tour kicked off in North Carolina on May 26 and coincided with another Rush-produced tour, Dope Jam, which featured artists such as Eric B. & Rakim.

For Run-DMC, the Run's House Tour was a fresh start. Their lawsuit with Profile was finally settled in May of 1988. Although the group had accused Profile of ripping them off for $7 million, their contract had so many loopholes that they were forced to re-sign for another ten years. On May 16, Run-DMC finally released their long-awaited fourth album, *Tougher Than Leather,* but Run worried that he had "slipped," recalled Chuck D. The two rappers had bonded during the Run's House Tour. "[Run] damn near had a nervous breakdown that summer," Chuck recalled. "I was like, 'What are you talking about? You're doing great! You guys ain't slipped at all. If anything, you guys are better. To me, it's a better album than *Raising Hell.*' "

For Chuck, the tour offered a major discovery: "It was an incredible experience. Being on that tour showed us how a tour should operate: it has to be run from within, and the artists have to be very integral to tying a continuity of the tour together." What's more, all the artists got along like never before or since. "We all ate together, we rode together, we enjoyed working together, we enjoyed performing together," recalled Chuck. "We all supported each other after the we came off the stage."

Back at Elizabeth Street, the summer of 1988 was turning out to be hectic, and there was not enough manpower to handle the roster of twenty-seven Rush-managed artists, of which eleven were signed to Def Jam. Many of these were big names and required a lot of attention. There was Run-DMC, LL Cool J, Beastie Boys, Whodini, Eric B. & Rakim, Public Enemy, Jazzy Jeff and the Fresh Prince, and EPMD. And then there were the "baby" acts: Nikki D., Whistle, Davy D, Derek B, Original Concept, Serious-Lee-Fine, Law & Order, Cookie Crew, DST, King Sun–D Moet. There were only two full-time staff people to handle all of these artists: Lyor Cohen, Rush's chief operating officer, and his recently appointed right-hand man, Chris Lighty.

Lighty needed extensive convincing before he accepted his job at Rush. He had had success managing his own artists, such as De La Soul and the Jungle Brothers, who were part of the ever-growing Native Tongues family that was ushering a more edgy, soulful sound into hip-hop. "We were making money without the Rush logo, and so [Lyor] presented an opportunity," recalled Lighty. Cohen, it seemed, wanted to monopolize the hip-hop management market and needed Chris Lighty—and his artists—on Rush's side. Cohen called up Lighty one day to make an offer: "You guys should come and align yourselves with me." But Lighty resisted. "Why would I need Lyor?" he thought. "Lyor is a big, tall Israeli and looks like the evil empire."

But Cohen persisted. He said that Lighty should at least sit down with Russell, and a meeting was arranged at Nell's. Hip-hoppers like Lighty preferred grittier spots like Union Square and Latin Quarter. "Nell's was the weirdest fucking place he could have possibly decided to take me," Lighty recalled of his meeting with Simmons. "He had me in this fucking weird-ass room with weird people, snakes, and all types of bullshit going on. Russell's talking a hundred miles a minute." It wasn't Lighty's scene, so he concluded that Rush would not be his scene either. "I don't care if you're Run-DMC's manager, I'm not fucking with you," he said to Simmons, and left. A week later, he got a call from Cohen, who apologized for Russell's hyperactive behavior and the inappropriate meeting place. Lyor suggested they meet at the Elizabeth Street office. Once they sat down together, it didn't take long for Cohen to get Lighty to accept a job at Rush. In exchange for the opportunity to work with the biggest hip-hop artists, Cohen convinced Lighty to give up most of his standard 15 percent management commissions for an annual salary of $40,000. Cohen claims he had no ulterior motives. Convincing Lighty to take the salary "had nothing to do with 'I was gonna receive more money,'" Cohen points out. "It was just out of necessity. I lent artists so much money or would forgo commissions so often that no one was getting rich."

In lieu of commissions, Lighty received priceless management advice from Cohen. "Don't worry about the flash, worry about how much cash you got at the end of the day," Cohen would tell him. "Let's focus on building the company and making something out of it, and getting paid *that* way."

Cohen found that one of the easiest and fastest ways to get his artists paid was by setting up 1-900 numbers, which became an enormously popular marketing tool in 1988. Everyone from Santa Claus to Freddy Krueger had a 1-900 line, along with pop stars like Tone-Loc, Samantha Fox, New Kids on the Block, Bobby Brown, and Al B. Sure! Usually advertised during after-school hours on TV, these phone lines hooked young schoolkids, who called while their parents weren't looking and would often spend $20 on each $2-a-minute phone call.

In July, Rush created 1-900-909-JEFF for Jazzy Jeff and Fresh Prince at the peak of the duo's popularity and aired the commercial incessantly on TV. The 1-900 numbers made up for lack of rap radio play by giving the artists exposure and connecting them directly to their audience. Checks were flying in so fast that people would be neglecting to bring them over to the accountant, Bert Padell. "You go into Lyor's office, and all this paperwork would be on the floor, and there'd be checks all over the room for that 1-900 number: $130,000, $180,000," recalled MC Serch, who along with his partner, Pete Nice, had recently signed to Rush under the name Three the Hard Way, which would soon change to 3rd Bass.

Checks were also coming in from touring. "Because they had the biggest acts in the world, you could tour," Serch pointed out. "They had the biggest machine, so they could get you out, and they got you worldwide recognition. Because of Sony, they had successful places all over the world, so you could get promoted in Europe at the same time as New York. Touring was major: that's how you got paid!"

After three months and sixty-eight shows, the Run's House Tour concluded on August 28 in Virginia. By the end of the tour, it was hard to deny it: Public Enemy had become the hottest group in hip-hop, eclipsing Run-DMC. On August 12, they did their third performance in front of prison inmates, this time at Rikers Island. During the uplifting forty-five-minute set, the group played tracks from their second album, *It Takes a Nation of Millions,* which had already sold 750,000 units since its release in mid-July. Public Enemy were undeniable.

•   •   •

Nearly two years after production first began, *Tougher Than Leather* had its anticlimactic premiere in theaters in September of 1988. Carmen Ashhurst, fresh from her stint on the Run's House Tour, was immediately hired by Bill Adler to help with the film's premiere and party. When it opened, *Tougher Than Leather* seemed somehow surreal, frozen in time. The Beastie Boys, who played a new group and at the time of filming were yet to become stars, had already become superstars and moved on to a new record label.

That the film didn't go directly to video was a miracle. All the synergy that had originally been planned—with the *Tougher Than Leather* autobiography written by Bill Adler, the film itself, and Run-DMC's new album of the same name—never materialized. Rubin didn't even bother to attend his own premiere. The critics panned it. "Vile, vicious, despicable, stupid, sexist, racist, and horrendously made" was one typical reaction.

The list of offensive content was long. There was Rubin's generous use of the word *nigger.* "Never thought I'd die on account of a nigger," his character, Vic, says during his death scene. The nudity and violence seemed gratuitous. In another scene, Vic kills a man by firing a gun into his mouth. In an eerie foreshadowing of his future execution-style real-life murder, Jam Master Jay—who played an exaggerated version of himself—is threatened with a gun to his head and the words "I like you, Jay. I'm gonna kill you, but I like you."

Simmons thought the movie bombed because expectations had been so high. "Now I think it's great: it's kinda funny, it's charming, it's ridiculous," he said in the fall of 2003. "The only problem with *Tougher Than Leather* was that people were so excited, there was so much hype, and it kept getting delayed. So when they finally saw it, it wasn't a smart-budget, creative film. It was now expected to be something bigger." Others agreed. "The movie was corny, but if it came out when it was made, it would've been incredible," said Glen Friedman.

Despite all its flaws, Rubin saw *Tougher Than Leather* as a precursor to the "new wave of black films, like Spike Lee's, Hughes brothers'," he said. "In some weird way, that movie opened the door for this new kind of black film. The movie kind of took the Hollywood out of the independent black film." He also took pride in that the film had been made completely on his and the crew's terms. "It was *our* movie, even though it wasn't good," he said. And although it was a critical failure, *Tougher Than Leather* stayed in the black, grossing $20 million on a $2.8 million budget.

By then the Beastie Boys had accepted an offer from Capitol Records to sign for $3.6 million. "I remember feeling sad," recalled Rick of his falling out with the Beasties. "There was so much potential—I already knew what the next single off the next Beastie Boys album was gonna be and what the video was gonna be. The continuation of where we were and where we were going was very clear to me, and it was really frustrating that we never got to do it." "If you don't deliver your record a certain amount of time after your first record, they suspend your contract, and they don't pay you royalties," as Scott Koenig explains. "They hold everything up until you deliver that record. And they walked away from those royalties."

Rick was also walking away. "We'd been stepping on each other's toes a lot, kind of growing apart creatively, no communication," Rubin recalled. "I felt like my vision was being compromised and I was sure he felt like his was. It just made sense." Rubin suggested that they meet for lunch at the NoHo Star to talk about their inevitable split. "I was sad," Rubin recalled of the meeting. "I was thinking he might say, 'Cool, I'll leave.'" But Simmons had no intent to leave Def Jam. It was agreed that Rubin would still have a large stake in the company, but would separate himself creatively and as a manager, although the agreement was never formalized on paper. "Business never came first," Rubin explained. "Our focus was on doing good work and moving forward, not on looking back and signing documents and arguing."

The following week, they had a 3 a.m. meeting with Bill Stephney at a diner on Fourteenth Street to tell him about the split. "I felt like my parents were divorcing," he recalled of the news. "They had been fighting for years, and finally there was a resolution." No formal announcement was made to the rest of the staff or the industry, because "it was such an inevitable thing," says Stephney. "They had been so psychically and cosmically separated [for so long]."

Indeed, by the time Rubin and Simmons had their meeting, Rubin was already negotiating with Geffen Records president Ed Rosenblatt to start an imprint that Rick planned on calling Def American. Andrew "Dice" Clay, Danzig, and Masters of Reality—acts that Rubin had previously signed to Def Jam—would now be distributed through Geffen. Rubin had already been living in L.A. for at least a year, staying at a posh suite at the Mondrian hotel, while keeping his apartment in New York, and was completely bicoastal. Rubin found that he was in his element in L.A. He was hanging out at the Rainbow, spending time with the guys from Guns N' Roses, who were on Geffen.

Because the "divorce" between Rubin and Simmons was so stress-free and amicable, most of the staff and artists speculated that "Lyor was one of the big reasons that Rick left," as Glen Friedman pointed out. Chuck D. thought that Cohen and Rubin definitely had a conflict, with the two of them "trying to do not the same thing but *their* thing." While Rubin tried to push the art, Cohen's focus was on marketing and making the most money for the artists. "I think that the thing that also wore Rick out was that he saw no concern [at the label] for the elevation [of hip-hop]," said Chuck. "So he opted out. And I understood that."

According to Danny Simmons, the artistic conflict was really between Russell and Rick. "I've never known Russell to jump a whole lot of boundaries—his boundaries," said Danny. "Russell's thing is to perceive what is and gonna be mainstream culture, and he exploits it:

'If most kids are not gonna get it, you don't wanna be bothered with it.' "

Over at Columbia, reactions were undramatic. Ruben Rodriguez, Columbia's VP of Black Music, had no doubts that Simmons could run the company without Rubin. "Russell's been a winner since day one," he said. "Plus, the face of Def Jam was Russell. You never want to see a combination like that break up, but I didn't worry, because I felt Russell could stand on his own."

It's also possible that the individual differences that made the Rubin/Simmons partnership so dynamic in the beginning pulled them apart in the long run. As Carmen Ashhurst points out, "There was nothing about Russell that was a rocker, and there was certainly nothing about Rick that was from the streets of Hollis, Queens."

CHAPTER 8

Rush
Communications

When Rick Rubin left 298 Elizabeth Street for good in the fall of 1988, he didn't even bother to pick up his belongings. His entire apartment on the fourth floor remained untouched; the equipment that he had been setting up in the basement studio was abandoned. ("Every once in a while he would just give up on something," notes Scott Koenig. "Leave it for dead.") Rubin decided to start completely fresh and opened an office right in the heart of Hollywood, on the Sunset Strip, where he was planning on running his new label. Just as in New York, Rubin bought an apartment mere blocks from the office, also on Sunset—this time, though, it was a spacious two-story Mediterranean-style place. He was all of twenty-six. The possibility of replacing Rubin at Def Jam was never discussed. Simmons wanted to prove to his staff and to Columbia that he could run the company solo. "I made a lot of hit records before I met Rick," he said, confidently.

Besides, Simmons was getting a lot of help from Lyor Cohen, who was now working out of the second-floor space that was originally occupied by the squatter. Cohen was so busy that he never bothered to get a desk, opting instead to work from his big couch, littered with paperwork, or right on the floor.

Cohen took his take-no-prisoners attitude into the office when he started working full-time at Elizabeth Street. There was a tremendous "fear of failure," he says, in the wake of Rubin's departure, and Cohen didn't want to become known as the guy who sank Def Jam. On his ship, there would be little tolerance for sloppy work. "You were always concerned that [Cohen] would spot mistakes," Cey Adams recalled. "It wasn't uncommon for him to fling a project across the room if he saw a flaw in it. He had the worst temper back then."

Lyor could be tough and abrasive, but some thought the behavior was justified. "Lyor's a yeller, but when he *has* to yell," Tony Rome pointed out. "There's a soft-spoken side to Lyor that understands the artist and the artist's perspective. And he will definitely handle you with kid gloves." Sometimes to make his point to corporate executives who doubted hip-hop's potential, he had to use intimidation. "You can't have a bunch of pussies [running the company]," as Chuck D. pointed out. But if intimidation worked in the corporate world and on his competitors, it wasn't always effective on Def Jam's own staff.

"When I first met Lyor, he was a sweet, great, nice guy," recalled Glen Friedman. "But then, as soon as he became part of the management company and the groups started to make money, he was the biggest asshole I ever met. He treated everyone badly who was trying to work with the groups, who was trying to make fair money. I never forgave Russell in those years for having Lyor do his dirty work for him." Yet, despite his ruthless behavior, Cohen actually showed signs of vulnerability when he would ask a staff member, "Am I really a bad guy? What are people saying about me?" as Cey Adams recalls. Bill Adler was known to curse and praise Cohen in the same breath. "I love Lyor like a brother, but he has a treacherous streak," Adler would say.

In November of 1988, *The Great Adventures of Slick Rick* finally hit stores. It was long overdue. Slick Rick had been working on his debut album since November of 1986, but was "getting nowhere, and they were getting nowhere for a long period of time," recalled Hank Shocklee, who became privy to company details when he took over publicity at Def Jam while Bill Adler was on sabbatical writing his biography of Run-DMC in January of '87. Shocklee thought Slick Rick was a special artist who deserved more of Def Jam's attention. "You guys got Slick Rick signed—what are you doing with him?" Shocklee finally asked Simmons, who suggested that Shocklee should meet with Slick Rick. So Hank convinced Chuck to come out to the Bronx with him—where Slick Rick still lived with his mother—and talk to the young rapper. The meeting went well, and Slick Rick agreed to start working on some tracks with the Bomb Squad. Those tracks became "The Moment I Feared" and "Kit (What's the Story?)." Rick Rubin had also contributed production prior to his departure with the track "Treat Her Like a Prostitute"—although Slick Rick claims that Rubin's famous "touch" was not that impressive. "I think the words carried [the song] more than the production," he says.

Perhaps one of the reasons for the delay of Slick Rick's album was his sometimes unpredictable behavior which could make working with him difficult. One day, he walked into 298 Elizabeth Street, and after being unable to get the staff's attention, took out a pistol and fired three shots into the ceiling, yelling: "Attention, peasants!"

By that time Carmen Ashhurst had been hired full-time as an assistant at Rush, doing administrative work, and helping out in the publishing department by doing things like typing up lyrics for albums. Since Russell never came into the office and it was hard to get directions from him over the phone, Ashhurst suggested that she should just bring her computer to Simmons's house and work out of there. "Well, if you want to," he said. Although the apartment was hardly conducive to work—Ashhurst would often come in the morning to find guests from the previous night lying around the living room—she and Russell worked hard. For three hours straight, nearly every day, Simmons would call up radio programmers, dialing the numbers completely from memory. "He would just sit down on the sofa, get a bag of potato chips, and just call one right after another and pump them to play the records," Ashhurst recalled.

Simmons also made sure that Columbia's promotions staff were

GLEN E. FRIEDMAN

Slick Rick had a Dr. Jekyll and Mr. Hyde personality: one moment he could be jovial and carefree; the next, he could be firing a pistol into the office ceiling.

working hard to get Def Jam's records played. Usually on Wednesday evenings, he showed up at the Black Rock building—the day after radio stations decided which records they were adding for the week—to see how many ads Columbia had gotten for his artists, by sneaking a peek at a blackboard that was kept in the promotions department. Each time a radio station called in with an ad, the promotions director would put those call letters under the titles on the board.

This was still several years before the creation of Broadcast Data Systems (BDS), a sophisticated airplay measurement system, which used precise technology to monitor radio airplay in the 100 top markets in the U.S. In 1988, hip-hop promoters had to still rely on sometimes dishonest program directors to report how often their artists were played on the air, especially when these programmers were often bribed by industry executives and independent promoters.

"People began to realize that Russell was walking around and looking at the blackboard, and seeing that there were no stations on certain records," Columbia's former Core Marketing executive Karen Duran recalled. "They wound up moving the board to someone's office."

But keeping track of radio play was not Simmons's only problem. There was a structural disarray at Rush and Def Jam, one of the biggest problems being that Rush was using its money for Def Jam–related affairs and vice versa. "It's like they were all one," Carmen Ashhurst said to Simmons one day. "It's gonna get us into trouble after a while." The bookkeepers often complained about trying to keep track of the two accounts, because money was constantly being moved around from one account to the other. "No one paid attention to the comingling, because the attitude was, we'll do whatever is necessary to get the group out," Ashhurst explained. "No one had ever bothered to backtrack and fix the administrative glitches. People didn't get the corporate implications of what growing was."

Ashhurst suggested that starting a parent company for Rush, Def Jam, and other Simmons ventures would help business run more smoothly.

"And that's how we got Rush Communications," she recalls. Under its umbrella, Simmons would ultimately include all of his multimedia companies, including fashion (Phat Farm), talent management (SLBG), advertising (Rush Media), Music Publishing (Rushtown Music), Film (Def Pictures), Publishing (*Oneworld* magazine), Television (RSTV), and Philanthropy (Rush Arts). The formation of the parent company was a key step in Simmons's career, and would directly affect Def Jam's growth. Simmons was now getting closer to becoming the media mogul of his dreams.

For Def Jam, the birth of Rush Communications signified a more mature way of handling business, and the formation of more imprints. Anyone who knew Simmons was not surprised that his first choice for an imprint was an R&B-only label. After all, this was the music that he had loved long before hip-hop: the Chi-Lites and Delfonics were two of his all-time favorites. Simmons finally got the little label of his dreams. But he wasn't interested in the new jack swing trend that was happening in black music, with artists like Guy, Keith Sweat, and Johnny Gill. Simmons looked ahead by looking backward, into classic soul. He called his label Black Gold, signing Alyson Williams, Chuck Stanley, Oran "Juice" Jones, Tashan—all of whom had previously recorded for Def Jam—and a new group called Blue Magic. "We're splitting Black Gold off from Def Jam to develop a special aura for the artists and the label," Simmons told *Billboard* magazine in November. "Our artists' images will be very strong."

Faith Newman was promoted to Black Gold's A&R director, in charge of overseeing the label's debut album, Alyson Williams's *Raw, Gutsy R&B* (which was retitled *Raw*), set for January 1989, and the Black Flames's self-titled album. Marketing a mature R&B artist like Williams to a hip-hop audience would prove to be a challenge. Newman tried to give the Black Flames, for example, a fresher image, "young them down a bit," she recalled. But to her, the music spoke for itself and it was "dated stuff. It just wasn't what people wanted to hear at the time." But it was what Russell wanted to hear.

Meanwhile, MC Serch and Pete Nice of 3rd Bass were still waiting for their big break. Although some former staffers have claimed that the two didn't like each other from the beginning and were put together by Lyor, Serch and Pete insist that—while they did start out as solo artists—they teamed up in 1986. "Originally I went to Dante [Ross], through a couple of other people, and got him my tape," Pete recalled. "And that's when he hooked me up with [producer] Sam Sever." Sever had already worked on some beats with Serch and he played them for Pete. One night, Pete and Sam met up with Serch and Dante at the World nightclub, "and just kinda hit it off," recalled Pete. He and Serch started getting together and driving around in Serch's blue Ford Granada, which they dubbed the "think tank." There was no radio in the car, so the guys were forced to create their own music by freestyling.

Sam Sever encouraged them to become a group instead of continuing as solo rappers. "You guys should put your heads together and work together," he said. Finally, they decided to just go into the studio and record a few tracks. "I played the shit for Russell," Sever recalled. "He flipped and said he loved the shit." Sever also came up with an idea for the group name: Three the Hard Way. It was three, because Pete and Serch wanted Sever in the group.

"We presented the name to Russell, and he was like, 'Whatever,' "

Sever recalled. "He came back to me the next day—and this is Russell jacking an idea, because he's good at jacking an idea—and was like, 'I'm doing a Run-DMC movie called *Three the Hard Way.* You can't use the name.'" Sever decided that unless he could keep the name, he wouldn't stay in the group. So Serch came up with 3rd Bass instead, and it stuck. "Once I got down with Pete, it was definitely me and Pete—I loved that dude," says Serch. "I loved him like he was my brother. We were down for the ride."

Together, they got a management deal with Rush in the spring of 1988. But it would take a while for things to happen. Serch even sought advice from Mike D., who lived a few blocks from Simmons. One day, Serch was coming from Russell's house and decided to stop by Mike's house. "He gave me really good advice," recalled Serch. "And then he started to throw shit at me [from the window]. He was just being Mike D., doing it to be playing around. And he just had this big grin on his face. I was like, 'All right, later.'" The incident foreshadowed a war of words between 3rd Bass and the Beastie Boys on future records.

In the meantime, Serch and Pete hustled. "We did nothing but just be on the street," recalled Serch, "and make a name for ourselves, so that the label would finally do what they needed to do." They wrote for other artists, like Whodini, and hosted hip-hop showcases like the rap battle at the New Music Seminar in October of 1988. Pete hosted a radio show on Columbia University's WKCR FM 89.9, paving the way for future star DJs Bobbito and Stretch Armstrong and their famed underground show, *Stretch Armstrong/Bobbito Show.* At WKCR Pete met DJ Red Alert and gave him some promos of him and 3rd Bass's DJ, Daddy Rich, to play on KISS FM on Friday and Saturday nights. "When you don't have a record out and you got promos playing, that's like you've hit the big time," Pete explained. "That was impressive on the résumé at the time."

Still, the waiting was taking its toll. "It was fucked up—counterparts of ours were coming out, dudes we used to hang out with in Latin Quarter and the Rooftop, at Union Square," recalled Serch.

"Kid 'n Play went from being those dudes that we used to see at the Quarter to having a huge hit record. We were like, 'We're getting passed.' " Pete and Serch were so frustrated that they started taping their meetings with Cohen as evidence of his many promises to them. Still, Serch admits Cohen was doing his job. "He was trying to do what managers did: hype us, keep us motivated, and also get us prepared for what it was gonna be like if shit fell through."

With his mind heavily on R&B and building Rush Communications, getting Simmons to focus on signing a new hip-hop group to Def Jam was not easy either. "There was a point when me, Serch, and Dante and Sam, we were like at every club every night," recalled Pete. "Russell would always see us around, and he just kind of looked at us as crazy white boys." Simmons told them he thought that Serch was trying too hard to be a B-boy, and that their songs were not that great.

By then, Dante Ross had left Rush to join Tommy Boy's A&R department and wanted to bring 3rd Bass to the label. Arista Records, which had just signed the much hyped but failed Rush-managed act Serious-Lee-Fine, was also interested in 3rd Bass. Then smaller labels like Sleeping Bag also came calling. But nothing seemed to be happening. Perhaps it was Cohen's "very abrasive style," as Serch called it, which would alienate certain people in the business, or that 3rd Bass was a low priority for him. "He wasn't focused on us; we were his baby project," said Serch.

At one point, Serch and Pete were so broke that they sold Slick Rick promo cassettes that they got from the Def Jam office. They helped open mail for Slayer, who were still getting all of their mail at 298 Elizabeth Street. "We used to call up mad obscure girls in Ohio and be like, 'I'm Tom Araya from Slayer, thanks for loving our record,' " Serch recalled.

"Let's just put this out on Def Jam," Cohen finally said to Pete and Serch. He had heard enough of the material that the group had done with Sam Sever to see that they were worthy of a Def Jam contract. "We got your basic start-off Def Jam artist deal," says Pete Nice of their $150,000 deal. Indeed, a standard contract for a new artist on a label is really no different from any other entry-level job in the business. "There was nothing to write home about, but there were all the incentives in there. We had less than three points to split, plus recoupment."

Like many other rappers, 3rd Bass hired accountant Bert Padell, who also handled Simmons's finances. "You could always go up to Bert's office and there'd be some hip-hop character there waiting for some sort of check," Pete recalled. Padell also represented pop stars and Hollywood actors: Madonna and Robert De Niro were some of his more famous clients.

At Def Jam it was customary for artists to give up half of their publishing. Those were simply the rules—no exception. Under the guidance of their "piece-of-shit lawyer," as Serch called him, 3rd Bass decided to ask for all of their publishing. "We thought we were playing hardball with them," Pete recalled. But Simmons was not interested in negotiating; he said if they didn't give up half of their publishing, they weren't getting a Def Jam contract. Pete and Serch got creative. They found a pair of sneakers in a garbage can, put them in a brand-new shoe box, and delivered it to Russell's door at Barrow Street. "We're steppin'," the attached note read. (They had pulled a similar prank a few months earlier, when they left a box from Tiffany, where Pete worked as security guard part-time, with a pair of fake ears inside and a New Year's note: "Hey Russell. Happy No Ears.")

But Russell wasn't amused. Maybe their prank reminded him too much of the Beastie Boys' break from Def Jam, and the lawsuit he was about to file against their new label, Capitol.

Def Jam had already sued the Beastie Boys for breach of contract, and the Beasties had countersued. Simmons alleged that during their negotiations back in November 1987, the Beasties had demanded "three times as much money" for the new album. Five months later, Capitol Records went behind Def Jam's back and offered "to pay the Beastie Boys an advance which was far in excess of the amount which the Beastie Boys would have received from Def Jam," as stated in the $20 million lawsuit filed by Def Jam against Capitol Records on December 21, 1988.

Def Jam was asking for $5 million in actual damages and also asserted that Capitol was liable for punitive damages of no less than $15 million. Def Jam was also asking for possession of and rights to all "master recordings of the Beastie Boys' musical compositions, and all copies derived therefrom." Simmons didn't hide his feelings about the entire fiasco. "I hate this, I really hate this situation," Simmons said to a reporter. "I see Mike D. in the street and say, 'Hey, Mike!' and he just runs away because obviously he don't wanna talk to me." Rubin, looking back, blamed the deterioration of their relationship with the Beasties primarily on the poor advice he and Simmons received from their lawyers: "Things that we were told to do by our lawyers and businesspeople—they're common practices in the music business, but they're not common practices for being friends with people and working together and really set up 'us against them' kind of scenarios; really foolish and unhealthy."

The lawsuit was a sour beginning to the new year ahead.

•   •   •

Russell was also concerned about a few of his new releases in 1989. Slick Rick's *The Great Adventures of Slick Rick* was underperforming and *Walking With a Panther*—the album that LL had been working on since December of 1988—was still incomplete. Simmons knew that Def Jam needed a hit in the fourth quarter, the music industry's most profitable sales period. LL had tried producing the album himself, but quickly realized that he needed help. Simmons set him up with Hank Shocklee, who produced two songs, "It Gets No Rougher" and "Nitro," but they didn't sound like hits to Simmons.

"You don't have that big song!" he kept saying to LL. "You need the big song!" On a flight back to New York from Los Angeles, LL started writing *that* song as though "it just came to him divinely," recalled his former manager Brian Latture, who was on the flight. By the time they landed, LL had the lyrics to "I'm That Type of Guy" and wanted to record the song right away. Together with L.A. Posse's Dwayne Simon producing and Steve Ett engineering, LL recorded "I'm That Type of Guy" at the only studio they could find that night— Sorcerer Sound, which specialized in rock recordings, on Mercer Street in SoHo.

Simmons counted on *Walking With a Panther* going platinum and yielding radio hits, but felt that ever since the sale of CBS to Sony, Def Jam's albums were not getting enough "white sales." He was concerned that Def Jam was being "marginalized" under Sony's new structure, being delegated solely to the Black Music department. "We know that we also need the help of the staffs who work the rock and pop acts," Simmons wrote in a memo to Tommy Mottola in early February. "Def Jam does not just make Black music, we make hip music which appeals to a broad audience." Simmons wanted Def Jam to have the same treatment as the pop megastars on Columbia's roster, like Bruce Springsteen. Instead, he found that his staff was routinely not consulted on print advertising, commercials, and artwork pertaining to their artists.

Even as the nineties approached, rap was still not being taken seriously by the music industry. This was evident on radio more than anywhere else—especially on black radio, whose program directors thought that rap was "too black," as Ruben Rodriguez, the VP of Columbia's Black Music department, explained. Black radio was fond of dayparting hip-hop in the eighties, which meant that rap records were not allowed to be played before a certain hour. "It was hell," recalled Lindsey Williams of the hard time he had as a promotions assistant at Def Jam trying to convince black radio to play Def Jam artists.

Rodriguez had the tough job of trying to convince black radio to play Def Jam records at a time when these programmers "were older, they were conservative," recalled Tonya Pendleton, who helped promote records nationally for Def Jam. "Black executives back then wore suits; they were mature." In their world, Def Jam represented hip-hop, which "was really reviled by most urban professionals," recalls Karen Duran. "Many restaurants and clubs in New York didn't want us to come in with the Def Jam jacket. Jezebel on Forty-ninth Street, for instance, would not allow [us] to wear the jackets—even when Russell came in."

While Def Jam was trying to solidify its place in the new Sony system, Pete Nice and MC Serch of 3rd Bass, who became one of the first groups signed under the new Sony regime, searched for their own respect in the music community. At first, no one quite understood what to do with these two white rappers, "who knew nothing about the art of making records," said Hank Shocklee, who had been approached by Serch and Pete about producing a few tracks for their album.

3rd Bass was also paired up with producer Prince Paul, whom Serch already knew from hanging out at Latin Quarter. After his success producing De La Soul, Paul got signed to a deal with Rush Producers Management, headed by Lisa Cortes, and was given opportunities to produce for artists in the Rush stable.

Serch and Pete told Paul that they wanted to do their version of "Buddy," the famous posse-style cut off De La Soul's 1989 classic *Three Feet High and Rising*. After two sessions at Caliopee Studios on West Thirty-seventh Street, Paul produced a "Buddy" for 3rd Bass. It was called "Gas Face," and would become the second single off the album. "I don't think 3rd Bass was a priority for Def Jam," says Paul. "I think they cared about them, but I don't think they saw them as a supergroup." The majority of the production on *The Cactus Album* was done by Sam Sever. "It was very spontaneous stuff," Sam recalls of those sessions. "I didn't really know what being a producer was. I was just doing what I loved to do." (His work with 3rd Bass, however, eventually created a falling-out between him and the Beasties, who would have a conflict with Pete and Serch.)

Meanwhile, Def Jam's staff continued to expand. Twenty-two-year-old Bobby Garcia—known today as writer/DJ/sneaker aficionado Bobbito Garcia—was hired in early 1989 as a messenger, a position with a lot of potential for growth. Russell Simmons took a special shine to Bobbito, noticing his talents for promotion. Often, Bobbito would have to run to the store to buy Newport cigarettes and carrot juice for Russell. He called it "the grand paradox of Russell Simmons"—mixing healthy habits with unhealthy ones. Garcia, a graduate of Wesleyan University in Connecticut, would soon be responsible for creating Def Jam's first college radio department.

Also hanging around the office was twenty-one-year-old Steven Carr, a recent graduate of New York City's School of Visual Arts, and a childhood friend of Scott Koenig's. Carr had no other employed friends, so he relied on Koenig to buy him lunch almost every day. "The only other guy who was waiting for lunch was Cey [Adams]," Carr recalled. "We were both really hungry, and we didn't have jobs." One day, Carr got an idea: to start Def Jam's first in-house art department, and have Columbia pay for all the art. Adams thought it was a great idea, and together they wrote a proposal for Russell.

But getting him to sit down and talk about creating an art department at Def Jam was nearly impossible. He was relaunching Black Gold under a new name—Original Black Recordings (changed for copyright reasons)—and grooming his R&B stars. Russell was looking forward to the third album by Oran "Juice" Jones, *To Be Immortal,* and Tashan's second album, *On the Horizon.* But the press didn't seem as excited about these acts, focusing instead on Def Jam's state post-Rubin. One reporter even described Def Jam as a "seething rubble." The Def Jam logo was losing its potency, and CBS sent out an internal memo saying the company could no longer count on people buying Def Jam product purely on the strength of the logo. Carmen Ashhurst, now working closely with Simmons on developing Rush Communications, was concerned about the fate of the label. "If we [didn't] look like we could do this job, [CBS] was going to take advantage of us," she said.

Furthermore, Def Jam could no longer count on touring as a surefire revenue source. Ever since Eric B. & Rakim's infamous show at Long Island's Nassau Coliseum on September 25, 1988, when one concertgoer was killed and fifteen others were assaulted by gangs, venues, insurance companies, and promoters had gotten nervous about working with rappers. Trans America, a major insurance carrier for rap shows (without insurance, a show cannot take place), was considering a blanket ban on insurance coverage for rap shows, and taking "a long, hard look at [rap]," said a spokesperson. Managers and promoters got worried that the ban could signal the start of a trend among other insurance companies. "Any ban on insurance for rap shows would damn near close my company down," said Russell Simmons in *Billboard* magazine. Promoters would now be forced to tour acts outside of the country as much as possible, and rap artists would piggyback on rock groups if they wanted to tour.

By the spring of 1989, Def Jam had clearly outgrown its Elizabeth Street office. Because of the huge soundboard that had been installed by Rubin, Def Jam couldn't expand into the basement. The soundboard could not be removed unless the concrete outside the building was broken, which required a city permit. Instead of undertaking that, Def Jam decided to move to a loft space at 652 Broadway. There was just one problem: the building was exclusively an artists' live/work space, so Carmen Ashhurst had to convince its board that Simmons was also an artist—not a business owner. While they waited to secure the space on Broadway, which was "a lot of drama," Ashhurst recalled, Def Jam moved for a few months to a temporary office at 6 East Forty-fifth Street between Fifth Avenue and Madison, just a few blocks from CBS's building, Black Rock.

After numerous failed attempts, Steve Carr and Cey Adams finally got a last-minute meeting with Simmons in May to discuss their art department idea. They ran down to his home on Barrow Street, amateur portfolio and proposal in hand to convince Simmons that Columbia should pay him directly to create all the art, and to let Adams and Carr be the creative directors. "Okay, Russell, we want to do something!" Steve told him excitedly when they finally got to his house. "Shut up! Don't worry about it," Russell shushed, as he skimmed through the portfolio and proposal. "He couldn't have been turning the pages faster," recalled Carr. "Aight," said Simmons after a long pause. The word changed Carr's life. "It was staggering to me, because Russell did that stuff five or six times a day, where he just changed somebody's life," says Carr, who today is a Hollywood director of such films as *Daddy Day Care* with Eddie Murphy.

Simmons instructed them to see Lyor for the money. Lyor, incidentally, lived right upstairs from Steve Carr and his roommate, Scott Koenig, on Ludlow Street. Scott helped Steve get a meeting with Lyor, at 8 a.m. in Lyor's apartment. "So I get all dressed up, walk up the stairs to his apartment," Steve recalls, "and he's just coming out of the shower."

Carr was a little uncomfortable and suggested that they meet at a better time. "No, come over to me now," said Cohen. "Come sit. Tell me what you intend." Cohen sat down on the couch, his torso draped loosely with a damp towel, right across from Carr. "He's in a fucking towel, no shirt, his nuts hanging out the bottom," Carr recalled. He thought the look was all part of Cohen's negotiation tactic to intimidate and distract. Finally, they agreed on a budget and Def Jam suddenly had its own art department. Getting the job had been so stressful for Carr and Adams that they took off for a two-week vacation to California to visit the Beastie Boys.

When they returned in late June Steve and Carr discovered that the office had already been moved to the third floor of 652 Broadway. (The artists who lived and worked in the building "were pissed off," recalls Carmen Ashhurst. "Because obviously we were a business, and obviously Russell wasn't living there, and neither was Rick.") Carr and Adams got left with a tiny space that had no windows and just enough room for two chairs and a filing cabinet. They also realized immediately just how ill-prepared they were to handle the technical aspects of graphic design. So they hired someone who was more experienced to do most of the work. Once they learned all the design tricks they needed, Carr and Adams fired their assistant. At Def Jam, it was truly about survival of the most cunning.

The first six months of running Def Jam's virgin in-house art department proved tough on Steve and Cey. For one thing, their salaries were only big enough to cover bills and rent; Steve even considered moving back in with his mother. But more importantly, this was the precomputer age, so everything—from spec type to color—had to be done by hand.

For the most part, Cey and Steve had creative freedom, since neither Lyor nor Russell hardly ever stopped by the office. The occasional times when Lyor did pop in, it was either to yell about a job, or to share an idea, "which was equally bad," says Steve. "It was double the amount of work, no matter what. If he had a brand new idea, we'd have to sit there and try to make sense of what the fuck he was saying. 'You must do technetronic backdrop!' We're like, 'What?' "

But he does give Lyor credit for being "a very free thinker. I think he's really open, and he'll take chances. If that's the definition of creative, then maybe he is. He wouldn't care about the design; he wanted to make sure that when he was driving down the street, going forty miles per hour, he could see the name of the album. Which, in retrospect, was something he was right about." Simmons, on the contrary, "had a much more eclectic view of what stuff could look like," according to Carr.

Cohen continued running his management company out of 298 Elizabeth Street. His schedule was so hectic that sometimes he wouldn't see Simmons for an entire week, catching up only during Friday or Saturday night car rides club-hopping around the city. Never much of a partyer, Cohen liked to unwind by simply lighting up a joint (or a cigar), reading, or calling up a friend to hang out. Scott Koenig remembers Cohen usually "with a book in his hand." Sam Sever often got invited to Cohen's house for Sunday brunches. "He would be calling me up, wanting to talk all the time," Sever recalled. " 'Sam, this is Lyor, I am smoking a turkey in the backyard, and I would like you to come.' "

Def Jam's new space wasn't a huge improvement over the old one, because when "you walked down the hall to go to the bathroom, it's like you just walked through three departments," as one former staff member recalls. Plus, the only windows on the floor were at the end of the hall, so there was hardly any natural light. Soon, the space would come to symbolize the general feeling at Def Jam in the early '90s—"a really dark time," as Faith Newman puts it, when the work "wasn't fun anymore."

CHAPTER 9

Damage
Control

By the spring of 1989, Public Enemy had eclipsed most of their competitors, becoming the biggest hip-hop act in the world. But jealousy within the group threatened to jeopardize their success. Ever since the Run's House Tour in June of '88, Professor Griff had been putting pressure on Chuck D. to make him a more vocal member of Public Enemy; he was, after all, their "minister of information." Even though Griff was "reckless with his tongue," says Hank Shocklee, Chuck tried to appease him.

On May 22, 1989, *The Washington Post* published what should have been just one of the many articles Public Enemy had done over the past year; instead it began a national debate about black nationalism and anti-Semitism. In the piece, Griff talked politics and then said, "Jews are responsible for the majority of wickedness in the world." "I was angry," Hank recalls of his reaction. "I don't think [Griff] understood the severity of what he was saying. I don't think he did it with any genuineness. I think that Griff was kinda pissed off at the group, that he wasn't getting the attention that Flava and Chuck was getting. I thought what he did was an act of sabotage."

Chuck tried to act fast to defuse the situation. He called a press conference in New York on June 21, to assure everyone that Public Enemy were not anti-Semitic, and to apologize for the remarks made by Griff, whom Chuck said he was firing. The public's approval of the group was important, because they were about to start promoting "Fight the Power," a song that they'd recorded for Spike Lee's *Do the Right Thing,* which was opening in theaters on June 30. "Fight the Power" was such an indelible part of the soundtrack that it came to be identified with the film itself, which, in Shocklee's opinion, was hurt by the Professor Griff controversy. Danny Aiello, who played the complicated owner of Sal's Pizzeria in Bed-Stuy, even declined to be photographed with Public Enemy on the set of the film. "It was that deep," says Shocklee of the situation.

No sooner did the film hit theaters than the militant New York–based Jewish rights group Jewish Defense Organization (JDO) jump on Public Enemy and everyone associated with the group. They began distributing leaflets denouncing Public Enemy and picketing screenings of *Do the Right Thing.* JDO even went after the Jewish staff at Def Jam who worked with Public Enemy, such as Bill Adler, whom they called "a self-hating Jew," and Rick Rubin, "self-hating Jewish trash." They blamed Rubin for Public Enemy's outspokenness. "He could have put a crimp on [Public Enemy] in the first place," said JDO spokesman Leonard Fineberg. "We're going to punish him for his lack of morality through strong but legal and effective means."

The staff at Def Jam were forced to take sides. Faith Newman, who was Jewish and had previously been close to Griff, recalls that "the whole incident really threw me." She decided to write Griff a letter and tell him about how his statement made her feel and try to examine why he'd said it. (He wouldn't apologize to her until several years later.) "The whole group felt like they were ambushed, so when you feel like you're being pushed into a corner, you're not gonna start apologizing," says Faith.

Over at Sony, President Walter Yetnikoff took Griff's remarks personally. "My first instinct was to can Public Enemy and throw Griff in the East River," he would recall years later in his autobiography. "But that wouldn't work. Their *It Takes a Nation of Millions to Hold Us Back,* a brilliant work, sold millions and their new single,

'Welcome to the Terrordome,' was poised to sell even more. I had a responsibility to CBS shareholders."

Amidst the Public Enemy controversy, Def Jam had to send out LL Cool J on the Nitro Tour, which he was headlining in July. His supporting acts included De La Soul, Slick Rick, NWA, and Too Short. When the artists assembled at La Guardia Airport for their early-morning flight to Louisville, Kentucky, the first stop on the tour, a new face was in the mix: Don Newkirk, or Newkirk, as he would be known. He was going to be Def Jam's next star, as Russell Simmons was announcing to everyone, hip-hop's answer to Prince.

Sitting next to Simmons at the airport, Newkirk felt like the mogul's little brother. He was being whisked away by Simmons for the first five days of the tour without even having signed any contracts. "I don't know if he took me under his arm because he thought I was gonna be his golden egg," he says, "or if he just genuinely liked me as a person. But I think it was a little bit of both."

Suddenly, an argument erupted. "Yo, keep my name out of your mouth! I'm serious!" Jam Master Jay, who came along on the first couple of dates of the tour, was standing over Slick Rick and yelling in his face. "Don't be talking about me!" Rick had said some scathing things about Run-DMC to *Word Up!* magazine a few months before, which hurt Jay. ("They're garbage," Rick said. "[Russell's] little family is out of the game.") As Jay kept screaming, Rick stayed in his seat, next to his mother/manager Veronica Felician, seemingly unaffected. "Man, nobody's worried about you with your little beat records," Rick shot back. "Nobody cares!"

DJ Hurricane started to get in between them to break up the argument, which continued to escalate. When Jay saw that Rick was reaching for his forty-ounce bottle of beer—he had been drinking, even though it was only eight-thirty in the morning—he got even more furious. "You're gonna hit me with a bottle, Rick?!" he yelled. Simmons nudged Newkirk, who was stunned by his first experience with hip-hop thuggery, and said, "You R&B guys don't do this shit, right?"

The altercation between Slick Rick and Jay was surprising because

many, like Hank Shocklee, believed that "Jam Master Jay was instrumental in making sure that Slick Rick got over to Def Jam." For his
part, Slick Rick says that the argument was "juvenile stuff. Young,
silly testosterone stuff: 'Your group is wack, our group is hot.' It was
just childlike competition. It wasn't nothing *major*."

The argument at the airport was an appropriate beginning to the
Nitro Tour, which was marred with bad press, poor ticket sales, arrests,
and interartist conflicts. In New Orleans, LL Cool J almost got into a
fight with Rakim by the hotel elevators. Another time, Newkirk, the
Black Flames, and Greg Nice, of Nice & Smooth, were spending an
afternoon by the hotel pool when Slick Rick showed up with a stable
of girls. "You want some of this?!" Rick started yelling across the pool
when he noticed Newkirk looking. The guys tried to ignore him, re-
calling how Russell once told them that "Rick was a little out of it or
whatever." But Rick continued, "You want some of *this*?!" Newkirk
got nervous. But there was no fight. Rick soon became distracted by
his women.

But a bigger problem than the ego clashes was the undersold venues that were booked by the promoter, G Street Express (its owners,
Darryl Brooks and Carol Kirkendall, would go on to manage Salt-N-
Pepa), at enormous stadiums with a minimum capacity of eleven
thousand people, while the tickets were too pricey for an average kid.
"We would have to literally fly in early sometimes to do prepromo-
tions just so that we can get those ticket sales," Brian Latture recalls.

No one was more hurt by the fans' response than LL Cool J. By the
time the tour hit the road, some of LL Cool J's hard-core fans had
abandoned him, thinking he had become too "soft." At one outdoor
concert, fans even threw objects at him. "It was awful," recalls Faith
Newman. "They felt like he was a sellout." I've heard crowds booed
Sugar Ray Leonard," LL later justified. "I've heard they booed Michael
Jackson. This happens." Perhaps LL's massive overproduced stage show,
full of explosions, and a souped-up Camaro driven onstage at the start
of "I'm Bad," turned off audiences that were used to seeing LL make a
show entertaining just by virtue of his presence and voice.

Simmons would later admit that he didn't steer LL the right way when it came to picking the first single for *Walking With a Panther.* "The worst advice I gave him was to use 'I'm That Type of Guy' as the first single, instead of 'Big Ol' Butt,' because I thought it was a much darker record than it was. I don't know if it was for everyone of his core audience." Brian Latture concurs, "We had more of a pop smash than we did an urban smash, and it backfired." Because the other artists on the tour were "really producing urban records for an urban audience," as Latture points out, "all of our marketing catered to the urban audience. But at that particular point, that wasn't LL's audience. There was very minimal promotional steps in terms of getting his full audience there."

Besides trying desperately to sell more tickets, Def Jam also had to do damage control during the tour. Someone in LL's entourage was arrested and charged with rape during the Minneapolis date. The victim was a fifteen-year-old winner of a backstage pass from a radio show. On August 14, LL Cool released a statement, in which he claimed that he was not present during, nor did he know anything about, the incident. "I want everyone to know that the young men involved will never again be associated with me or any project bearing my name," he said.

The Nitro Tour ended in September, and with sales of *Walking With a Panther* falling below expectations, LL Cool J paid a visit to Prince Paul to see about working together on LL's next project. "It was a big deal when he came by my house," Paul recalls. "The whole block transformed into a parade. 'Wow, LL Cool J's here! Look at that car!' "

"Yo, Paul, man, you give me a hit!" LL pleaded.

"If I get you a hit, I want one of *those*," said Paul, pointing to LL's white Benz with a blue top.

"I'll get you the best 1-90 you've ever seen," LL said.

"What? 1-90? I want one of *those!*"

Paul comments, "That's one thing about LL, he's smart. He kinda just talked around it." The collaboration never materialized. Marley Marl, the producer behind Big Daddy Kane and Biz Markie, stepped in to do the remix to "Jinglin' Baby," which "turned the whole thing around," recalls Faith Newman, who suggested that Marley do LL Cool J's entire next album. Simmons agreed and promoted twenty-four-year-old Newman to vice president of A&R, where she would oversee the release of Newkirk's debut R&B album, *Funk City,* scheduled for October.

Like De La Soul and the Jungle Brothers, Newkirk was part of the new, more playful and peaceful style filtering through rap. Newkirk had gotten signed to Original Black Recordings (OBR)—also home to Tashan, Black Flames, and Chuck Stanley—which he was "not too ecstatic about," he says. He wanted the Def Jam logo on his album, "that Def Jam stamp, that seal of approval." OBR became Russell's way of giving the R&B artists "more definition," says Tashan, because "once people saw that it was from Def Jam, they expected it to be rap."

Newkirk did not become Def Jam's answer to Prince, like Russell had hoped. The main problem, he says, was Def Jam's "choice of bad singles," and "bad marketing," including a "weird neon" album cover with a giant peace sign that Newkirk says he "kinda got talked into." Even though he had three videos from the album, which was a lot for a new artist, the Prince comparison was not good for his career. "Don't worry," said Simmons to Newkirk when the album's sales fell below expectations. "You made the wrong album this time, but we'll make another album."

Two weeks after Newkirk's release, 3rd Bass's debut album *The Cactus Album* followed in late October of 1989. The album was pure New York City carefree hip-hop: creative and fun. "But we had worked our asses off—from hosting and being on MTV," recalls MC Serch, "even before we were up and running, just from the battles we were doing, we were creating a buzz on the street."

Overseeing the project at Columbia Records was Angela Thomas, who had recently replaced Jeff Jones as the label's new product manager (Jones left for MCA Records, where he would work projects like the teen queen Tiffany). Thomas became the key liaison between

Def Jam and Columbia's top dogs: Tommy Mottola, president of CBS Records, U.S., and Columbia president Don Ienner. Thomas's job was to make sure that Simmons's and Cohen's visions were absolutely clear to Sony, especially since the parent company sometimes had trouble taking Def Jam's requests seriously. Thomas recalls the issue of manufacturing 12-inch vinyl and maxi singles. Vinyl was a crucial element in hip-hop's DJ culture, and maxi cassettes were important in underground and college radio play. "[CBS] didn't understand how important it was as a DJ marketing tool," she says. Thomas fought to get Sony to manufacture more vinyl. Even Chuck D. got involved at one point, telling Angela to talk to the head of sales at Sony, Rich Kadoler, and explain to him how important the maxi cassette was. In the end, Def Jam got the vinyl and the cassettes.

"I think Donnie [Ienner] was a big supporter [of Def Jam]," says Thomas. "He didn't always understand it, yet he did absolutely allow us to do what we had to do, even when it was a fight. And usually, it was always about money, and that's just normal in a corporation."

The promotion of *The Cactus Album* stayed within the cactus theme, with the press receiving mini-cacti with their advance copies; and there were parties in New York, L.A., and London—all decorated with cacti. Def Jam even took out a double-spread ad in *Billboard* to advertise the album—something they had only done for four other groups. "That blew me away," recalls Serch. "It made a huge statement. That's when we were like, 'They're really gonna pay attention.' "

The album cover, created by Steve Carr by a fluke, was one of the year's best. "They had done a photo session, and I was just doing this drawing for the inside of the album with photocopies and hand-coloring them," Carr recalled. "Russell came in, saw it, and went, 'That's the cover right there!' Serch was pissed, because he's like, 'You can't even see my face!' [On the cover, Serch has the back of his head to the camera.] But ultimately he warmed up to it." (In the acknowledgments Serch thanked one "Leo Cohen." That was not a typo; Steve Carr had purposefully misspelled Lyor Cohen's name, which was one of the ways Cey and Steve liked to amuse themselves at work. He would continue to give *Lyor* interesting spellings in future credits.)

The first 12-inch single was "Steppin' to the A.M.," produced by Hank and Keith Shocklee. "We had it out for a couple of weeks, and it wasn't really doing too much anywhere," recalled Pete. The guys shot a video for "the song and then flew to London for some performances." By the time they returned to the States, the video had debuted and "all of a sudden, there were significant [album] sales of like twenty-five thousand a week," recalls Pete. "And it just started to take off from there."

Sales continued to grow with the next single, "Gas Face," produced by Prince Paul. On the record, 3rd Bass famously dissed MC Hammer, something he wasn't too happy about. "We had a whole situation where Hammer had put out like a hit on us," recalls Pete. "Hammer's brother had called up [Def Jam] and he had gotten a copy of an album before the video, and this one song we did 'The Cactus.' His brother called up going off on Serch. All of a sudden, this whole beef started. Word got back to Russell from some gang people [in L.A.]. Russell actually had to step in and defuse that."

Along with those videos, Def Jam also put out two more, for "Triple Stage Darkness" and "Words of Wisdom." But the critical and commercial success of 3rd Bass's debut would become tainted by copyright lawsuits. "We thought we were smarter than the average band," says Serch. "Pete thought that we wouldn't get sued for samples that we wound up getting sued for. He thought they were so mad obscure that nobody would know about them. What little [money] we had got taken in lawsuits."

•   •   •

Meanwhile, Public Enemy were gearing up for the release of their third album, *Fear of a Black Planet*. But Chuck D. was still trying to defuse the Griff situation. While his black supporters urged him to stand by his group member and brother, Jewish groups threatened to boycott the group. Chuck chose his black supporters and brought Griff back into the group as "community liaison." The move, says Hank, brought "a dark cloud over Def Jam, and it brought out the fanatics." Indeed, staff sighted snipers outside the office, and Hank started getting bomb threats at his studio at 510 South Franklin in Long Island, where he employed a few young mothers to help with administrative work. "So now everybody's on nervous alert. Lives are being jeopardized and families. And all for what?" says Hank. Chuck also couldn't make up his mind about keeping Griff in the group—firing and then rehiring him several times—which made the situation more "ugly," says Hank. "[Chuck] made the whole thing linger on, rather than making a definitive point. That was just hate and it was stupidity. One thing about Public Enemy, it was never about stupidity and it was never about hatred. It was about uplifting, it was about empowerment."

Out of frustration, Hank wrote "Welcome to the Terrordome" in early fall, and by December the single was in stores, while Griff was again back in the group. Reaction to the song and its controversial lyrics, which compared the attacks on Public Enemy by the Jewish community to the crucifixion of Jesus Christ, was swift. Walter Yetnikoff, the chief executive at CBS Records, soon received a letter from the Anti-Defamation League describing the organization's "dismay" with CBS's decision to release and distribute "a hate-filled recording by the rap group Public Enemy." Soon, Public Enemy product started getting banned.

In Canada, the MuchMusic video station, executive-produced by Moses Znaimer, who was Jewish, decided to ban all of the group's videos, even though the controversial lyrics—"They got me like Jesus"—in "Welcome to the Terrordome" were missing from the video. The ban was lifted three weeks later, most likely for business reasons, although the network still refused to air the "Terrordome" video. Columbia even talked to their retailers about pulling Public Enemy's product off the shelves. Some of the Jewish marketing people at the parent company refused to work on Public Enemy product, while some salespeople refused to carry the records and sell them to stores. "So now, within the record company, there was a division," recalled Hank, whose involvement with the group declined drastically after the incident. "It's amazing that the group even lived through it."

They had to: a new album needed to be set up. "The best thing about working for Chuck was that he would basically sketch everything out," says Cey Adams. "Most [artists] would just leave it up to you to decide. He was a real stickler for detail." When the time came to create the artwork for the *Fear of a Black Planet* album cover, Chuck and Steve Carr were having lunch at a diner, waiting for a meeting, and Chuck started sketching his idea for the cover on a napkin. "The earth is getting eclipsed by the PE planet, and I want some spaceships floating out here, and I want that *Star Wars* type."

Carr liked the idea of an illustrated album cover, especially since it was so rare in hip-hop. He decided to call NASA and find an illustrator there who specialized in painting space images, and B. E. Johnson got the call. He agreed to look at Chuck's napkin sketch, but decided to pass on the project, because "the logic of Chuck's idea wasn't scientifically sound," as Carr recalls. But Steve kept calling, "begging this guy to go against the physics and science to create a painting." Finally, B.E. conceded. "But this is just wrong," he said. "I've just committed intergalactic faux pas." (Fifteen years later, the painting would be displayed proudly on B.E.'s website, with a caption: "One of the greatest album covers of all time.")

Carr and Adams were indeed designing some of the best album covers in the business, but they still worried about getting fired by Cohen, who constantly gave them mixed messages. "Whenever he would introduce us around [to an artist], he would be like, 'These are the best in the world.' And then he'd come back later and go, 'This is the biggest piece of shit, this cover! I could shit this out and make it better!'" Often, they sought refuge in Simmons, who was more lenient. When Cohen literally fired them one day, after another angry outburst, they tracked Simmons down at a club after work, panic-stricken. "Get outta here! Don't worry about it!" he told them. The next day, Adams and Carr showed up at work, as though nothing had happened. "We never talked about it again," Carr recalled.

On February 7, 1990, all the members of Public Enemy—including Griff, who was now back in the group and working on a solo album for Skywalker Records, run by 2 Live Crew's Luke Skywalker—gathered at the Def Jam office to shoot the back cover for *Fear of a Black Planet*. The concept had the group looking down at a large map. In the middle of the shoot, however, 3rd Bass showed up to take care of something in the office.

Although Def Jam had by then learned to schedule artists' meetings in the office around their respective conflicts, this time they had miscalculated. Griff didn't waste any time; he confronted Serch about the video for "Gas Face," in which 3rd Bass satirized Griff and S1W's. "Fucking Jew bastard," Griff reportedly screamed at Serch, along with various physical threats. Suddenly a huge fight broke out in the office, with the photographer who was there for the cover shoot documenting the entire thing. "It was a complete mêlée," recalled Cey Adams. "The office was trashed and it delayed the shoot for two hours."

The timing of the incident couldn't have been worse, since 3rd Bass and Public Enemy were about to embark on a European promo tour, scheduled for March, and Russell worried that the tension between the groups would become unmanageable. Serch said that 3rd Bass would not tour with Public Enemy as long as Griff was in the group. The following week, Russell released a statement to the press that addressed the incident between Griff and Serch. "I don't like Professor Griff and I hate what he stands for," wrote Russell. "He's not allowed anymore in the offices of Def Jam. Griff's wildest imaginary Jewish conspiracy could not have done more damage to Public Enemy than has Griff himself." Russell made clear, however, that his dislike of Griff did not affect his love for Chuck D. and Flavor Flav, because "Public Enemy has had a more positive influence on today's young black Americans than has anyone else."

The next day, Griff answered Russell's press statement with one of his own. "Does this mean my contract with Def Jam Records is over?" Griff wrote in his statement. "Anyone with eyes and ears knows what this is all about. I am tired of all of the back and forth conversations and accusations about what I said and meant. Stated simple, as a strong Black man, I can not and will not allow any actions that disrespect Black people to go unconfronted. 3rd Bass was out of line and I called them on it. Case closed!!!"

But it wasn't. Griff got banned from the Def Jam offices and did not appear in the publicity shots of the group for the new album. He was not allowed to go on the tour, and 3rd Bass joined Public Enemy as the supporting act.

CHAPTER 10

RAL

"W hat are you gonna call it?" Russell Simmons asked Lyor Cohen. It was March of 1990, and hip-hop's two biggest movers and shakers were on the phone discussing the name for their new venture. Simmons wanted a separate label that would house the various imprints that he and Lyor had started handing out to Def Jam's more profitable artists and producers. This entity would essentially become Def Jam's own production label, which would produce and market various artists that could otherwise be getting signed to other labels. Chuck D. was one of the first to get his own imprint, which he called PRO-Division, "basically so I could do something for Terminator X," he explained, "who wasn't written into the Def Jam contract."

Jam Master Jay had been handed his own label in late 1989, JMJ Records, which he had started with his childhood friend and business partner, Randy Allen. They had already signed a group called the Afros, led by DJ Hurricane, and his friend and former Def Jam artist Davy DMX, as well as a trio of young brothers called Fam-Lee, who modeled themselves after the Jackson 5. There was also former Disco Fever owner Sal Abatiello's Fever Records, which would house dance artists, as well as Jazzy Jeff's label DGF.

Lyor Cohen thought that Rush Associated Labels would be a

good name, and Simmons agreed. Whether it was "Lyor's way to gain more control of Def Jam," as Chris Lighty puts it, or an effort to "empower the artists that were bringing in the money," as Angela Thomas points out, RAL was, above all, the partners' main point of renegotiation of their Sony deal. They were talking about doing a 50 percent co-venture deal, in which Columbia would put money up front for marketing, promotion, and distribution to RAL, while Russell and Lyor retained creative control. It was a more lucrative deal than Def Jam's former arrangement with Sony, in which Columbia only promoted and distributed Def Jam and OBR product, while keeping a large percentage of the profits.

By March of 1990, the paperwork for this new deal had been drawn up, and everyone was waiting to sign on the dotted line. "Are the papers signed yet?" Simmons would phone Cohen to ask almost every day. In early April, formal contracts were finally signed, while Russell renegotiated his partnership with Lyor, in which each would have 50 percent ownership of RAL.

The next artist to receive his own label was twenty-year-old Prince Paul, who was already signed to Rush Producers Management. Paul was "a hot ticket," as he puts it, in hip-hop production, but he wasn't interested in having his own imprint. He was content with just being a producer. "I turned [the offer] down a bunch of times," he recalled. But Lyor insisted, calling Prince Paul constantly and pushing the idea, until finally, Prince Paul conceded and received a $50,000 advance. "They could have given me a dollar and a sandwich, and I would have been, 'Oooh,' " he says. Prince Paul met to discuss the label name with Simmons, who was under the impression that the label would be called Prince Paul Records. But Paul corrected him, " 'Nope! I wanna make it Dew Doo Man!' I remember he just looked and just kinda frowned." "Nah, nah. Prince Paul Records, right?" said Russell. "No," Paul insisted. "Either I make it Dew Doo Man, or I'm not doing it. I got the logo and everything." "All right, man, do whatever you want," Simmons agreed reluctantly.

As part of the deal, Prince Paul had to demo-up the artists and give them to Def Jam for their approval before he could sign them. He ran the label right out of his house on Long Island and picked a trio called Resident Alien—his friends from the neighborhood who "really didn't rhyme," recalled Paul—as Dew Doo Man's first artists. "I don't know what I was doing," he remembered. "I was a kid. I was in the spotlight all of a sudden, so everything kind of moved quickly."

By then, Def Jam had renegotiated its contract with Columbia for a pressing and distribution deal, which meant that Def Jam would now have to start operating like a real label, with a bigger staff and much more defined departments, like A&R, artist development, and promotions. Columbia could no longer work with Def Jam being a company of eight people, where "whoever we get on the phone is the one who does the job," pointed out Carmen Ashhurst, who was appointed vice president of operations and, in that capacity, set up the artist development department.

Simmons did not want to put a cap on the number of labels and production companies that would ultimately be signed to RAL. But for now he had seven: Fever, No Face, PRO-Division, JMJ, True Blue, DGF, Pump Up, with several of the labels committed to releasing at least three records per year. But some could foresee problems within this new structure. "There's bound to be chaos and disorder when you're creating a lot of different things at a rapid rate," noted Chuck D. In addition to RAL, Simmons had a vision of power that only a handful of music industry executives had achieved. "I want a film company big enough to make the next *Raiders of the Lost Ark,* radio stations that make up radio networks, record companies, associated radio," he told *Paper* magazine. Specific projects included a weekly music-video show called the *New Music Report,* and he was also in negotiations with Columbia Records to create Russell Simmons Visual Productions (R.S.V.P.), with two films already in preproduction (one starring Oran "Juice" Jones, and Doctor Dre and Ed Lover in the other). Simmons was also launching Rush Broadcasting, which would acquire radio stations in New York, L.A., and Chicago.

With his new deal with CBS finalized and a check in the bank, thirty-three-year-old Simmons moved in June to a penthouse triplex in the Silk Building co-op at 692 Broadway and West Fourth Street (the location of Tower Records' flagship store). The apartment was once owned by Cher and had been featured in *Architectural Digest* magazine. Simmons paid $1.6 million for it, but he didn't need to spend a dime decorating it—Cher had left behind all of her furnishings when she'd moved. "He just added some phones," as one friend remembered, and replaced Cher's Aztec art with African works (along with some framed photographs of models like Naomi Campbell and Beverly Peele). He also added a gym on the third floor.

Some people in the industry thought that Simmons had sold out. ("Hip-hop died when Russell bought Cher's apartment," wrote one critic.) But Simmons could care less about what others thought. The physical move also marked a social step up into a stratosphere of new wealth and success, one inhabited by downtown showbiz royalty like Robert De Niro. "I'd like to be him," he said of De Niro. Within a month, Russell was a partner in De Niro's trendy eatery Tribeca Bar and Grill, after Quincy Jones pulled out.

Like his new environment, Simmons's look had also evolved. Now it was "downtown casual" meets B-boy preppy: a polo shirt, chinos, and sneakers. Like the wild clothes and Stetson hats he'd worn in the late seventies, the penny loafers and argyle sweaters in the early eighties, the head-to-toe Adidas gear in the mid and late eighties, the most recent look became an indelible part of the Russell Simmons persona at that time. He was becoming a brand unto himself, perhaps even more recognizable than the Def Jam logo. "I want to be compared to powerful people," he said. "I don't want to be compared to Berry Gordy, I want to be compared to [the now deceased former Warner Communications chairman] Steve Ross."

As he got richer, Simmons became healthier. In the late '80s, Columbia's Ruben Rodriguez had introduced Simmons to the Tenth Street Baths, a Russian bathhouse in the East Village that had been around since the 1890s. Simmons visited the no-frills spa weekly, spending hours sweating away in a stone sauna, plunging himself into

Russell Simmons kicking back at his newly purchased penthouse apartment on Broadway and West 4th. He was entering a new stratosphere of wealth and success, and on his way to becoming the mogul of his dreams.

a thirty-seven-degree pool, or receiving a "platsa" massage, which consisted of getting beaten by oak-leafed twigs soaked in olive oil soap. Simmons was at the baths so often that he sometimes even conducted interviews there with reporters. He was also experimenting with a healthier diet, eating a lot of sushi at a time when sushi "wasn't in," recalled Don Newkirk, who was initiated into the baths by Simmons on one winter evening in 1990. "I remember when I came out, I felt like a god," Newkirk recalled. "I wasn't cold, my pores felt really open and refreshed." Simmons needed that kind of release to keep himself balanced. "I think there's a small aspect of manic depression in Russell," says his brother Danny. "I think Russell has periods of very highs and very lows."

Simmons continued conducting most of his business out of his Broadway apartment. Instead of going to the office for an A&R meeting, for example, the whole department came to him. He visited the Def Jam office so rarely that he didn't keep track of the new hirings and didn't even keep an appointment book, because he enjoyed the excitement of starting each day without knowing what could happen. Nonetheless, he continued to be actively involved in his artists' lives. When he wasn't on the phone making deals, Simmons harassed Columbia's and Def Jam's promotions departments to make sure his records were charting. When he found out that not enough stations were playing the new Black Flames single "Watching You," he didn't hesitate to leave an angry message in Def Jam's promotions department's general mailbox one February of 1991. "I don't know what the fuck y'all doing, but if we don't fucking chart this Black Flames record this week, everybody's fired! Everybody!" he screamed into the phone. Thomas Lytell, who had recently joined the staff as a regional manager and was celebrating his birthday that day, heard the message and ended up canceling his plans and calling program directors all night. Simmons's threat yielded results: "Watching You" finally charted on the *Billboard* R&B Top 20 singles.

Lytell and Vice President of Promotions Wes Johnson were responsible for getting the records to a certain position on the charts, at which point Columbia would take over. "Then they would kinda try to take all the accolades of taking the record to the next level, when we did all the groundwork," says Lytell. Def Jam always knew how to sell records without radio, but in the early nineties that task was becoming increasingly difficult. The touring market for hip-hop continued to decline and insurance prices soared. The Spectrum in Philadelphia, for example, required Public Enemy to take out a $3 million insurance policy that cost the band $35,000 for its first U.S. tour as a headliner, Tour of a Black Planet, in late June. Madison Square Garden, which had always welcomed rap performances in the 1980s, did not host a single rap concert in 1990; neither did The Ritz, which was a major venue for hip-hop acts. The Apollo only had six rap concerts during the entire year.

●   ●   ●

Despite all the controversy and turmoil surrounding the group, Public Enemy's *Fear of a Black Planet* went platinum within just one week of its April 10, 1990, release date, a first for a rap act. Although it took him longer—nearly two years—Slick Rick also went platinum and started working on his follow-up album. But his personal life was about to interfere with his professional one. In late April, Slick Rick was shot, along with two other people, during a "wild gun battle" outside The Castle social club in the South Bronx. At least twenty shots were fired at Slick Rick's Nissan Pathfinder as he sat behind the wheel. The gunmen fled, and Slick Rick was taken to Bronx-Lebanon Hospital for treatment. He signed himself out of the hospital a few hours after being treated, against the wishes of his attending physician, according to police.

Less than three months later, on July 3, Slick Rick again got into trouble. He was with his pregnant girlfriend in a borrowed car on White Plains Road in the Bronx when he spotted his cousin Mark Plummer and Wilbert Henry—one of the two men who had allegedly fired at Rick's car outside The Castle nightclub back in April. Rick pulled up beside them, on the corner of East 241st Street, and opened fire, hitting Henry in both feet and Plummer in the leg and abdomen. Dozens of people in the street—the location was across the street from an Off-Track Betting parlor—ran for cover. Someone called the police; by then, Rick was gone, speeding down the Bronx River Parkway, weaving in and out of heavy preholiday traffic for more than two miles, as police trailed him. The chase ended when Slick Rick crashed into a tree while trying to exit the highway, breaking his and his girlfriend's legs. Six loaded weapons were reportedly found in the car.

Rick was arrested and taken to the Bronx Municipal Center with his girlfriend for medical treatment. "I just panicked," Rick would explain years later. "I should have just stopped and pulled over or whatever." Rick was charged with two counts of attempted murder, two counts of assault, and six counts of criminal possession of a weapon. He pleaded not guilty and was held in a prison near his home in the Bronx on $800,000 bail. Although he had sold more than a million copies of his debut album by then, Rick didn't have that kind of money, and neither did his family.

The arrest interrupted Rick's work on his second album, scheduled for a January 1991 release, so Simmons paid Rick's bond, so he could be released and finish the recording sessions for his new album. Simmons asked Faith Newman to scout studios in upstate New York, where Rick was being locked up, and they had to be close to a hotel where he could stay while recording. "I'm not surprised that the record didn't come out as good as it should have, because this is a guy who had an armed marshal on him the entire time," Newman recalled. Indeed, armed guards would keep watch outside Rick's hotel room, never letting him out of their sight.

In late August, the video for "The Boomin' System," the first single off LL's upcoming fourth album, *Mama Said Knock You Out,* slated for release in September, was completed—a big video with corny video-game special effects and an underground arcade called Rushland. Even LL's voice sounded different, almost unrecognizable: deeper, less energetic. "After 'The Boomin' System' was lackluster, LL was mad, LL was tight," recalls Chris Lighty. "And dealing with LL was like trying to put control over a tornado, because you're dealing with [a young man] that has never really had a straight job." Lighty recalls that during that period LL's relationship with Lyor was "super love-hate." It would remain that way for years.

•   •   •

When CBS Records officially changed its name to Sony on January 1, 1991, it signaled the start of a new era. For Def Jam, it would be a difficult year. Lyor and Russell would miscalculate single choices and the timing of releases, like they did with Nikki D. In February, her first single, "Daddy's Little Girl," finally hit the streets and stayed in the number one spot on the Hot Rap charts for two weeks in April through the beginning of May. But the single "came out too soon," says Nikki. "This is really where Lyor and Russell bumped heads. Lyor didn't want to put it out then, he wanted to wait for the album. Russell wanted to put it out then, because he was so geeked off the song." Ultimately, the single's coming out a full eight months before the album hurt album sales. "We sold the single, but not an album," she says. "The single was so huge that when it dropped, we had pre-orders in the South alone for like half a million in 1991."

When the album was finally released September 3, 1991, Nikki D.'s *Daddy's Little Girl* album finally hit stores, but Nikki was no longer the only female signed to Def Jam. There was also a duo called Bytches With Problems, who had been stirring controversy since June with their raunchy single "Two-Minute Brother." BWP were even invited to *Larry King Live,* where they were introduced as "rap's nastiest duo." During the interview, the two MCs, Lyndah and Tanisha, couldn't have been more different from their oversexed, gritty image. Before they started rapping, as they revealed to Larry, Lyndah was actually a computer operator and Tanisha was a dance teacher. The girls were incredibly soft-spoken and polite, and their feminism was inspiring. "They were bright, they worked hard, they really wanted to make their album a success," recalled Angela Thomas. But with virtually no radio play (even the songs' clean versions were being refused airplay), it was hard for the duo to sell records.

By then Nikki D.'s hit single "Daddy's Little Girl" had fallen off the charts. The next two singles—"Hang On, Kid" and "Wasted," both of which had videos—did not perform as well. Nikki had spent the summer on the road with EPMD and LL Cool J, riding the success of "Daddy's Little Girl." When she got back to New York, Nikki stopped by Elizabeth Street, and the promotions department. Wes Johnson pulled her into his office and said, "Babygirl, I have to tell you: we lost your record." Nikki didn't understand. "Okay, where'd you lose it at?" "We lost it at radio," Wes said. "We had it up there, it was up there and we fucked up. It fell. So now we have to work on another record."

When it came to pushing her debut album, which entered the *Billboard* charts at No. 70, Nikki says that Def Jam "fucked me up." But people like Hank Shocklee believe that Nikki's lack of charisma and connection to her audience were to blame. "You either have it or you don't," Shocklee points out. "The success is based upon whether or not people really like you, and they identify with you as a person, as an artist. You make them laugh, you make them feel good." He feels Nikki D. lacked those qualities. "I know the beat's gonna be dope, but if you can't bring anything to the table, then I have to say that you have no talent in that aspect. And that, to me, was Nikki's problem."

Def Jam's other baby acts were not being nurtured enough. Prince Paul's group on Dew Doo Man Records, Resident Alien, would have been a perfect tie-in to the growing Native Tongues movement, but in the Def Jam pantheon of big, loud hip-hop, its sound didn't seem to fit. "They weren't paying any attention to Dew Doo Man, because it was too out there," says Leyla Turkkan, Def Jam's former publicist. "Resident Alien was genius. So ahead of their time! That stuff always freaked [Def Jam] out: A Tribe Called Quest, all that stuff. They were very focused on this OBR thing. They saw Uptown was making all this money on this new jack R&B thing."

Indeed, Def Jam poured an enormous amount of money into an R&B project: the soundtrack for an obscure urban film called *Livin' Large* about an aspiring news anchorman—played by future *Living Single* star T. C. Carson—who rises to stardom. Michael Schultz, Simmons's old friend from the *Krush Groove* movie days, was the film's director, but the movie was a mess. Def Jam's marketing budget for that project approached an astounding $800,000 as they filmed videos for four of the singles released—including Newkirk's "Small Thing" and Alyson Williams's "She's Not Your Fool." There were two release parties, one in L.A. and one in New York, and Def Jam spent a boatload of cash on advertising. It was big risk that ultimately would not pay off.

Def Jam could have invested that money into Nice & Smooth and their sophomore album and Def Jam debut, *Ain't a Damn Thing Changed*. "Hip-Hop Junkies," the first single, was already making noise, as was the video, which was completed on August 30. The track was an instant hip-hop classic, a true gem. Smooth B. and Greg Nice had two of the most original flows in hip-hop; their voices— Greg Nice's singsongy cadence, and Smooth B.'s mellow twang— became instantly recognizable. Greg rapped "I got a funky rhyme with a funky style," and he was right. On "Cake and Eat It Too," off the *Ain't a Damn Thing Changed* album, the guys actually sang. Their lyrics didn't always make sense—"A teeny weeny midget fell in a well / I knew way back that my shit would sell" was one example— but they were funny and lighthearted.

On October 22, 1991, Nice & Smooth's video for "Sometimes I Rhyme Slow" directed by Eric Meza, was completed. It was the second single off the duo's album. With a solid budget of $50,000, the video was, without a doubt, one of that best of that era (despite the requisite girls in tight dresses dancing around, which, regardless of a song's subject matter, seemed to be a must in any hip-hop video in '91). Although Greg Nice and Smooth B. were charismatic on camera, behind the scenes they turned into two fairly irresponsible young men. "Greg Nice wasn't very nice!" recalls Leyla Turkkan, who handled their publicity. "They had a lot of talent, they were just ornery." According to Angela Thomas, they were "the most challenging group" that she worked with at Def Jam. "I don't know what was going on in their brains, but to do an event with them was like making a motion picture. They were their own worst enemy."

"Sometimes I Rhyme Slow" was a "huge" record for Columbia, says Thomas, but most of the promotion and marketing was done without Greg and Smooth present. Don Ienner loved "Sometimes I Rhyme Slow" so much, he begged Angela to get the DAT from Smooth B., which he planned on taking with him overseas to get the whole world on board with the record. "I'm coming down!" Smooth told Angela when she called him to hurry up with the DAT. But he never showed up. "They could have gone so much further," she says of Greg and Smooth.

The duo even ruined an opportunity to headline at the coveted *Showtime at the Apollo* slot on Thanksgiving night in 1991. "They would not go onstage, because they insisted that they have fourteen people onstage with them," Angela recalls. But Apollo could only pay for eight people onstage, because on television you have to pay per person shown on camera. So the group simply refused to do the show. "They really hurt themselves," she says. "Even Lyor couldn't control it." On the contrary, the "least stressful" artists at Def Jam, in Angela's experience, were Chuck D., LL Cool J, and Slick Rick. "The reason why they're so big is because they're the whole package: they're personable, they take care of their details with work, they know what they have to do."

Public Enemy's fourth album, *Apocalypse '91 . . . The Enemy Strikes Back,* hit stores on September 24, 1991, and Chuck D. had by then added two more acts to his PRO-Division roster: Total Look and Style as well as Juvenile Delinquinz. Public Enemy also spent the entire summer of 1991 on tour with Heavy D., Kid 'n Play, and Digital Underground. They had a lead review in *Rolling Stone* and *Spin* magazines and were guests on *Yo! MTV Raps* for an entire week to launch the first video, *Can't Truss It,* off the album. On September 28, Public Enemy performed on *Saturday Night Live*'s season premiere— hosted by Michael Jordan—and the following week went out on tour with Anthrax. Pairing up their hip-hop acts with a rock act seemed Def Jam's best solution to the grim touring market for hip-hop acts in 1991. Meanwhile, all of New York City was being sniped with flats and cover blowups, and preparation for the group's next two videos—"Night Train" and "Shut 'Em Down."

By the end of October, LL Cool J had completed thirteen tracks for his upcoming album, including "Pink Cookies in a Plastic Bag (Getting Crushed by Buildings)," "Fantasy," "Strictly Business," and "Christmas Song," which was to be used as promotion. A remix album was planned for the first week of January 1992. By a "total fluke," nineteen-year-old Tracey Waples, who joined the company in the summer of 1991, ended up playing LL's girlfriend in the "Pink Cookies" video. Waples served as the liaison between Rush and Def Jam and assisted Dawn Womack and Faith Newman in the A&R, which was still performing the duties of a product manager, a position that did not exist at Def Jam.

"The lead girl caught cold, didn't show up, and they grabbed me out of my sweatpants," Waples recalled of her unpaid "Pink Cookies" gig. "I was mortified." She was put in a tight white dress and did her best job portraying LL's girlfriend. The story had LL taking a bus, because his car broke down, to meet his girlfriend, played by Waples. The video, directed by Brett Ratner, became a centerpiece of a huge marketing campaign that Columbia and Def Jam launched for LL, filling his schedule with nonstop interviews, appearances, and performances.

In early November of 1991, Def Jam released Slick Rick's "It's a Boy" 12-inch, hand-delivering vinyls in diapers to all major program directors and DJs. Right before Rick was going to jail in September, Def Jam shot some blue-screen footage for "It's a Boy," but still had no treatment for the video. Everyone was gathered in the conference room to discuss ideas and the director. "I had an idea that, because obviously we couldn't use Rick, we would have this rappers' playground and we would have all these kids dressed as rappers," Steve Carr recalls. There was a young Kool Moe Dee, a young LL Cool J, and even an eight-year-old Chuck D., and they would be in the rappers' playground. "That's great! Who are we gonna get to direct that?" everyone said. "It's my idea, I wanna direct it," said Steve. "Nigga, you don't know how to direct," said Russell. "No, no, I do. I can do it," said Steve. "I've done stuff like this before." Simmons looked at Steve and said, "Aight." Suddenly, Steve Carr was a music-video director. "Again: one second in his life changed mine," he said.

Cey Adams painted a big graffiti piece that said "Rappers' Playground." "I got onto the set and yelled 'Action!' and 'Cut!' indiscriminately," Steve Carr recalls. "I'd go into the bathroom, throw up, and come back out. I tell this advice to every director who asks me: If you're really confused, and you don't know what to do, just go to the bathroom. By the time you come out, the crew will have already figured out what to do. And it always works."

Resident Alien's album, to be called *It Takes a Nation of Suckers to Let Us In,* was due out in early November, but kept getting pushed back. The 12-inch had been doing well in the streets, but the album was taking a long time to finish. Columbia planned on releasing another single in March and, depending on its success, the album right after it. There was some press anticipating the group's arrival. "We been doing that W-word: waiting," Mr. Bug, one of Resident Alien's three MCs, told a reporter. One reason for the delay was that Prince Paul remembers Russell saying, "I need a pop hit!"

"What's a pop hit?" Paul asked.

"Well, you made them before!" Russell would say.

Paul was like, "I made them by chance. There was no formula, especially for rap music back then. How do you make a pop record?" While Paul was trying to come up with what his vision of a pop record was, Def Jam was losing more and more interest in Dew Doo Man, pushing it lower and lower on the priority list.

Around that time, Def Jam hired an A&R rep named Jeff Trotter, who, according to Prince Paul, "turned out to be the guy to put the knife in my back." Paul was convinced that Trotter told Cohen and Simmons to reconsider releasing the Dew Doo Man acts. Paul sensed that Def Jam was also ignoring most of the other new acts, like Downtown Science and Nikki D., so Paul tried to "pull all of us 'little guys' together, so we can have a unified voice," he recalls. "Individually, we don't have a voice, but collectively we do." Ultimately, though, fearing being dropped by Def Jam, all the artists backed out, leaving Paul alone to have a meeting with Cohen.

By then, it seemed inevitable that Paul was going to be dropped. "At first I didn't take [the label] seriously, but then I became passionate about it," he says. "I was banking on those records coming out, and that was gonna be my claim to fame." None of his artists ever got to see the light of day, which was a shame. "They made some big mistakes," says Leyla Turkkan, pointing to the failure of Resident Alien and Dew Doo Man Records. "They were pushing some shit that was so-so." A lot of the "baby" acts, the new groups signed up in various imprints, like Newkirk, The Don, and Fam-Lee, were struggling.

The experience of failing at Def Jam was like a music industry "crash course," says Paul. "At that time, it was one of the most oppressing things I went through, but it kinda made me realize who's in your corner, who's not in your corner, just the morality of the business, or the lack of. It's good to have talent, but it's really about num-

bers at the end of the day." Cey Adams felt that some of the new
A&R staff did not have the same kind of commitment that Rick
Rubin did back in the eighties. "When Rick put a band together, he
was thinking about the logo, the sound of the music, who they would
go on the road with," says Cey. "So after Rick left, it seemed that
artists weren't getting the attention that they deserved."

"It was a time of flux," Faith Newman recalls of the period when
Def Jam was trying to find a middle ground between being a boutique company and a legitimate record label. "It really felt like the
label had lost its way." As a liaison between Def Jam and Columbia,
Faith noticed how relieved the Columbia staffers seemed to be each
time she came by—one of the few organized staffers in an otherwise
"jumbled" company. "They always felt like Def Jam was like the Wild
West out there somewhere," she recalls. Newman liked coming over
to the Sony building, because it was "*so* organized there," she says.

Russell Simmons's own career, however, was flourishing, and he
used his artists' CDs as mini-billboards to advertise his many ventures.
Along with the logos for RAL, Def Jam, and Rush Management, he
also put information about the *New Music Report,* his syndicated
music-video show, on the back of most CDs put out. One of the few
albums out that year to bear only the Def Jam logo was 3rd Bass's
Derelicts of Dialect, released in mid-June.

Bobbito Garcia remembers trying to turn Russell on to the underground hip-hop movement starting to take place, but Russell
passed on everything, including Simply Too Positive MCs, which featured Pharaoh Monch and Prince Poetry, who later became Organized Confusion. "I begged Russell to sign them," says Bobbito, but
Russell was "not concerned with heavy lyrical shit, just someone
who was more marketable," says Bobbito. While doing his radio
show with Stretch Armstrong on WKCR 89.9 FM—which he
started in 1990—Bobbito had gotten hold of demo tapes by rappers
Akineyele and Nas. He met with both of them, but took a particular
liking to Nas. But he didn't even bother bringing it to Russell. He
knew he would turn him down. Nas wasn't that "animated" or
"comical" enough to grab Russell's attention. Months later, Bob-

bito's prediction turned out to be correct: MC Serch brought Nas to Russell, who promptly turned him down, comparing him to a "wannabe Kool G. Rap."

Lyor Cohen shared Simmons's aversion to more left-of-center hip-hop acts, focusing on more commercial-sounding acts. His latest pet project was The Don, a cartoonlike nineteen-year-old L.A. rapper whose real name was Donald Saunders. "The Don, he's fucking incredible, he is the fucking Fresh Prince put together with fucking Big Daddy Kane," Lyor would announce to anyone who would listen. There was a big push behind this rapper who came out of nowhere (and went nowhere). Def Jam put together a twenty-minute EPK (electronic press kit) for him in September, which was produced by Brett Ratner and edited by Glen Friedman, and shot an expensive video in L.A. for his single "My Big 12-Inch" that same month. Certainly, after the heaviness of Public Enemy, The Don brought a welcomed lightheartedness. "Lyor had The Don ready to be the next Michael Jackson," recalls Pete Nice, who was sent out on a promotional tour with The Don for 3rd Bass's *Derelicts of Dialect*. But "My Big 12-Inch" was not doing well on radio. Don went out to L.A. for several weeks in November to work with a marketing firm. Unfortunately, he just couldn't find an audience: he was not pop enough for fans of MC Hammer and not street enough for fans of LL Cool J.

But you couldn't tell Cohen that. "It was very difficult to talk to Lyor in those days," Faith Newman recalls. "Lyor didn't do a lot of talking; he did a lot of yelling." When Newman's assistant, Dawn Womack, accidentally sent a defective tape that Cohen had ordered for LL Cool J in L.A., he told Newman to fire her assistant, and she refused. After a screaming fight with Cohen, she hung up the phone, called Columbia, and told them she was quitting Def Jam. "You're making a huge mistake!" Simmons yelled at Newman after she told him in May of 1991 that she was leaving. "If you stay at this company for ten years," he said, "you're gonna get a piece." But Faith had made up her mind. She was twenty-five years old and ready to experience something new. "Russell was big on loyalty, and he took it very personally when I left. *Very.*"

When Faith left, she took Newkirk with her, and Def Jam didn't mind transferring his contract over to Columbia. He was going to get dropped anyway. "That was when Columbia was like, 'You spent too much money on this stuff,' " recalls Newkirk. "Russell was like, 'I'm gonna have to cut a lot of these artists.' He started making the cuts: the Black Flames got cut first. I was like, 'Here it comes. I'm feeling it coming.' " Newkirk would end up having a short career over at Columbia, and recording an album that never got out of the gate.

3rd Bass was also at a crossroads. Although they continued to perform together, Pete and Serch had already decided to part ways, and Columbia was starting to strategize ways of dealing with their upcoming solo projects. Their temporary breakup would become permanent. Some thought that Serch's wife, Chantel, created the tension in the group. When she went on the road with them during their last tour in support of *Derelicts of Dialect* with fellow Columbia act Cypress Hill in September of '91, "[Chantel] started acting like a manager," Sam Sever recalled. "She wanted to tell the dancers how to dance, and it just became a point of contention. They started fighting." "That was the tour when everything went nuts," recalls Pete. "Serch was accusing me and Rich of rigging his mike so that it would sound worse during shows to make him look bad, and that we were giving secret signals to our dancers to screw up to make him look bad. A lot of drama." Angela Thomas remembers the "trying times" when Serch would be in a car with Chantel, following the tour bus.

Thomas was often at Cohen's house downtown, going over marketing plans. Simmons was never present at these meetings—just Thomas, Cohen, and Carmen Ashhurst. The typical album setup consisted of saturating the market for about three months with a 12-inch and a CD promo, before going to radio. "Then, the objective was to go to crossover radio, because at the time, crossover radio was more open to hip-hop," notes Angela Thomas. "And then from crossover, we go back to urban radio. College radio always played an important role; street DJs, record pools, always played an important role. From there, we would do trade advertising. In setting up the album, we'd always do snipes, postcards, we'd have a video. Def Jam always did most of their videos, and they would just deliver it to us. Depending on what artist it is, we'd do a different campaign."

Cohen would go through the marketing plans with his usual keen eye, approving certain expenses and rejecting others. "Lyor was always focused," recalls Angela, who would then have to go back to Sony and explain to them what Def Jam intended to do. "And nine times out of ten," she says, "[Sony] were in agreement with almost everything." Ultimately, Sony would always foot the bill for Def Jam's demands. Still, she admits that with artists like The Don, Def Jam "spread itself too thin."

CHAPTER 11

Hard-Core

On a cold day in February of 1992, Tracey Waples stood in the lobby of Russell Simmons's building for an A&R meeting, where she was going to introduce Simmons to an artist that she was interested in signing. Just before being buzzed into the building, Waples noticed a strange-looking character crossing the street, heading right in her direction. He was wearing a bright orange leather jacket, his hair in an unruly, bushy Afro, his eyes hidden behind "Tom Cruise *Risky Business* shades," Tracey recalls, and a tissue was sticking out of his nose.

Waples realized that it was Redman, the Jersey rapper she wanted to sign. She knew he was a character, but she wasn't prepared for just how different he was. "I'm ready to put Reggie on," Eric Sermon of EPMD had said to her a few weeks earlier, and handed her a home-made demo tape. Reggie was Sermon's twenty-one-year-old pro-tégé, Reggie "Redman" Noble, and the five-song demo was his. The two of them had been good friends; Redman even lived in Sermon's apartment for two years after getting kicked out of his parents' house.

Tracey listened to the demo, and one track, "Redman vs. Reggie Noble," really got her attention. She thought it was genius. "It was like he was battle-rapping to himself," she recalls. Waples knew Redman would be right for Def Jam. After all, the label needed an artist who was not only talented, but could also bring it a much needed boost of street credibility. Waples could tell that Reggie was a star, and soon Russell could, too. "He knew Redman was gonna be off the hook, there's no question," says Tracey. "[Russell] knew he was insane, but in a good way."

Meanwhile, Parrish Smith—the other half of EPMD—was trying to persuade Simmons and Cohen to sign his own protégés: a duo called Das EFX. Lyor passed on them and picked Redman instead. Within a few months, Das EFX would sign with Elektra and release their hit album *Straight out da Sewaside,* which would become one of the biggest hip-hop success stories of 1992. "The word right around then was 'Lyor played himself. He should have signed them, too,' " David Belgrave, Def Jam's former artist development executive, recalled. Lyor stood by his decision. Redman had that "it" factor. "There was a mystique around Reggie," as Belgrave recalls. Redman would come by the office and intimidate the staff with his cryptic, thuggy persona, strolling around in a hoodie and Carhartt's, with a tissue in his nose. He would hardly say a word to anyone. "I think some people were legitimately scared of him," David recalls.

Def Jam was about to add another hard-core artist to its roster. Foreseeing the popularity of West Coast rap, Simmons discovered a twenty-one-year-old female rapper from California who went by the name Bo$$. She rolled with a sidekick, a kind of hypewoman named Dee, who also rapped. Russell heard a demo tape Bo$$ had made and immediately wanted to sign her. "He was just floored by her," Tracey Waples recalls. "That's all he could talk about." Simmons also thought Bo$$ was pretty, and many agreed.

But you'd never know it from press pictures and by the way she carried herself. She looked like a female thug, as unladylike as they come. (Ironically, when she first started rapping at the age of fourteen, her moniker was Lady.) Bo$$ dressed like a man and even sounded like a man when she rapped. Her outfits—a skull hat, dark shades, and saggy jeans—had been her dress code since she was a college student in Detroit, where she'd met her partner, Dee. Together,

SUNNY BAK

"Jam Master Jay was my teacher," said Lyor Cohen of Jay—shown here, taking a break on the Together Forever Tour in '87. Much more than just a DJ for Run–DMC, Jay played a key role in Def Jam's growth. He headed one of the label's most successful imprints—JMJ Records—responsible for such platinum acts as Onyx.

they left school to pursue rapping in L.A., and that's when Bo$$'s image became even darker. Homeless, "walking around in night-time," remembers Bo$$, the girls "wanted to blend in. We didn't want to look like no girls." It was truly survival of the fittest, and of the most masculine. *Them rapping bitches from Detroit, we should rape y'all bitches,* the local guys would say. So at night, the lipstick and the earrings all came off, and the skullcap, jeans, and gym shoes came on.

Bo$$ kept the look, and that's when Russell discovered her. En-couraging Bo$$ to exploit her good looks was useless. "I didn't want to be *seen,* I wanted to be *heard,*" she says. "I felt like I was saying some deep shit. I put a lot of time in them flows, perfecting that shit." And Def Jam didn't push her to exploit her good looks either. "To play up that aspect really would not be the Def Jam way," says David Belgrave. "She just happened to be [pretty]."

Bo$$ was surprised that Def Jam, the quintessential East Coast label, was interested in working with her. "Because Def Jam was nothing like my rap," she says. She was right: Def Jam had never signed a rapper before who hung around gangs in L.A. like Bo$$, who had moved around L.A. constantly, eventually ending up in Compton, notorious gang territory. "So who we hang with? Gang motherfuckers," says Bo$$. "The bitches we was hanging with was gang bitches. It was like shit after shit after shit. Like one big day, one big zone—years. It was like out-of-body." The girls even slept in a car at times. "It was all for the rap shit," she says.

All Bo$$ ever wanted to do was rap, and when she signed to Def Jam, she turned a deaf ear to the business aspects of being a recording artist. "It gave me a headache," she recalls. "I just wanted to do the artist part." She let her manager pick her lawyer, which was "a dumb-ass move on my part," she would later admit. "Just 'cause they're your manager don't mean they ain't jacking your ass." Years later, she would learn the price for ignoring the business of being a rapper.

Bo$$ joined Def Jam during a time of camaraderie between the artists. "Everybody was cool, which fucked me up," she recalls. "I thought people was gonna be stuck-up acting and shit. Chuck D. was cool as hell! Redman was *so* cool. He was like, 'Just do your thing.' He always had little words of wisdom and shit. Jam Master Jay was cool as hell." Bo$$ also got along with Nikki D., which she hadn't expected. "'Cause, you know, female rappers usually have a little thing with each other," says Bo$$. "I didn't meet nobody up there that was like fucked-up, from the staff to the artists."

The feeling was mutual. "Bo$$ was a major priority for Def Jam," recalls Brett Ratner. "That was when Russell was really involved in the day-to-day operations of picking the singles." Russell was so fond of Bo$$ that he let her and Dee stay in his vacant apartment on Barrow Street. The girls had been in New York for two months, living at the Gramercy Park Hotel since March of 1992 and working on Bo$$'s album. Russell doted on Bo$$, spending a lot of time around her and Dee, which was something he didn't do for just anyone. Sometimes he would pull up unannounced in front of their apartment in his white, bulletproof Rolls-Royce. "We need to hit this party," he would summon them from downstairs. "Y'all need to come down!" On other nights, he would take the girls out to dinner, "and order fettuccine with salmon, his favorite dish," recalls Bo$$. Russell gushed to everyone about what a great artist Bo$$ was, calling her album-in-progress one of the "best albums I've been involved with in five years."

Sometimes Lyor would also come along. "He was cool," Bo$$ recalls. "He seemed like a damn dictator and shit. He pretty much stayed to himself. I was like, 'He must be doing a lot of work or something,' because he pretty much stayed in his office. I just thought of him like, 'Oh, this is that mean motherfucker.'" When Russell was unavailable to entertain Bo$$ for the evening, he would send over someone from the office—such as David Belgrave. "I had to take her out to a BDP show at the Roxy," remembers David. "I still had my car from college, a 1978 AMC Concord two-door, left door that worked. I remember I piled them all into the junk mobile."

Also dropping by often to see Bo$$ and Dee was Jam Master Jay, who lived downstairs at 111 Barrow. He sometimes brought a new group on his label, Onyx. "Okay, listen to these beats," he would say to Bo$$ and Dee. "If y'all need some help writing, Onyx can write with y'all." Onyx were a group of four MCs from New York who previously had a one-single deal with Profile records, the same label that Run-DMC recorded for. Cousins Fredro Star and Sticky Fingaz fronted the group, with backup from Big D.S. and Jun See.

When Jam Master Jay had heard "Stickin' Move," a song from a demo that the group passed on to him, he knew he might have found in Onyx the star group on his JMJ label. "Give me ten of those," he said to the group.

Onyx signed an EP deal with Def Jam, but they recorded so many tracks that they quickly re-signed to an album deal. For then-fifteen-year-old Sticky Fingaz, the signing was a big deal. "Def Jam was it— the biggest, greatest, largest, most potent label at the time," he says. "All of the big stars." He was so young, in fact, that he didn't even know who Russell Simmons was. "We're at Def Jam in the lobby, looking at all the plaques on the wall, and saying to ourselves, 'I can't believe I'm fucking here.'" he remembers. "And there's this guy that's walking around that everybody seems to come to attention

PAUL NAJERA

When Def Jam launched Def Jam West, the emphasis was on hard, grimy rhymes and flows, even if you were a female. Bo$$, Def Jam's first successful female rapper, was much more Onyx than Foxy Brown. Some felt she should have exploited her good looks more.

when he comes around." Sticky asked Fredro who it was. "You idiot!" Fredro exclaimed. "You don't know who the fuck that is? That guy's Russell Simmons."

But it wasn't Russell who Sticky and the rest of the group were most concerned with impressing—it was Jam Master Jay.

"Jay was hands-on everything," recalls Sticky. He even gave Sticky Fingaz specific instructions about how to act: " 'I don't want you to say one word. When it's time for interviews, don't even talk, just sit there. You don't talk; you just rhyme,' " Sticky says Jam Master Jay would direct. "Jay, he's a positive dude. He's a gangsta, too, don't get it twisted. I went to nigga crib one day, the nigga showed me like ten automatic weapons. I'm like, 'God damn!' Niggas from the hood like guns. We collect them shits. But he was definitely a good-hearted motherfucker though."

The recording of Bo$$'s album dragged on for more than six months, as she tried to settle on the right style of beats. "In L.A., I liked slow beats," she says. "And then in New York, their beats were kind of more up-tempo. I was like, 'Damn, you got me having too many words in my rap!' " After experimenting with a few different producers, Bo$$ settled on MC Serch, who "did some real nice shit," she says of the songs "I Don't Give a Fuck," which would become the album's first single, and "Diary of a Mad Bitch." Eric Sermon also ended up producing two tracks, as well as Jam Master Jay.

But most of the production was done by a young producer from L.A. called Def Jef. He produced the album's biggest chart-topping single, "Deeper." The song was recorded with a sample from Barry White's "I'm Gonna Love You Just a Little Bit More, Babe." At first, Barry White refused to clear the sample. Then, he gave them a figure that was considered astronomical for sample clearance in 1992: $10,000. "Russell believed in the record so much that he really fought to get that cleared," Tracey Waples recalls. "When we got that clearance, boy, we thought we were like up, up, and away!"

"It was like a factory," Bo$$ recalls. "Everybody was moving fast; I wasn't used to that shit. With the rap industry, it's twenty-four hours!" Def Jam was also launching Def Jam West; along with Bo$$, they added two more artists: MC Sug and Mel-Low. But since there was still no West Coast chief or staff, Russell wanted to keep Bo$$ close. Meanwhile, Redman was in the studio, doing more work on his songs for the upcoming album. His album was pushed back until after the release of EPMD's new album, which was scheduled for May.

•   •   •

When Lyor Cohen realized that he needed another assistant, Seena Greenwald, who was an intern in the office, thought that her older sister Julie might be right for the job. Having come home to New York after doing Teach For America in New Orleans, where she was planning on returning after the summer, Julie was looking for a summer job.

When Greenwald first walked into the Rush office for her interview, she remembers being greeted by "this tall dude" with "jet-black, curly hair with this 'fro going on," with skater sneakers on. It was Lyor, of course. The only thing that she could think was *You run a record company?*

"Why should I hire you?" Cohen asked her with "this crazy accent," Greenwald recalls. "'Cause I'm smart, I've got a great work ethic, I'll be able to do whatever you need me to get done."

"Can you type?" he asked.

"Yeah, fifty words a minute!" she said, lying. Ten years later, she would admit from her twenty-eighth-floor corner office as the president of Island Records that she's still a lousy typist. "I was not a hip-hop chick at all," she says. "I came from the Catskills. [The job] landed in my lap, and I quickly learned about [hip-hop] and really just started immersing myself into it. I had a lot of interns from Howard University; I surrounded myself with young kids."

Greenwald was hired and immediately put to work in Cohen's messy office. "I never saw something so disorganized and disheveled," she recalled. "There was just product everywhere: old posters, point-of-purchase items, records, CDs. I literally had to sit on the edge of a couch with a makeshift shelf—that was my station." Cohen sat a few feet away, in his favorite lime green chair, screaming at people most of the day, while Greenwald would sit with her shoulders hunched over, thinking, *Please don't let it be me.* She didn't know that just two days before she'd started her job there had been a bloody altercation in this office. Big Daddy Kane, who had been on tour promoting his latest album, came by one sunny afternoon and beat up Big D., who was Lyor's tour manager and a liaison between the artist and the booking agent. Big D. had recently started his office job after being on the road for a few years. Apparently, Kane had gotten stranded in North Carolina after a show; the bus had broken down, and for some reason Kane did not get timely attention. Sheryl Konensburg, who also assisted Lyor and was Julie's cousin, found herself in the middle of the fight. Kane simply picked her up, moved her out of the way, then blocked her in her cubicle. Big D. was pushed against the computer stand and cut his back; bodies were moving, people were yelling. "It could've been a lot worse," Sheryl recalls. "If anybody really wanted to do anything bad, it wouldn't have been just a fistfight." Still, she says, "it was bad." Scott Koenig was downstairs when the fiasco took place. "I remember being at the foot of the stairs when they were all rolling out the door," he says, "and Kane had this hood on, and he gave me a black-power sign. But with a smile on his face."

Three weeks into Greenwald's new job, Cohen walked up behind her and shouted, "You don't know how to type!" But he wasn't mad,

because, as Greenwald puts it, "he already fell in love." And when
Cohen got a good vibe from someone, he befriended them right
away. "One of his best qualities [was] he could look you up and
down, and ten seconds later he knows your whole rap," says Scott
Koenig. "He knows if he can manipulate you. Some people he will
yell or scream at to motivate; some people, he'll never scream at."
One of the people Cohen never screamed at was Julie Greenwald.

As Greenwald was discovering, Def Jam was going through serious growing pains. Where once five-figure checks would be lying on
the floor, now company credit cards were routinely being declined.
"We were ice-cold," says Chris Lighty. One day, David Belgrave
came by the office of Profile Records, just a few blocks up from Def
Jam's, and someone asked him, "How do you keep a beer cold?"
"How?" David asked. "Put it in between two RAL twelve-inches!"

But it wasn't funny. "Things were fucked-up!" recalls Brett Ratner. "The record company was in the toilet, shit was hittin' the fan.
Russell became an insomniac around that time." Even Danny Simmons thought that his brother was acting "withdrawn a little bit," he
recalls. "You could tell he'd be sort of distant, he wouldn't be connecting fully with stuff." Danny wasn't the only one who noticed.
Stan Lathan, Simmons's partner in Def Jam Pictures, and Carmen
Ashhurst also worried that Russell didn't seem "balanced" and called
Danny for a meeting. "I told them that whatever it was, Russell could
handle it; that he was just going through a bad period. That I think it
would be a mistake at that point to confront him with that."

The transformation into RAL was confusing for those working
for the company, as well as those working with it. "We were RAL,"
says Julie. "It took a minute for us to get back to being Def Jam. We
stopped being Def Jam." The famous Def Jam logo had practically
vanished from business cards and company letterhead. Instead, everything read "RAL," alongside seven different logos: JMJ, PRO-
Division, Outburst, Def Jam. "It wasn't sexy," recalls Julie. "Here I'm
working for this great-ass company, Def Jam; everybody wants my
jacket. I'd call people, tell them I'm from Def Jam, and then I gotta

send them shit with RAL on it. I'm thinking I'm the coolest moth-erfucker in the world. And my business card says RAL." Cohen loved the colors he'd picked for the logo: orange and green, an homage to his alma mater, Miami University.

Although there were suddenly handfuls of Def Jam flops, what was happening at the label was not unique. Theirs was a fairly text-book example of a record-label growth spurt. "There's a variety of is-sues that have an impact on whether or not you succeed. Sometimes it doesn't have that much to do with 'Are you good?' " says Leyla Turkkan. "It's a matter of where in the cycle are you released, what are the budgets like, what's going on at radio."

But in spite of the flops, there were enough street and commercial hits to keep the label afloat. On July 28, after a two-month delay, EPMD's *Business Never Personal* hit stores, with two standout tracks: "Crossover" and "Head Banger," which featured Redman. The al-bum's release meant that the door was open for Redman to finally make his debut as a solo artist. His single "Blow Ya Mind" was set for an August release. Six weeks later, in September of 1992, Redman's *Whut? Thee Album* hit stores.

"His album was a masterpiece, a work of art," says Tracey Waples. "It was what Nas's [debut album] *Illmatic* was to his time period. From the interludes, to the skits, it was just a masterpiece." The setup for the album took place rather organically, since "we never expected records to get played on the radio," recalls Tracey. Def Jam marketed directly to the streets, Redman's core audience, "to make sure we had visual impressions that would play to that audience," says Waples. One of the promotional tools that Def Jam had become fond of using were long-form commercials. To capitalize on Redman's already massive buzz, Def Jam decided to shoot one for him.

"It was the coldest freaking day of the winter that year," Tracey recalls. "We shot on this dirty, crunchy, abandoned yard; [Redman's] nose was running endlessly, so a tissue stayed in it the whole time, but for me that was part of the whole thing. I wanted to showcase that." With a snippet of "Blow Ya Mind" running through the clip, Redman walked around the burnt-out neighborhood, pushing the guy holding the camera. The clip accurately captured the real-life Reggie Noble. "Redman still lived at home in Newark, and he was real," says Brett Ratner. "He was a guy who carried a pistol, and all of his friends carried pistols. And he smoked a lot of weed. And the way he spoke: he was so unarticulate, but smart though. So smart!"

The same month, Public Enemy went on tour as the opening act for U2. When Public Enemy finished their set, and U2 came on, Russell said to Brett Ratner, who accompanied him to the show, "Let's get outta here." "Wait a second, it's U2," Brett said. "Who the fuck are U2, man?" Russell responded. "Russell was very much isolated," Brett recalls. "What he knew about was what he knew about."

In October of 1992, EPMD set out on their Hit Squad Tour, which proved a success; there was a strong buzz on their single, "Head Banger," and the album went gold in just thirty days of its release. (But the tour became tainted by the potential of Eric and Parrish breaking up.) *Whut? Thee Album,* was also doing well and Redman's performance was a highlight. There was a strong focus on college radio with Redman, with a college advertising plan scheduled for November of '92. There was also a major tour, featuring Redman, being planned by ICM for January, and a minipromo tour with video, press, and radio being discussed. Tracey Waples also helped promote the record through her valuable connections in the industry. "Puffy would give me the Jodeci stuff and I would give him the Redman stuff," she recalls.

During EPMD's tour, Def Jam also serviced to radio a white label 12-inch of "Head Banger," off their album. "Crossover," meanwhile, was number one on the CMJ charts, and on October 9, it took the award for Best Rap Single at the 7th Annual New York Music Awards. LL Cool J was given the award for Best Rap Artist.

"Back to the Grill," the second single from MC Serch's solo album, *Return of the Product,* was also released in the second week of October, moving the album up to No. 4 on the CMJ charts. Serch performed with Nas at the nightclub Shelter to a house of seven hundred. It was also the CMJ Marathon, and Def Jam had a whole batch of new artists to promote. On October 28, 1992, CMJ Music Marathon held a Def Jam/Rush show-case at the Muse nightclub in New York, at Tenth Avenue and Thirteenth Street, formerly Mars. Redman, who was sell-ing forty thousand copies of his *Whut? Thee Album* per week, was the biggest marquee act, performing his hit "Time for Some Akshun," Bo$$ per-formed her second single, "Deeper," and Onyx—whose album was bumped to the first week of November—did

CAROLINE TOREM-CRAIG

Redman brought the street credibility back to Def Jam when it needed it most.

"Throw Ya Gunz." Funkmaster Flex deejayed. The next day, CMJ hosted a "Columbia Night" at the Muse again, during which Bo$$ performed "I Don't Give a Fuck."

•   •   •

In November of 1992, Onyx's "Throw Ya Gunz" single was deliv-ered to radio, and although it was getting played, program directors "were complaining" about the profanity and violence in the lyrics, as Sticky Fingaz recalled. "Nobody wanted to play [the video]," ac-cording to Julie Greenwald, who had by that time been promoted to promotions coordinator, "but the places it *did* get played, it was so re-active, and so potent. We circumvented it with the vinyl out on the streets and with the video at the local video outlets, and we got such major response off that, and we knew that we were developing some-thing so cool.

"It was so exciting, because back then breaking an artist on such a big level, and getting into mainstream and MTV and having people play your record on radio, it was such a huge deal," says Julie. Bo$$, in many ways, was like a female version of Onyx: just as hard and tough, but less hyper. And because Onyx's debut was released within three months of Bo$$'s *Born Gangstaz,* the two acts were promoted together, even when it came to merchandising and promotional items such as T-shirts (one featured Bo$$ on the front and Onyx on the back) and tapes (Bo$$ on one side and Onyx on the other). Both acts were taken to every radio station possible.

Because Onyx and Bo$$ both had a hard-core image, Cohen thought it would be a good idea to package them together by putting them on the road for a promotional tour for a month. It was Lyor's "Rush Management philosophy of touring, and he was dead-on," says Tracey, "especially knowing that we are putting out records that we are not getting on the radio with. So we put all the groups on a bus together and just worked the pavement."

The two acts went on a number of promotional tours together. The crowds were responsive, because luckily both acts were electrifying performers. Bo$$ and Onyx also got along well, having already spent plenty of time in Russell's apartment, writing raps and getting to know each other. One day on the bus, Tracey Waples—who came along on a promo tour—overheard Sticky Fingaz playing an instrumental that didn't sound like anything she had heard before. He kept rewinding the record over and over, and writing rhymes to it. "It's my man and them," Sticky told Tracey. "They got this new group called Wu-Tang." "Wu-Tang? Are they Asian?" Tracey asked. "Nah, nah. But they're on it like that. It's a bunch of guys from Staten Island." The instrumental, he told her, was of a track they recorded called "Protect Ya Neck."

"Redman's debut was made successful due largely to an all-out retail and street campaign, which created a buzz in retail and the street like no other I have ever experienced," wrote Thomas Lytell in his end-of-the-year report on December 22, 1992. "It's this kind of excitement that retail hopes to generate on every new release in 1993. The RAL/Def Jam New Music Seminar sampler played an enormous part in creating the aforementioned buzz on Redman, as did the Triple Threat sampler for Onyx." According to Lytell, the "buzz surrounding Onyx is good, not as big as Redman experienced, but we are continuously doing things to build on this already-existing level of excitement."

Russell, meanwhile, also had big plans for 1993, inspired by the success of his hit HBO show, *Def Comedy Jam,* which had been on the air since August. The premise was simple: four stand-up comics perform during the thirty-minute show to a live audience. The language was raw, the subject matter adult, and the tapings quickly became a hot ticket in New York, attracting urban royalty: Spike Lee, Rosie Perez, and Heavy D. The show became an instant smash hit for HBO, regularly beating out *The Tonight Show* in homes with HBO.

An HBO sitcom was also being negotiated, called *The Johnson Posse*—"*Married . . . with Children* in the projects with real language," as Russell described it—as well as a TriStar film about a white boy who grew up in the ghetto and has to adjust to an Ivy League college (working title: *Clown Prince*).

In the midst of pushing their new crop of hard-core street acts, Def Jam had a bit of a dilemma with the newly solo Pete Nice. In his video for "Rat Bastard," Pete decided to make fun of his former groupmate and picked Brett Ratner to direct his vision. "We got a real fat kid and inscribed '3rd Bass' on the back of his head," Brett recalls. The video was quite violent; it was back when artists could put guns in videos. "It was Russell's favorite video!" Brett recalled. "This guy would show it to chairmen of companies, people off the street. He would bring people to his apartment and screen the video over and over. 'Brett Ratner's a genius!' " But Serch was not crazy about it. In fact, according to Brett, when Serch saw the video, he "literally stormed up to Def Jam and just started crying in a staff meeting with all the A&R's. He said he was gonna beat me up! He felt really humiliated."

But there were doubts about the success of the project. Even Russell worried about how well Pete's album would sell and had regrets about picking "Kick the Bobo" as his second single, especially after "Rat Bastard" was not a big hit, despite the infamous video. Pete Nice was now Pete the entrepreneur. He was living in "a junior version of Russell Simmons's crib," as one journalist pointed out, downtown. The upstairs level of the duplex functioned as the office of the newly formed Hoppoh Records, the result of a deal that twenty-six-year-old Pete had negotiated with Columbia/Sony. Bobbito Garcia was helping Pete run the label. The first artist was supposed to be Bobbito's longtime friend and neighbor from uptown named Kurious George. Pete and Bobbito were also running a management company called Hit-U-Off, which looked after artists like H2O, Artifacts, and a production crew called SD50s.

Serch was also more than an artist. He had formed a production company called Serchlite Music, overseeing the debut album by Nas (or Nasty Nas, as he was called then). It was the new era of the hip-hop businessman. Serch's own solo effort, released a year before Pete's, sold a dismal 250,000 copies.

Having sold 12 million albums worldwide, LL Cool J was still very much a priority artist at Def Jam. Still, he was nervous about how the public would receive his latest effort, *14 Shots to the Dome,* which was ready to hit stores in March 1992. One day, he came into the office to get an opinion about his album-in-progress. Chuck D. was also in the office that day, and LL wanted his reaction to a new song he had been working on. David Belgrave and Jordan Sulmers, a Def Jam A&R rep, were close by and also slipped into the conference room.

"What's going on, Mr. Belgrave," Chuck D. greeted him, as he usually did. They didn't mind David and George being in the room, but David quickly became horrified. "What if this song sucks?" he thought. The beat dropped, and the song turned out to be merely "aight," as David recalls. "And so, I don't want to leave in the middle of it, but I didn't want to get polled at the end." The song finishes, and LL turned to Chuck: "So, man, whatcha think?" Chuck looked at him and said, "Hey, you LL Cool J! I can't be mad at anything you do." Then he hugged LL and left. "That was the whole thing about Def Jam—it was total access," David points out. The song did not make LL's new album.

Def Jam also pushed Onyx's *Bacdafucup,* which hit stores in May 1993, with all its power. They shot a unique EPK, in which a kid in a barbershop gets his head shaved. "We could only do one take, where they grabbed him and put him down on the chair and just started shaving his head," recalls Belgrave of the clip. "They took it back to the basics," recalls Sticky, "where you go meet the retailers, you go to the one-stops, you meet the guys that run the one-stops, you make it a little bit more personal. You shake hands, you sign autographs, take pictures for the kids. That way, they feel like they know you." Another tool that Def Jam utilized, which was so rare among hip-hop labels back then, were reps, also called regionals. Most labels have a regional in one or two states, but Def Jam made sure it had a rep in every major city in the country. "A regional is a person that lives in the state and knows everything about it: where the barbershop is, where the clubs is at, where the bad bitches is at, where the liquor store at, where they sell weed at," Sticky explains.

One of Onyx's favorite regionals was a twenty-five-year-old Baltimore native named Kevin Liles. "He was dope regional!" Sticky recalls. "I could see how he got to a high position—'cause he was going extra. We would come to town, he would check us in the hotels; I go in my bathroom, my sink is filled up with ice and forty-ounces and Hennessy bottles. Blunts laying on my bed with like a quarter of weed! All the people he had working for them was females, bad chicks. It's good when you get off a five-hour flight to go to the hotel to see that they really care."

Kevin Liles was Def Jam's freshly appointed mid–Atlantic regional. He had started as an intern in 1991, reporting to then mid–Atlantic regional Kevin Mitchell, who would eventually be hired as the national college rep. "Kevin, why don't you interview for the job?" Thomas Lytell said to Kevin when Kevin Mitchell's former position opened. Liles, who came from a business background, showed up to the interview in a suit with a briefcase full of marketing analysis. "In marketing and sales I was like a wizard: pie graphs, numbers. I was very analytical," he says. One of the people interviewing him was Lyor Cohen. Kevin's competitors came in with just résumés, while Kevin was "overprepared," as he remembered. Kevin did his presentation and went back to Baltimore. "I nailed it," he recalls of his interview. He didn't hear from anyone for two weeks.

He wasn't too worried; after all, he was making enough money in Baltimore, had two cars, a house. He was still collecting royalty checks from the massive hit song he co-wrote in 1990, Milli Vanilli's "Girl You Know It's True." One day his phone rang and it was Julie Greenwald. "We wanna hire you," she said. "But we wanna pay thirty K a year." "I make more than that here!" Kevin said. "Well, it's what we have to offer, and we think you'd be a great asset," she replied. Kevin asked if she could hold, then thought about it for a minute. "I can work with y'all for that," he said when he got back on the phone. "No, you won't be working *with* us," Julie clarified. "You'll be working *for* us."

•   •   •

It was important for Julie Greenwald to keep doing events that kept the "Def" logo relevant, piggybacking off *Def Comedy Jam* and putting together "huge flyaways" from the shows, and bringing in program directors, not just contest winners; and then doing a big brunch, with a huge video presentation, to tell them about upcoming acts. She was given free rein to plan these events. "Tell me anything," Lyor would say to Julie, and she would. When it came to innovative ideas, the two thought alike. "He's one of the most creative people you will ever meet in your entire life," she says of Lyor. "He was so open to anything that was different, that would get the kids excited, that would get the DJs excited, that would get the retailers excited. He never wanted to do anything the same way." The two of them worked to make sure that no two marketing plans were alike.

When radio and standard video channels such as MTV and BET failed to deliver, Julie relied on the Box, a kind of pay-per-view video program, in which viewers paid several dollars to see their favorite video, as an effective marketing tool. "My God, did we use the Box," she recalls. "I used to sit at Lyor's house till three in the morning and just call. We were the original jackers of the Box. We would just sit there with two phone lines and hit them." For about $10,000 for a video, Def Jam was able to get all of their new videos into the homes of their target audience: teenagers.

"There were pockets of radio stations that were our friends, that definitely played rap, were proud of it," says Julie. "And for our friends, we treated them superwell and we made sure we catered to them and really got the artists down there and supported the stations and did whatever we needed to do."

But with the creation of Broadcast Data Systems (BDS), radio was already changing. BDS was a sophisticated airplay measurement system, which used the same technology that the military first developed to detect submarines, to monitor radio airplay in the one hundred top markets in the United States. Each time a record aired, the system would detect it, register the time of day, and cross-reference it with the Arbitron rating system for each radio station, producing precise airplay information about every song played in major markets.

Despite the effectiveness of radio and music-video programming in breaking Def Jam's artists, nothing compared to the relationship between consumers and the club DJs. "When you put a record on vinyl, and you send it to the DJs and they're playing it in the clubs, and it's on their mix shows, they have such an honest relationship with their consumers," says Julie. "If they're putting out records at two in the morning and the place is erupting, you got something. If it's clearing the dance floor, you know you're in trouble."

Def Jam knew they were on to something when they released Onyx's "Slam" single. "We needed something that we could kill them with, but dominate radio," recalls Sticky Fingaz. "That's when we made 'Slam,' which was just as hard [as 'Throw Ya Gunz'], but more [radio-friendly], and it had a concept to it." Def Jam also released

Bo$$'s "I Don't Give a Fuck," followed by "Deeper," which had a video, as well as "Recipe of a Hoe" and "Progress of Elimination."

Bo$$ and Onyx were finally sent out on a real tour in October of 1993: the Chronic Tour with Doctor Dre and Snoop Doggy Dogg. It was an opportunity to make solid tour money. Unfortunately, the tour was halted after only four dates, when some of the participants got out of hand. Onyx had arranged a big merchandising deal, and after the tour was shut down, the merchandiser tried to sue them.

Tracey didn't forget about the Wu-Tang Clan instrumental, "Protect Ya Neck," she'd heard coming out of Sticky Fingaz's stereo on the tour bus. When she got back to New York from her promo tour with Onyx and Bo$$, one of the first things she did was to get hold of Wu-Tang, who were already recording in their producer RZA's basement in Park Hill, Staten Island. Tracey didn't waste time and went to meet with them in their neighborhood. For a few weeks, she went out there as often as she could, getting to know the members, and trying to figure out which one she wanted to sign to Def Jam. "Please, y'all, don't let me get robbed," she thought as she drove her white BMW through the dangerous streets of Park Hill. She took the risk, of course, because "when you're serious about an artist and pursuing them, you want to get into their world." She would often pick up a drunk Ol' Dirty Bastard, who would be singing old songs that he said his mother used to sing.

Although Waples liked the entire Wu-Tang crew, she gravitated to ODB and Method Man, the ones with "far more star potential," she says. Finally, she set up a meeting between the group and Russell at Time Cafe on Lafayette Street. Wu-Tang, all seven of them, gathered at a table, along with a few friends from the neighborhood, excitedly waiting to meet the famous Russell Simmons. "He walked in, and the look on his face was priceless," Tracey remembers. "He was like, 'Who are all these people?' "

After the meeting, Russell told Tracey that she had to pick either ODB or Method Man. "I really had my heart set on Method Man *and* Ol' Dirty Bastard," she recalls. "Look, I don't have money to sign both of them," Russell told her. So she went out to Staten Island again to make her decision. As she sat in the basement of RZA's house, she knew that everyone else was waiting on her decision, too. She could feel RZA's eyes "burning the back of my neck," wanting to know whom she was going to pick. "I was observing Method Man do something a little bizarre, but for whatever reason, it was an indication to me that he was the one," she recalls. "[Tracey] was credited as the A&R person, even though Lyor really signed Method Man," says Chris Lighty. "Sometimes he had great ideas, sometimes he had shitty ideas. He loved the whole Wu-Tang situation, and the fact that they were able to do solo deals. He jumped on Method Man, because he felt Method Man was the star."

But one artist wasn't too excited about Method Man's arrival: Redman. Having spent nearly every day with Tracey as her star artist, Redman started to feel that "he was gonna get kicked to the curb," Tracey recalls. One day, he came into her office "beefing," she recalls, and complaining that Def Jam hadn't been paying enough attention to him. "You're still a priority at this company, and you're definitely still a priority for me," she assured him. "Y'all haven't even met yet! Y'all are just alike. You and this guy can fuck around and be like brothers if you give it a chance."

Redman, Bo$$, and Onyx became the trinity of new, more hard-core Def Jam acts to rescue the label from its slump. It was "the big turnaround" for Def Jam. Now with Method Man added to the roster, Def Jam was really going back to the streets.

Part Three

Fast
Company

1994–2004

CHAPTER 12

The Lyor Show

Written over twenty-three hundred years ago, *The Art of War* by Sun-Tzu is considered the oldest military treatise in the world. It is filled with compact views on cunning, integrity, deception, manipulation, and advice such as "Lure them with the prospect of gain, take them by confusion." American officers during World War II read the book closely. The Japanese army studied it for decades, and many twentieth-century Chinese officers are said to have known *The Art of War* by heart.

Lyor Cohen lived by that book. He had long been using its principles in the trenches of artist management at Rush. Now, as he was leaving management to move in with Def Jam in its new office at 160 Varick Street, Cohen was ready to apply the "art of war" to running Def Jam. Of all the numerous moves that Def Jam had gone through since its inception, the one to Varick Street on June 1, 1993—office number four—felt most like a new beginning. Def Jam even ran an ad announcing their move, depicting two high-rise buildings next to each other: one was being demolished ("Outta There!" the caption read); the other was standing tall, shiny, and new ("In There!" the caption proclaimed).

Rush Management, and whatever remained of its already tiny staff, was left back at Elizabeth Street. Chris Lighty was put in charge

Looking ahead: The future king of Def Jam, Lyor Cohen, during a stop on the Together Forever Tour (the destination on the bus behind him reads: "Shousurtitz.") "He is the general leading an army in the war to maximize profit," said former art director Eric "Haze" Lieber. "Loyal, efficient soldiers will be taken care of and treated with respect. Incompetence isn't tolerated."

of winding the company down and, as a bonus, was given his own imprint—Violator Records—under the RAL umbrella.

Having launched Phat Farm clothing in the spring of 1993, Simmons had mostly removed himself from the day-to-day business of the label. Both the staff and the artists respected his priorities. "You don't never call Russell, 'cause he is like Lady Eloise," pointed out Sticky Fingaz. "More than anything, it's just his face on the product." And the face was now even more famous than the Def Jam logo. Simmons's weekly TV show, *Def Comedy Jam,* was a huge hit, and magazines like *Vanity Fair* published flattering profiles of him. The now defunct *Mademoiselle* magazine even ran a page in its April 1993 issue covering a day in Simmons's life. "Rap mogul goes camera crazy," the piece proclaimed, and featured thirteen candid photos of Simmons living the good life: hanging out with Alan Grubman, Robert De Niro, and Naomi Campbell in St. Bart's, mugging for the camera with actor Forest Whitaker in New York. "The only reason we were sexy is because Russell was sexy," says Chris Lighty.

Lyor Cohen's job now was to take hold of the reins at Def Jam and make it sexy in its own right. "[Def Jam] got real mature, real quick," recalled producer Kaspa, who was managed by Rush Producers Management. Cohen's office reflected his new status in the company, too: although still small, it was now outfitted with "exceptionally fine Italian furniture," as Cohen's former business manager Todd Moscowitz recalled, along with a premium humidor always by the ashtray. Occasionally, Simmons would step in to oversee special projects, but "for the most part, it was Lyor's company," said Julie Greenwald, who stood right by Cohen's side, devising innovative promotional events and marketing campaigns that would become her forte. It was Julie's idea to send out invites to a Christmas party inside a mock pill container, or to print invites on the tag of a mini, burgundy Def Jam T-shirt.

Another marketing brainchild of Greenwald's, designed to help Onyx move units, was called "Slam Censorship," which was put together for the Black Radio Exclusive (BRE) conference in Washington, D.C., in July of '93. "Slam," which was released as an Onyx single on June 22, was selling well, and Julie came up with the idea of doing an event that would play up that the single was called "Slam" while they were in D.C. "All these congresspeople were really going after hip-hop at that time," Julie explains. "We were such an easy target."

Steve Carr directed a promo of various artists speaking against censorship, and the final result got plenty of praise. The event cost practically nothing—$30,000, which was pennies for a major label. "We were so nickel-and-dimed back then," says Julie. Indeed, while there were plenty of good ideas at Def Jam, bringing them to fruition—with the budgets that Sony allotted for marketing—was a constant struggle. "You almost felt that you had to beg," recalls Julie. "You just felt like, 'Why can't we be in control of our own money? And we should be controlling the budgets.'" She would sometimes hear about Sony's big sales conferences at which Def Jam product was not even discussed. "We need to be treated like the big boys are treated," she thought. Lyor, too, was growing tired of the struggle of being "in a relationship where you're constantly fighting and arguing," as Julie points out. "You wanna be *partners* with people." Furthermore, Sony "tried to internally build an urban music department," recalled Todd Moscowitz. The label they created was called Chaos, and Sony staff that had previously focused on Def Jam product exclusively was forced to juggle both. "We were doing so well that we dwarfed [Sony's] urban experience and business," Cohen explains. "Instead of taking pride, they took it as competitiveness."

Cohen knew that Def Jam was at the end of its road with Sony, and started looking into new distribution. But there were no takers. He called Joe Galante, who was the head of RCA and today remains the chairman of the RCA Labels Group, "begging him," as he recalls. "I didn't tell any of the staff. And he sent me a fax to the general fax machine, saying that RCA wasn't interested in Def Jam. That was terrible." Especially since there were hot records. By midsummer of 1993, Redman's *Whut? Thee Album* had gone gold and was fast approaching platinum. This was great news. Onyx going platinum, meanwhile, was amazing news. *Bacdafucup* shot up the charts, even outselling LL Cool J's *14 Shots to the Dome.* (Sticky never forgot what Russell said to him one day when Sticky started complaining about certain marketing and promotional issues. "Listen, man, don't give me a headache," said Russell. "Until you got platinum, don't give me a headache.")

Lyor also got Onyx on a soundtrack for a film called *Judgment Night,* starring Emilio Estevez and Cuba Gooding Jr. A unique mix of rappers collaborating with heavy-metal and rock bands, the soundtrack was released by Epic, a division of Sony, so when it was being put together in the summer of 1993, Lyor and Russell decided to jump on board. Sticky remembers that the idea of pairing up Onyx's vocals with Biohazard's music was Lyor's. "They actually had to force us to do it," Sticky recalls. "We wasn't really trying to cross over. Hell, no, we from the streets. We hard-core: guns, money, drugs." But ultimately, Biohazard "turned out to be cool dudes," says Sticky.

"We hung out with them before and after the thing. It was a good move."

Others disagree. "Biohazard ruined Onyx's career," says Scott Koenig. "It's obviously a lot more than that, but that was the catalyst." But Sticky thinks the collaboration was "icing on the cake. 'Slam' was already platinum, then we did it with Biohazard, and it's double platinum. So, yeah, it helped it a little bit." As for street credibility, working on a song with a rock artist had no bearing, says Sticky. "It's hard to destroy the street credibility when your first impression is 'Throw Ya Gunz,' " says Sticky. "We saved Def Jam, actually. We sold two million singles, and we sold two million albums."

But the success that Def Jam had with Onyx in 1993 would pale in comparison to that of a twenty-one-year-old kid from Long Beach, California, named Warren G. On June 29, 1993, the soundtrack to the John Singleto–directed film *Poetic Justice* was released. The standout track was "Indo Smoke" by L.A. rapper Mista Grimm, which Warren G. guest rapped on. Warren had been one of the earlier producers for Tupac and already had production credits. "Indo Smoke" became an L.A. hit, selling in excess of two hundred thousand copies in L.A. alone. Those kinds of sales figures were rare for a local hit and caught the attention of Def Jam. Paul Stewart was a VP at Def Jam and also a partner with Singleton in a management company. The two of them entered into a management agreement with Warren and introduced him to Def Jam.

Warren had a group in the late eighties called 213, which he produced and deejayed with. Nate Dogg sang in the group, while Snoop Doggy Dogg rapped. Though 213 had a great underground buzz in L.A., it never got radio play. Still, they sold a lot of tapes. Warren G.'s older brother, Doctor Dre, meanwhile, was having success with NWA but not making any money, so when he met Suge Knight, the two decided to start their own label, Death Row. They were interested in Warren's group, 213, but ultimately signed only Nate and Snoop.

Warren remembers when Chris Lighty called him in L.A. for the first time. "We like what you're doing," Lighty said. "We're inter-ested in signing you to Def Jam." Warren was excited, but had been so sheltered inside his Long Beach bubble that he didn't even know who was signed to Def Jam. "I always thought the artists I was trip-ping over were signed to Rush," he recalls. (Indeed, all of Def Jam's albums carried the Rush Management logo, so it was easy to get con-fused about Def Jam and Rush.) "They told me: LL Cool J, Beastie Boys, Public Enemy, Slick Rick," he remembers. "I was kinda freaked out. 'They can't be interested in me with all those talented groups.' " But Warren's lawyer assured him that Def Jam was serious.

In mid-October, Def Jam flew Warren out to New York. "I think it might've been my first time flying," he recalls. As soon as he ar-rived at his hotel, a car picked him up to take him down to Varick Street to meet everyone at Def Jam. "I heard these guys in the room, like they were arguing," recalls Warren. "And that's when I first met Lyor, doing business."

Lyor took Warren around the office and introduced him to every-one. *Wow, this is really serious,* thought Warren. After he left, Cohen picked up the phone and called up LL Cool J. Later that day, back at the hotel, Warren got a call. "This is LL. I'm downstairs," the caller said. "Who?!" Warren asked, stunned. "LL Cool J," the caller said. LL had recently come back from the summer's Superfest Tour and was getting ready to perform at *Showtime at the Apollo.* His newest video, for "Backseat of My Jeep," was one of the most requested on the Box, and he had recently finished the third video off *14 Shots to the Dome,* "Stand by Your Man," remixed by Teddy Riley, a new jack swing–sounding, sleek rap ballad.

"I almost shitted myself," recalls Warren when he got the phone call. LL had been summoned by Lyor to take Warren around the city. "I guess he was just welcoming me to the family," recalls Warren. "He took me shopping down in the mall to go get me some gear, took me all around the whole Jamaica, Queens; took me to [his] house, showed me his old Samurai from back in the day. Showed me his grandmother's house, the basement where he started—the whole nine! I thought I was dreaming. I was like, 'Wow! LL Cool J!' 'Cause I'm a humongous LL Cool J fan, so I was starstruck." Later that night, at a party for the New Music Seminar, Warren was introduced to Russell Simmons. Warren remembered him from *Krush Groove,* and he was in awe. *I can't believe I'm sitting here with Russell Simmons,* he thought. "It just freaked me out," he recalled.

By the end of his whirlwind trip to New York City, Warren had made up his mind about Def Jam. "I just met so many nice people. They just extended all the love to me. When I got back on that plane, the deal was closed. I didn't even want any conversations with any of those other companies. I'm with Def Jam." When he got back to L.A., a contract was negotiated. "They decided to put him on Violator, to give Chris Lighty's label a little push," says Wron G., Warren G.'s manager and uncle.

Like many new artists, Warren G. was unfamiliar with the business side of music. He didn't even realize that he was going to get an advance for signing with Def Jam. So when he got his first check for $50,000—of a $350,000 deal—he "freaked out," he recalls. "So young, getting a check like that! First thing I did, I gave everybody in my family some money, then I bought myself a car. Then, I bought a whole studio [worth of equipment]. Got me an apartment and started recording *Regulate . . . G-Funk Era.* I hired a personal engineer; he would come to my house."

• • •

Warren was at his new house in Long Beach on a Monday afternoon in December when he heard a knock on his door. He opened it and there stood a tall white man. He recognized him right away: it was Lyor Cohen, his new boss. "I was tripping: Lyor came all the way down here to hang with me and see what it was like where I'm from," recalls Warren. "I took him up in the room where I was doing my thing. That's when I let him hear 'Regulate.' " The track had just been finished two days earlier. "He couldn't believe it," Warren recalls of Lyor's positive reaction to the track. "Then I played 'This DJ,' and he went nuts. Everything I was playing was a hit. And he was just so pumped up and so happy."

Later that day, Warren's friend Snoop Doggy Dogg was filming a video for "Who Am I (What's My Name)?"—off his platinum-selling *Doggystyle* album, which was released that November—and Warren decided to bring Lyor to the set with him. "He hung out with me the whole day; I introduced him to a lot of the hood," recalls Warren. "They was just looking like, 'Who is this white dude?' " But no one said anything, "out of respect for me. They were like, 'He's a cool dude.' "

When Lyor got back to New York, he was excited about Def Jam's upcoming Warren G. project. "Listen to this and let me know what you think," said Lyor to the staff as he walked around the office with a handful of cassettes. "This is Warren G., it's Dre's little brother. Just let me know if it's hot." Back in L.A., Warren played "Regulate" for Death Row founder Suge Knight and Doctor Dre. He didn't tell Death Row, however, that he had already signed with Def Jam. Besides, he says, "it seemed like [Death Row] weren't really interested" in him as a solo artist. "I knew they were doing a soundtrack, and I wanted to get my record on the soundtrack," Warren says of the *Above the Rim* soundtrack. "I didn't think they was gonna like it." But they did. A few days later, Warren got a call saying they wanted that record. "We gotta have that record" was the word from Jimmy Iovine, president of Interscope Records, which was putting out the soundtrack. Def Jam had no problem with Warren's song being on *Above the Rim,* as long as Def Jam got to keep the single rights. For Warren, it was a win–win situation: his single would appear on both the soundtrack and eventually on his own album.

Only after Death Row expressed interest in "Regulate" and put it on the *Above the Rim* soundtrack, "Def Jam stepped up and let them know what time it was," said Warren. "I just went my own way and didn't turn back." Once Suge found out, he didn't appreciate it. "Here we came [into his territory] and signed Warren G. We just went in and got him," says Julie. "We didn't ask permission and didn't talk to nobody. That was Dre's little brother, and Suge was

Even though they had signed Dr. Dre's younger brother, Warren G., at the height of the East Coast/West Coast fighting, Def Jam managed to avoid the drama. Warren G. yielded a monster hit for the label with "Regulate" in 1994.

really running the West Coast and had a lock on it, and then all of a sudden we're gonna put out a record that's gonna sell three million! I think he just felt it was inappropriate."

Russell actually offered Death Row a deal in which Def Jam would have the single rights to "Regulate," and Death Row agreed, not anticipating how big the record was going to become. By the time Death Row realized that Warren was talented, he no longer wanted to sign with them. "He knew the treatment over there," says Wron G. "And I think he wanted more. I think he was willing to have balls enough to say, 'I'm going to sign somewhere else, so I can make my own.' I think that Dre knew the type of environment [Death Row] was, and I think he didn't want his little brother over there. I remember Dre saying, 'Go somewhere and make your own.'"

Perhaps because Warren found himself right in the middle of the gangsta movement in hip-hop, Def Jam decided to make him look a little tougher. In his early publicity shots, Warren was photographed holding a gun. "I took all those pictures and destroyed them," recalls Wron G., who at that point stepped in as Warren's manager. "You have to remember the times: those were gangsta times." Although twenty-year-old Warren came from Long Beach, where he ran with the Crips, he didn't look like a gangster. "He's a nice guy, he's a smooth guy. I think what the rap industry hadn't seen yet was a guy who was good-looking enough from the West Coast. Warren was a good-looking guy with a baby face."

Still, Wron G. liked the energy at Def Jam. "They were masters at hitting the street with records and getting the word out and promoting their artists," he says. "It was like a college. They're running around, they're marketing, they're building plans. It was a cool environment, man, and I knew something was gonna happen big at Def Jam." Def Jam let Warren be more than just an artist, to also produce his own material. "They totally gave me the freedom," he says. "They didn't try to tell me how to do my record. That was one of the things that I enjoyed about them: they didn't sweat me; they let me do what I had to do." Def Jam also allowed Warren—"after a little bit of controversy," as Wron puts it—to retain all of his publishing for the record. "You know how big that is?" says Wron. "We were fighters, and they knew we were fighters. It was my idea to have Warren, when he got old and gray, have his publishing." The music industry was notorious for taking away song ownership from black performers, many of whom would end up going broke. Wron wanted Def Jam to understand that, and they did. "The one thing about Lyor and Russell is they have compassion," says Wron. "If you put down a great argument, you can win."

At the end of February, David Belgrave flew out to L.A. for a taping of the *Soul Train* Awards at the Paramount studios. David's job was essentially to make sure that Greg Nice got to the studio on time for his performance with Fever Records/Def Jam artist Lisette Melendez, who was singing her hit "Goody Goody." When David got to the greenroom, Michael McDonald, who sang "I Keep Forgetting," which was sampled in "Regulate," was also there. *Man, I hope they cleared the sample,* David thought, and decided not to say anything about the song to McDonald. Thankfully, the sample was cleared before the *Above the Rim* soundtrack hit stores on March 22, 1994. "Regulate," which was heard in its entirety during the movie's closing credits, helped the album quickly go platinum and eventually reach 4.5 million in sales. College-radio and mix-show DJs played the single the most.

Unlike many of the baby acts at Def Jam, Warren didn't do a promo tour. "I felt we didn't need a promo tour," Wron G. explains, noting that "Regulate" was already a hot record, thanks to the *Above the Rim* soundtrack. "What could you be promoting?" he asked Lyor. "It's time to take it somewhere else now. You're solidified in the U.S., why kill it?" Wron wanted to send Warren to Europe and meet with Famous Artists agency. "You can go to Europe, but first I want you guys to meet with Barry Hankerson, who manages R. Kelly," the agents at Famous said. After meeting with Barry, together with Lyor, Warren was put on the Budweiser Superfest Tour, which was headlined by R. Kelly, along with Heavy D., Da Brat, and Coolio. Wron did a big merchandising deal in New York "because we thought we could sell his face." The tour was a success, and it also brought in a mixed crowd thanks to Warren, who was "selling sixty-seven percent white at that time," according to Wron.

•   •   •

Meanwhile, unbeknownst to much of the staff and artists, Lyor had been closing a distribution deal for Def Jam with Polygram music. Polygram was a subsidiary of Philips Electronics that also owned Island, A&M, and Mercury. When Lyor and Russell went into talks about selling off half of Def Jam to get out of the $20 million debt they had with Sony, it was less than a year after Polygram acquired Motown Records. Clearly, Polygram was in the market for black music. "Lyor was so quiet about it," Julie recalls of the Polygram deal. "I remember being sworn to secrecy, and knowing that it's gonna go down. And you're looking at all these people in their faces, and you can't say anything. Until it was fully negotiated that we had a new home, he couldn't go stir anybody up. Once he knew he had the deal at Polygram done, then he went to all the artists before it was publically announced." The deal would include film projects, with Def Jam retaining all rights to its catalog, while giving Polygram equity stake in the company.

When it came time to announce the move from Sony to Polygram in early June of 1994, Lyor gathered the entire staff in the conference room and began describing what was about to happen to the company, as Steve Carr recalls. "Kind of really over-the-top and kind of like he's on his own soapbox. He's pacing back and forth speaking to everybody." Suddenly, Lyor stops and addresses the staff: "You know what is funny?" But before Lyor continues, Steve whispers, but loud enough for Lyor to hear him, "When a fat guy slips on ice?" Lyor heard Steve, but let him get away with it.

As a former marine, Wron could see the type of discipline that Lyor was bringing to the company: "I see Lyor around the company like a military officer, shouting orders, and it's like a whole organized chaos." Russell, on the other hand, was great at dealing with business. "I see Russell as the consummate businessman," says Wron, "who was smart enough to walk out on Sony, not knowing how it was going to end up, and being clever enough to take a chance with a West Coast artist and go over and sign a deal." Projects that were in midmarketing and midpromotion—such as South Central Cartel, Domino, and Lisette Melendez—would be completed by Columbia.

Right before Lyor closed the deal with Polygram, he and Julie met John Stockton at the Gavin Convention and shortly thereafter hired him as West Coast director of promotions, to work alongside Paul Stewart, who had PMP Records, in Def Jam West's Beverly Connection offices. Stockton was a man-about-town in L.A. who "knew everybody in the ghettos, and everybody in the clubs," as he puts it. Julie and Kevin Liles needed someone like that. Although John did not have extensive experience, he had the attitude that appealed to Lyor. "They look at the flavor, they look at other things than just experience," says John. "They don't like hiring people that are jaded by other record labels."

Stockton was trained by Kevin Liles, who was "the most thorough guy in the world," John recalls. "Everything that we did, we either sent out a page or set up a group call, so that everybody knew what was going on." Kevin took John on the road with him for a promo tour with South Central Cartel and Mel-Low. South Central Cartel was one of Russell's favorite projects in 1994. "Havoc [one-half of South Central Cartel] had a special relationship with Russell," recalls John. Their album, *In Gatz We Truss,* was an underground smash, scanning four hundred thousand units, which was "unheard of," says John. "No airplay. Still a classic West Coast album."

When they returned to L.A., they took part in a big conference call, and that was when they were told that Def Jam was making the jump to Polygram, and the Def Jam West office was moving to Sunset Boulevard. Meanwhile, John Stockton was moved, per Kevin's orders, into the corporate Polygram offices. "Kevin wanted me in the branch, because we were dealing with Polygram, it was a new deal, and all the distribution people were right there in the branch." The environment was exciting, with labels like Motown, Island, and Mercury all under one roof.

In the case of Warren G., the Polygram deal came at just the right time. "I remember being on the phone with [Island marketing executive] Johnny Barbis, and him saying, 'Okay, we're gonna roll out Warren, and you've got a million dollars,' " Greenwald remembers. She and Lyor sat for an hour figuring out the budget. "It just all started from there: okay, we're gonna be in control of our own destiny," she says.

The $1 million budget really paid off. One day, as the promotion for the album was starting, Lyor called Warren and Wron in L.A. "Warren, step out on your balcony and look up in the sky," said Lyor. Warren did. Above him, a plane was flying over, with a banner: "Warren G. Regulate, the G-Funk Era." "They got down," says Wron of the promotional push. "It was a new big marketing time for Def Jam. They moved into mass marketing."

On June 7, 1994, Warren G.'s *Regulate . . . G-Funk Era*—the first release under the new Polygram regime—hit stores, with his now hit single reissued on the album. The commercial response was instant, as the album debuted at No. 2 on the *Billboard* 200 charts. "We can all jump and take credit for 'Regulate,' but truth be told, 'Regulate' was just a huge single," says John Stockton. "It was just one of those records that just took off. Program directors, everybody that heard the record, loved it from jump." Still, Stockton admits that the Def Jam West team "worked our ass off on that record. No matter how much somebody likes the record, no record gets to four million without a lot of push."

"Def Jam, they weren't prepared for the type of success that they got," says Wron G. of *Regulate.* "I remember Russell estimated the record would sell eight hundred thousand, and if we got a million, we were blessed." By the end of August, the album was certified for sales of 2 million and would go on to sell nearly twice that amount worldwide.

After the Budweiser Superfest Tour, Warren G. headed to Europe. It was a good time to go away, because Warren was right "in the middle of the East–West bullshit," says Wron. "We were receiving a lot of death threats daily." But Def Jam was initially reluctant to send Warren to Europe, because "they weren't selling records in Europe," says Wron. But Warren went anyway and got some great promoters, who "took [him] under their wings." So Warren toured the U.K., France, Germany, doing TV shows, interviews set up by Ellen Zoe Golden, who was "one of the tightest publicists at the time for Warren," says Wron. "She got him into the mainstream: *Rolling Stone, Spin.*" Golden came from a background in rock, so she brought the crossover sensibility to promoting Warren. "The whole Europe experience was a humongous moment," says Warren, who had never been out of the country before. "Everywhere I went, I got so much love. It was people in front of every hotel I went to, just standing." "He was really huge overseas, on some Michael Jackson shit," recalls Wron.

On July 5, Def Jam released Warren's second single, "This DJ," and he headed off to Japan for a two-week mini-tour. "It was amazing," he recalls. "Didn't speak one lick of English, but they knew all my lyrics. Everywhere I went, there was a bunch of Japanese people outside with lowriders, dressed up like gangsters." Warren brought along with him the Twinz, the 5-Footers, and DJ Rectangle, all of whom would eventually land deals with Def Jam. "That was the beginning of Def Jam internationally," says Warren. To the credit of producers Tracey Jordan and Penny Macdonald, "MTV was playing Warren incredibly," recalls Wron. "That was part of the marketing strategy. ['Regulate'] was embraced by America, totally one hundred percent. So it put [Def Jam] in a whole new ball game."

The fact that Russell wound up with single rights for "Regulate" was ultimately what started the conflict between Def Jam and Death Row. Even though *Above the Rim* was a Death Row production, it was Def Jam that benefited from the release of "Regulate," as part of the soundtrack; it was Def Jam that benefited when they put "Regulate" out as a single, and then finally as part of Warren's debut album. "There were three paydays off of that record," as Wron G. points out, which, clearly, did not sit well with Suge Knight.

Although publicly Warren claimed that it was "all love" between Def Jam and Death Row, according to Julie Greenwald, the beef between the two labels was "real." At the 1994 Video Music Awards in early September, Lyor and Suge saw each other in the lobby of the venue. "It was very intense," Julie recalls. "I think they just really liked staring each other down, letting each other know, 'I'm here. You're here.' " The rivalry escalated to a point that Paul Stewart, who was working at Def Jam West at the time, checked out of his house and into a hotel for a while.

●   ●   ●

While Warren G. was reaping the rewards of his success, Nice & Smooth weren't as lucky. Their first album in three years—*Jewel of the Nile*—wasn't causing much noise after its release on June 28, 1994. After Columbia's previous experience with trying to promote *Ain't a Damn Thing Changed* with the uncooperative duo, the staff was being careful the second time around. (Warren G. and Nice & Smooth were pushed together in ads, since their release dates were so close.) Because Nice & Smooth had been "very unreliable regarding past album/single radio promotions," [Columbia Product Manager] Angela Thomas noted in a company memo, "promotions is not very willing to go out on a limb to have the group hurt established relationships by not showing up. With this in mind, we have arranged with the group to proceed with a slow, 'one toe in the water at a time' approach. It is understood that their failure to live up to commitments will result in negative promotional repercussions and a general morale drop by the promo staff."

In the case of Nice & Smooth, it was clear that Def Jam's job was to juggle not just the artists' careers, but also their personal lives. This all became painfully obvious one Friday in early July, when Greg and Smooth came by the office to prepare to shoot a video for their second single, "Hip-Hop Freaks," which would follow their poorly received "Old to the New" single. Everyone seemed in a jovial mood as Greg Nice, Smooth, and their posse gathered in the reception area.

"What's up, baby? What's going on?" they greeted David Belgrave, who came up to the front desk to pick up his lunch. *Rolling kinda deep,* David thought, but didn't pay it too much attention, since Nice & Smooth always traveled with a large group. "Yo, so we're getting to do the video?" David asked. "Yeah, no doubt, no doubt!" said Greg Nice. "Okay, cool, cool. Later. Peace!" said Dave, and went back to his office, dubbed the "meat locker" because it had no windows.

As he unwrapped his lunch, Dave kept his door open and suddenly noticed something that seemed a bit out of the ordinary. "I just happened to glance in my doorway and I see Smooth walk by, I see Greg walk by," David recalls. "Then I see another guy, another guy, like they're all walking single file from David's office to Lyor's office."

Scott Koenig worked right outside Lyor's office and could hear everything that was taking place inside. The group, apparently, was upset about Def Jam putting out "Old to the New" as the first single, instead of the catchier "Hip-Hop Freaks." "Motherfucker, if you ain't gonna use that gun, put it down," Lyor screamed. Although guns were being pointed in his face, Lyor knew that "if he was gonna shoot me, he would've shot me," as he told Scott Koenig, who marvels at Lyor's courage under fire. "Most people would never say that to anybody with a gun in their hand. And Lyor said he was scared as shit."

Russell Sidelsky, the office manager, quickly came around and told the staff that the office was being closed. Because it was a Friday, no one seemed to mind. After they finished with Lyor, the guys headed to Russell Simmons's house, where they had an argument but didn't draw guns. Not surprisingly, *Jewel of the Nile* would be the final Nice & Smooth album on Def Jam. "They started having security at Def Jam after that," recalls Brett Ratner. "I think [Nice & Smooth] thought Lyor was a thief. Lyor's not a thief. He's definitely un-scrupulous sometimes, and underhanded in the way he goes about business. But being a thief? All these artists can scream and yell about how they got ripped off. You're only as good as your lawyer. But rappers back then certainly weren't sophisticated enough to do that, and that's why they resorted to violence."

If Cohen was shaken up by the wrath of Greg Nice and Smooth B., Brett Ratner was about to find out what it felt like to be on the receiving end of Cohen's wrath. Cohen had asked Ratner to direct the first video, "Stay Real," from Eric Sermon's highly anticipated *No Pressure* album, which was released on Def Jam/RAL/Chaos on July 26, 1994. It was an ironic title for the album, because a lot was, in fact, riding on Eric Sermon's success as a solo artist. "Brett, this video is going to make or break his career," Cohen warned him cryp-tically. "But worse than that: if the video sucks, it will bury Def Jam! You have to bring us a hit. Because if your video is wack, it will brick everything. And you will destroy us! And we will be out of business."

Brett felt the pressure. But he did the video, on a budget of $30,000, and was happy with the results. Russell was happy, too. Brett showed him the video on their way to the Hamptons for the week-end with their girlfriends. By then, Brett recalls that "Russell posi-tioned himself so he didn't have to work so much. That was what Lyor was there for. Russell was really the mouthpiece, and Lyor was doing the actual work." Excited that Russell liked his video, Brett called up Lyor to make sure that he was okay with it. He got Lyor's machine and left a message.

After the weekend in the Hamptons, Brett and Russell headed

back to New York. Brett got behind the wheel of Russell's Rolls-Royce (Russell still didn't know how to drive). Brett hadn't heard back from Lyor, when suddenly his phone rang. It was Lyor and he was not happy. "You have fucked Eric Sermon!" he screamed. "You have fucked Def Jam! You have made the worst piece of shit ever! You have destroyed his career! He's a hard-core rapper, and you have him singing in the shower! You have bricked him beyond belief. But on top of it, you have buried Def Jam. We are going out of business because of you!"

Brett was pulling off the road, with the phone still cradled to his ear, while holding on to his chest with the other hand. "You stole our money! You're a thief. You're a criminal. You're the worst friend to Russell he's ever had!" Finally, Russell grabbed the phone. "Fuck you! Don't do that!" he screamed back at Lyor. "He did a good job!" Then Russell hung up, looked over at Brett, and said the words that changed Brett's entire outlook on the experience and his attitude toward being a video director: "It's just a video!" It was also a perfect example of the difference between Russell and Lyor. As Chuck D. puts it, "Lyor is a guy who cares and he's concerned, but somebody has to be the bad guy. Russell's such a nice guy, agrees with every fucking thing. Lyor had to be the bitch."

"Stay Real" was released, but the album was a minor hit. No high-tech, big-budget video could disguise that Eric Sermon did not have enough charisma to succeed as a solo act. Eric even admitted that himself: "I'm not really considering myself a solo artist," he told a reporter. As he explained, *No Pressure* was really "a compilation," since there were so many guest stars.

Eric Sermon was one of the many Def Jam artists who found the switch from Sony to Polygram disorienting and difficult. These artists were faced with a completely new company with its own set of rules. Some of the lesser-priority artists got lost in the transition, while star artists had to get used to a brand-new staff handling their product. Domino's album—after a promising start with his number one Hot Rap Singles track "Ghetto Jam"—stalled right in the middle of going gold. "He had two hits, and we were continuing to work the album," David Belgrave recalls. "But you have a major switchover like that. It's hard for a record to survive that."

No one felt more hurt by the transition, however, than Public Enemy. Their first album of new material in three years—*Muse Sick-n-Hour Mess Age,* released in August of 1994—fell right through the cracks of the new Polygram system. Chuck says that Lyor and Russell initially used the album to help seal the deal with Polygram and thus get them "out of the hole" with Sony. Lyor and Russell promised Chuck that if he came on board, he would retain the kind of autonomy that he had had at Sony, where he'd already started positioning the album with the staff as early as December of 1993. "Russell and Lyor would come out to [Public Enemy's] complex in Long Island and say, 'We need this record delivered and we're trying to stay with this Polygram move.' The whole Sony staff was really happy and energetic about [Public Enemy's new album]," recalls Chuck, who thought the first single, "Give It Up" was "incredible."

The American press, however, gave the album the worst reviews of any Public Enemy project. "What the fuck happened to hip-hop's most powerful voice?" wrote *Ego Trip* magazine. *Rolling Stone* gave the album two stars out of five. Chuck was upset about the unfavorable reviews and wanted to point fingers—at everyone but himself. "No artist ever wants to hear it's their record," she says. "It's always the record company, it's never the artist. It's hard. You wanna be told that your child's ugly? No. And they wanna blame you, so they wanna get angry at you. But you understand: they need to get angry at somebody, so you take it."

Chuck's lawyer at the time, Ron Sweeney, suggested that making a move to Polygram was a great move, because "It's a candy store, and being part of Def Jam will not hurt in the new situation. Meaning that I would have some autonomy and I could probably find a better place for artists that I was developing." Russell and Lyor even took Chuck with them in early 1994 to a corporate Polygram meeting in Indianapolis, for a presentation. "Russell and Lyor knew that it was important for me to be there in order for them to sell Def Jam as a burgeoning record label to the people who were now bailing them out of the hole," says Chuck.

But when Def Jam switched to Polygram, Chuck realized that Lyor and Russell did not keep their promise. "Somehow, Russell and Lyor said they didn't have to respect my musical judgment anymore," he says, "because basically I was over with. That was the attitude." Chuck no longer had the freedom he'd had at Sony; he now had to answer directly to Lyor, which he wasn't used to. "So that's pretty much what I got for being a team player," he says. The first real sign of trouble came when Chuck tried to set up his artist Terminator X's new album, which was released in late July of 1994. "It was just a disaster," Chuck recalls. "I knew no one [at Polygram], no one knew me, and there was a whole different set of rules. It was like being traded to another team. And my abilities to work directly with a situation were slashed with that transition."

"We all believed in that album," said Julie Greenwald of *Muse Sick*. "We spent a lot of money on that project. Like a million-dollar rollout. Put them on a huge promo tour across the country, organized in-stores, all these great things. Their album was coming out, and you didn't want them to get caught in the cold 'cause we were switching companies. I ran up a $96,000 American Express bill [for PE's marketing] that I couldn't pay. I still have a scar on my credit report for the rest of my life. Finally, Polygram agreed to reimburse me, but when I went to get my mortgage done, sure enough, there it was right there."

Julie says that the problem was that the album got "very little" radio play. " 'Give It Up' had a good video, but at the end of the day, we struggled at radio. The album went gold, but the singles are what drives things." But Chuck claims that "rap DJs across the country gave more love to 'Give It Up' than they ever gave before to any Public Enemy record." Internationally, the album was Public Enemy's and Def Jam's "biggest record around the world," says Chuck.

Whatever the critical and commercial reaction to the album, Chuck ultimately felt used and let down by Def Jam, and their relationship became strained. "And I think Chuck wanted to do different things, and music was changing so radically at that point," says Julie. "MTV was starting to play way more happier, friendly videos. Poppier stuff was really taking over."

The leader of this new trend in "hip-pop" was Sean "Puffy" Combs and his Bad Boy Records. If one moment signaled the beginning of hip-hop's "jiggy" era, it had to be Puffy's twenty-fourth birthday party at Roseland Ballroom on November 8, 1994. "There will be a formal dress code," the invite read. "For this event, anyone who disrespects the dress code will <u>NOT</u> be let in. The code is formal, this means no sneakers, jeans or T-shirts. Get fly! Do not get left outside. The code applies to everyone. P.S. There will be one exception, Russell Simmons."

In 1994, Russell was the kind of hip-hop executive that all of his peers in the industry aspired to be. He had the three desirable components: money, power, and respect. His Phat Farm clothing line made him a fashionista who hung out with models. His HBO smash, *Def Comedy Jam,* turned Russell into a household name among those who didn't listen to hip-hop. When he wasn't being driven around the city in his white Rolls-Royce, Russell was having lunch meetings at the chic Time Cafe or having drinks at the Bowery Bar, both right around the corner from his apartment. He now worried less about whether his Def Jam artists were getting radio play, and more about making money for Rush Communications.

With Russell hardly in the office and Lyor in the office full-time, Def Jam became divided into "a Lyor side and a Russell side," as Chris Lighty points out. "Lyor was trying to run a tighter ship in the building, [with a] clear chain of command," says Drew Dixon, who was an A&R director at Def Jam from 1994 through 1996. "And then Russell [was] just randomly out there, doing things that were actually in many ways really helpful, really creative, very valuable. But he didn't feel the need to check in. So if you came in through Russell, you were at a huge disadvantage, just politically, in the organization. All of the people in the building were Lyor's people."

"Lyor was Russell's point man for the ugly world of business," says Eric Haze, Def Jam's former art director. "And Lyor was uniquely suited for the role. When it came to dollars and cents, Lyor was hard-core. But he also had a big heart, and a genuine concern and interest for his artists as people. Lyor has a take-no-prisoners approach to business, and he is the general, leading an army in the war to maximize profit. Loyal, efficient soldiers will be taken care of and treated with respect. Incompetence isn't tolerated."

Drew Dixon, a twenty-three-year-old hip-hop fanatic with some administrative background in the music business when she was hired by Russell in July of 1994, would learn firsthand what it felt like *not* to be on the Lyor side of the company. Cohen didn't mince words. "If you see me in the hallway, the best thing you can do is go into the nearest office, so that I don't see you," he said to Dixon one day, "because I'm not checking for you. I don't need any more tall, skinny 'flavor bitches' at Def Jam. I'm trying to run a real company." But when it came to staff members that Cohen liked, such as Jason Jackson, who was hired for the marketing department on the same day as Dixon and given his own office, they were quickly pulled into "the inner circle."

Drew could have quit right then. But she loved hip-hop too much not to give it a shot. *There's a bigger goal here,* she thought. So when in August Simmons assigned her the soundtrack for the hip-hop documentary *The Show*—the first project started from scratch under the new Polygram system—Drew knew it was her opportunity to prove her loyalty to the company and her abilities as an executive. *The Show* was executive-produced by Russell, with Rysher Entertainment, a motion-picture arm of Polygram Filmed Entertainment. Because the soundtrack was a compilation, the music didn't have to be recorded from scratch. That also meant lengthy legal paperwork to license the songs.

•　　•　　•

In November of 1994, Polygram's acquisition of 60 percent of Def Jam for $33 million was finally made public. The distribution-deal contract was for five years, with Cohen and Simmons retaining their titles and duties. By then, Warren G.'s *Regulate* album had sold 2.7 million units. Def Jam was given a new life. "Here was this company that was saying, 'We love you, we appreciate everything you're doing, we're gonna fund you, you're gonna have your own autonomy, you're gonna totally have the ability to increase your regional staff,' " recalls Julie. Part of Lyor's agreement with Polygram included dissolving Rush Management, which would probably have gone out of business regardless. Rush was in serious debt, mostly from lending artists money that was never repaid. When Rush went out of business, Scott Koenig licensed the Rush name for $1: he was managing a few heavy-metal groups—Biohazard, Fear Factory, and Downset, among others—who were known under Rush Management, so he was allowed to use the name as long as he stayed in business with Lyor or Def Jam.

The deal with Polygram also helped tie up the loose ends, such as ownership points, that Def Jam still had with Rick Rubin. Lyor, Russell, and Rick split the money that was left over after they settled their debts with Sony. (Polygram paid $35 million for 60 percent of Def Jam.) "That's when that whole [issue with Rick] was put to bed and was settled," said Carmen Ashhurst. RAL was folded into Def Jam. Under their new agreement, Lyor would get a third of all advances and any money that came into the company. He and Russell weren't the only ones who got paid. "Those that were the true players, true soldiers for Lyor and Russell, we all were taken care of [with bonus checks]," says Chris Lighty.

"We were in control of everything," Greenwald recalls of Def Jam's new beginning with Polygram. "We had our own art department in-house, we controlled our videos, we controlled when we would ship a single, when we would work a single, when we would service a video. It was wonderful."

Redman and Method Man were two Def Jam artists who benefited from Def Jam's move to Polygram. Their albums—Redman's sophomore effort, *Dare Iz a Darkside,* and Method Man's debut, *Tical*—were released after the transition was complete, and just days within each other in November 1994. Julie Greenwald came up with the innova-

CAROLINE TOREM-CRAIG

At first Redman [*left*] felt threatened by Method Man's arrival at Def Jam, but then quickly warmed up. The joint marketing of the two stars in 1994 and for years to come would prove to be a clever and profitable move for Def Jam.

tive idea of dubbing November the "Month of the Man." Def Jam had been successful with marketing Bo$$ and Onyx as one package, and they decided to take the same approach with Redman and Method Man. After all, they were both solo artists, the same age, and with similar comedic, yet street, personae. (Although both were promoted with equal effort by Def Jam, Method Man's debut would outsell Redman's album. "Method Man was down with the Wu-Tang Clan, he was a phenomenon; he was a shining star," explains Kevin Liles.)

Method Man solidified his star quality with the video for his first single, "Bring the Pain," which would become one of Def Jam's most-requested videos ever. The shoot was also David Belgrave's first job as the head of the video department, and he chose Diane Martel to direct. The grimy, surreal clip featured Method Man and his friends riding in a "stolen" bus around a nighttime city, with Meth wearing a white contact lens in one eye. It was the perfect visual representation of the track itself: manic, dark, and very street. Many of the ideas that ended up on-screen had come from Method Man himself: from the bus to the white contact lens.

The action on the screen was also a good reflection of the real-life drama that took place during the Harlem shoot. "It was late at night," Belgrave recalled of the bus sequence. "We'd start from 110th Street on Lenox Avenue and take the bus up to like 125th.

Diane put a dolly on the bus that was going up and down the length of the bus, but every time the driver stopped, the whole dolly would come racing toward the front of the bus. And this shit is heavy!" Martel got in an argument with the dolly operator, who tried to convince her that the shot was impossible. "I need the shot! I need the shot!" she screamed at him.

The argument escalated until, somewhere around 117th Street and Lenox, the dolly operator told the bus driver to stop, got off the bus, and decided to walk ten blocks back to the trailers at two o'clock in the morning. "And for the rest of those takes, the members of Wu-Tang operated the dolly," Belgrave recalled. "Rae, [RaeKwon, Wu-Tang member], everybody, get around!" RZA would scream, as Method Man's supportive groupmates helped him complete the key shot. Even the homeless man on the bus was "a real bum," recalled Belgrave. "And I swear this guy smelled *so* bad. When you're seeing that on film, that's exactly the energy that was on the bus." When the video was finished, everyone loved it. "We stood in Lyor's office and watched it on the Box play over and over again," Belgrave recalled.

The shoot was a good example of the general "cultivated chaos," as Drew Dixon puts it, that defined Def Jam in 1994. "They believed that without the dysfunction and without the madness, you're not gonna get the kind of cutting-edge, irreverent, iconoclastic art and the marketing to support [the art] that you need," she says. The lack of structure worked for some, but Dixon found it intolerable. It was early December, and she worried that with only three finished songs— none of which were hits—Def Jam would miss their January 15 deadline to hand in *The Show* soundtrack. Dixon couldn't get beyond her personal oral agreements with artists' reps, because she couldn't get the legal process started—Def Jam's attorney, Frank Cooper, who was told by Lyor whom and what to prioritize, wouldn't put Dixon on his calendar. In Cohen's book, Dixon and her project "had no currency whatsoever," she says. "Russell hired me, and nobody else in the firm knew who I was, and Russell wasn't in the building." Drew tried her best to finish the project on her own: she called up Tupac, the members of A Tribe Called Quest, and Wu-Tang Clan, among others, and asked for records. Dixon even called Suge Knight and asked if Def Jam could use a Snoop Dogg interlude. "He was nice," she recalls.

Concerned that *The Show* soundtrack was simply going to "implode," as she put it, Dixon—"after several failed attempts to get [Lyor] to pay attention"—went directly to Simmons. She met with him at the Bowery Bar, his favorite spot, and laid out the situation with *The Show* soundtrack. "We're supposed to walk into Polygram in about three weeks with music and in about another two weeks with label copy and closed agreements," she said to Simmons. "And we have nothing! You guys are gonna lose credibility at Polygram, [and] in the film world. This is gonna be really embarrassing if you can't get this right, as a soundtrack. [Polygram] is gonna look at you, like, 'What *can* you do?'"

Finally, Simmons called Cohen and put the pressure on him to deliver the soundtrack on time. "Once it became clear that all I had was a stack of cassettes, 'cause that's all I could get from people without legal agreements, [Julie Greenwald], upon Lyor's instructions, was very cooperative. They stepped up, in the end," says Dixon, pointing out the track "How High," which paired Redman and Method Man. Still, Def Jam didn't make their deadline for *The Show* soundtrack, and Dixon had to stay up for two nights in a row, hand-typing all the lyrics to the songs and all the label copy. Those kinds of sacrifices were common practice at Def Jam; staff members often contributed not only overtime but their own earnings toward the company's good. "I don't know how much I spent of my own money to make sure that the job got done at Def Jam," says Thomas Lytel, who worked in promotions.

• • •

Redman and Method Man helped seal Def Jam's street credibility in 1994, but Russell Simmons thought the label needed an R&B single that could also win over radio. So when Lyor Cohen heard a song called "This Is How We Do It" by an L.A. artist named Montell Jordan, which was picking up buzz on the West Coast, he was intrigued. Jordan, it turned out, was using a sample of Slick Rick's "Children's Story" without Def Jam's consent, and it was obvious to Cohen just how to get Jordan to sign with him. "Lyor definitely thugged [Montell]," recalls Greenwald. He told the singer that he should either give up the "Children's Story" single or sign with Def Jam. Jordan signed. The song would become the first single off his debut album, *This Is How We Do It*.

Cohen's persuasiveness probably worked so well on Jordan because he "had no thugness to him at all," recalls John Stockton. "The guy with the college degree: graduated from Pepperdine University. So he was, in that respect, different from a lot of the artists at Def Jam, 'cause most of our artists were definitely street cats." And at nearly seven feet, Jordan stood out from the crowd. Although he came from South Central L.A., Jordan came from a "very sheltered" upbringing, points out Stockton. "He was the kind of kid who was in some kind of church activity every day." Montell was also married. His wife, Kristen, was known for taking care of business. "She was very hardcore business," says Stockton. "She studied Lyor, and I could tell some of the things she said [were things that] Lyor said. Montell needed that."

Slick Rick, the artist who'd laid the foundation for "This Is How We Do It" with his "Children's Story" single, was on Rikers Island, wasting away. Worse still, he didn't get paid what he "was supposed to," he says, for the use of his song. He says the trouble was in his publishing deal, which was "crossed with the record label," which made it impossible for him to get royalties until he fully recouped all of the label's recoupable expenses. "They get to take out your cut and their cut. They get fifty percent, you get fifty percent, but in all reality, they get one hundred percent, because they say that you're not recouped."

Meanwhile, LL Cool J was filming a movie called *Out of Sync*, directed by Debbie Allen. In this low-budget action flick, LL played a

DJ who was torn between his music and the street life. Although LL had "high hopes" for the film, his comanager Brian Latture, among others, disapproved. "The only thing memorable about it is that they talked him into removing his hat," says Latture. "It was the first public image of LL without his hat." But Brian felt that the reveal was premature and should have been saved for a more significant moment. Even the poster for the film looked low-budget, with the film title written in graffiti letters and LL flanked by a girl holding a gun seductively. "Out of money, out of time, out of sync," the copy read. The movie tanked at the box office, selling a mere $9,000 worth of tickets. LL later admitted that his "acting sucked" in the film. The only positive thing to come out of the experience was LL landing a starring role on a new sitcom called *In the House,* which was a Debbie Allen production.

The start of the new year also meant the beginning of an aggressive campaign launched by Bill Adler, who was running his own PR firm (he'd left Def Jam in 1990), to help Slick Rick get his parole. One of the things he wanted to do was to put on a "Free Slick Rick Concert" "as a way of demonstrating public support for Rick and applying pressure to the judicial system," he explained. The show would not be "a money-raiser," Adler said, but a "consciousness-raiser." For weeks, he had been reaching out to everyone and anyone—from Hot 97 DJ Fred Buggs to David Paterson of the New York State Senate, and even one official at Rikers Island who liked Rick—to testify on the rapper's behalf.

MTV also aided the campaign, filming an exclusive interview with Slick Rick at Rikers on January 11, which would be broadcast on the *Week in Rock* program on January 20, perfectly timed for the release of Rick's third album, *Behind Bars,* three days later. Although it was a Slick Rick album, it was hard to find Rick in the project; he seemed almost like a hip-hop phantom. Warren G. made a cameo appearance on the title track, a pairing that made little sense stylewise—especially since the two had never even met. The album wouldn't even reach gold.

Slick Rick's parole board review was scheduled for December of 1995, and Adler once again campaigned for Rick's release. He even got a detective from Mount Vernon to write a letter to the immigration judge in Rick's defense. The detective, Allen Ayers, was also the founder of a youth community-outreach program that counseled and tutored city kids, which Rick had visited in 1991 to speak about his mistakes and how to avoid them. "I was very impressed with him," Detective Ayers wrote in his letter. "Rick was quiet, sober, and serious." Flavor Flav of Public Enemy also had some legal trouble: he was sentenced to three months in jail for firing a gun at his neighbor in 1993 during an argument. He could have gotten a year behind bars under the original charge—attempted murder—but that was plea-bargained down to weapons possession.

Meanwhile, Montell Jordan's "This Is How We Do It," which was released on April 15, 1995, became an instant smash. "We went upstairs to Island," recalls Julie Greenwald, who asked the label's top-notch promotions department to cross the record over to Top 40. "I remember they did a really good job, and we were blown away by having so much airplay, [which] we saw in the album sales."

While it was a bona fide hit on radio, it wasn't Def Jam's biggest hit that year. That honor went to a track called "He's Mine" by a female trio from Compton who called themselves MoKenStef (a play on the names of the women: Monifa, Kenya, and Stefanie). "He's Mine" became Def Jam's biggest radio single to that date. But having radio hits did not equal having critical acclaim and street credibility. The trio's self-titled album, released in June on the Def Jam–distributed imprint Outburst (also home to rapper Domino), was considered corny by the same audience that used to buy Public Enemy albums.

Chuck D. also went on record to talk about his dissatisfaction with Def Jam. "I used to admire Def Jam for being innovators and trend-setters," he told the *Toronto Star.* "But they're nothing but followers. They're an irresponsible crackhouse of a record company." Chuck D. wanted out of his contract. "It was sad," says Julie Greenwald. "You don't wanna be out of business with them. It was Public Enemy. [Chuck D.] was very vocal, and when you read that he was upset or he was unhappy with us, it hurts, because we were a label that prided ourselves on treating artists really well and taking care of our artists, and spending money on our artists, and manpowering resources."

Just as Drew Dixon was finishing *The Show* project in February of 1995, she realized an important anniversary was approaching for Def Jam. "I was hanging out with some friends at home, and something came on TV, and one of the guys who was there said, 'That's so funny, it makes me think of something that I did back in the day, when I was hanging out with Russell. Oh my God, it's been ten years!' " Drew got an idea. "Ten years? That's a product! That's a box set." She called Simmons immediately and said in a message, "Are you aware of the fact that it's your ten-year anniversary, and you should maybe put a compilation together of catalog items that you already own and release them in a box-set format, and it's just like found money." Simmons raved about Dixon's idea and put her in charge of the project. Although she started putting together some songs, with the help of Chris Lighty, Dixon already had one foot out the door at Def Jam.

•   •   •

High off the success of "This Is How We Do It," the video department prepared for the video shoot for Montell's second single, "Somethin' 4 Da Honeyz," which was released on August 1, 1995. The video was directed by Hype Williams and produced by Philip Atwell. You'd never know by looking at the washed-out, sunny montages of posh rappers playing golf on beautiful green fields, surrounded by gorgeous women, that a person almost got killed that day on set. Or, as David Belgrave puts it, "It was the best video shoot of my life that turned into the worst."

The concept for the video—an afternoon of "hip-hop" golf—called for an assortment of cameos on the greens. (The entire shoot took place at a Sherman Oaks golf course in California.) Along with

Montell Jordan, a bevy of rap all-stars showed up on the set, including Nate Dogg, Warren G., Redman, and Method Man—and "like fifty ridiculous-looking girls," Belgrave recalls. But that wasn't enough for Kevin Liles, who insisted on also putting Snoop Doggy Dogg in the video. Snoop had the hottest hip-hop album in the country, *Doggystyle,* but he had a beef with two new Def Jam artists who were going to be present: BG Knockout and Gangsta Drester, the Def Jam imprint signed to Outburst. BG Knockout looked like a younger Easy-E, with the curls and the hat, while Drester was a big two-hundred-pound, "bulky, strong-ass dude," David recalls. They were down with Easy-E and had a song called "Muthafuck Dre," which was a direct dis on Snoop, who was loyal to Dr. Dre. "Kevin did not understand the West Coast," points out John Stockton. "I told him, 'You can't get all these cats together and it's gonna be peace.'"

With most of the shots in the can, Hype had time to shoot one more "special" scene, when all the rappers show up in these lowrider golf carts that jumped up like lowrider cars. "And something happened where maybe somebody looked at somebody the wrong way or it couldn't be contained," David recalls. "And people started to have words, and somebody tried to punch somebody else, and then this big ruckus broke out on the golf course." The commotion got so bad that the golf course security actually pulled out guns on people to control them for a moment. It seemed that the fight had been broken up.

Belgrave and Stockton were standing on a hill collecting themselves after the altercation, when "We see that Nate is coming down the hill and he's holding a golf club," David recalls. "And it registers to both of us that he's coming to fuck up Drester." As Nate approached, John and David tried to stop him, but to no avail. "Now he's starting to get close enough to us that we can see his nostrils flaring," David recalls. "And at a certain point, I'm like, 'You know what? Lyor don't pay me for this.'"

So he and John stepped to the side and watched in horror as Nate came up to Drester and swung his golf club as hard as he could. The only thing that kept Drester's head from getting cracked was that he put his hand up to block the swing, which "broke his arm instantly," David recalls. "But because of the force of the swing, the golf club snapped around his arm, but didn't break. And it formed a hinge around his arm, and the rest of the club swung around and hit him in the head anyway. I mean, if that was some 110-pound woman, it would have been like, 'Good night!' "

Finally, the bleeding Drester and the fuming Nate were separated, and everyone was prepared to have the shoot be shut down. Suddenly, they hear an announcement over the walkie-talkie: "We've got a code in the parking lot." David says, "Apparently, after Drester got hit with the golf club, BG was walking him up to the circle to go wait for the ambulance that was arriving to take him to the hospital, and when they got out to the circle, apparently Warren G. and the Twinz, and I think DJ Rectangle, were all out by Warren's Suburban, and when Drester walked by with Knockout, I think Warren looked at him and started snickering at him."

So BG picked up a Heineken bottle, cracked it, and started running after Warren in the parking lot. "And apparently had Warren hemmed up in some corner when Sherman Oaks police finally arrived," David recalls. Drester told the cops that Warren had pulled a gun on him. "Now the cops get on Warren and they pull him to the side and start pulling his truck apart," David recalls. By nightfall, with thoughts of "What the hell happened?" running through their minds, Hype Williams, Kevin Liles, and David Belgrave reconvened at Le Montrose Hotel to plan a pickup day to shoot additional footage at a new location.

For his part, Kevin Liles said he'd never expected there to be peace. "If I had to do it all over again, I would do the same thing," he says. "I'm about unification. And sometimes separation is necessary, but I truly believe that integration is the cure. Was it something that was gonna come to a head maybe in a worse way? I felt like I could make a difference. What if it was just on a street corner? What if it was at a club, where it wasn't controlled?"

Although delayed by several months and overbudget, *The Show* soundtrack hit stores on August 8, 1995, and by the time the film premiered in theaters—on August 25—it reached No. 1 on the Top R&B Albums chart and No. 4 on the *Billboard* 200. The soundtrack's sales were driven mainly by the Redman/Method Man collaboration, "How High," which was released as a single on August 15 and became a huge hit. The footage in the film, produced and directed by Brian Robbins (of *Head of the Class* fame), came from several concerts that had taken place in Philadelphia in December 1994 and featured a variety of rappers, such as Run-DMC, Notorious B.I.G., Naughty by Nature, and Snoop Doggy Dogg.

It was hard to believe that one of Def Jam's biggest highlights that year—*The Show*—was essentially put together by one recently hired woman, Drew Dixon. For her work, Simmons offered Dixon a job as vice president with a small raise of a few thousand dollars. "I just felt used, demoralized," she says.

Slick Rick—who was approached by Def Jam to be part of the film while still incarcerated—also felt exploited. He claims that Simmons refused to pay him "because *The Show* was a documentary" and essentially ordered Slick Rick to appear in the film. "If you don't, then you just anger us, and we just write you off as being hard to work with," said Simmons, according to Slick Rick.

So Rick appeared in the film's most sobering sequence, where Russell came to visit him in prison, then completely bad-mouthed him when they were not in the room together, calling Rick "as crazy as a bag of angel dust" and saying that he's only going to see Slick Rick because of the film. "Make sure you keep that in, I want it to be real," Russell said to the camera. Slick Rick never got over the feeling of being used by Russell for the sake of the movie. "You extend yourself to the label, you show all this love to the label," Rick says, "only for them to turn around and try to disrespect you."

CHAPTER 13

Sexy Again

"We were fighting against Puffy, just for survival," Chris Lighty recalled of much of 1995, when the hottest hip-hop label was Sean "Puffy" Combs's Bad Boy Records. Combs had long had a connection to Def Jam. Just three years earlier, he was interning with Russell Simmons's former employee Andre Harrell, at Uptown Records. Back then, he was a familiar face at the 298 Elizabeth Street office, which Rush Management still occupied, and once even hid out there after being chased by police for stealing something from a Broadway store around the corner.

Puffy continued to have a connection to Def Jam through its art department, the Drawing Board, who as independent contractors had Bad Boy as one of their clients. They worked on artwork for Bad Boys platinum-sellers like Biggie Smalls, Craig Mack, 112, and Faith Evans, including the classic cover of Biggie Smalls's debut album, *Ready to Die.* If five years earlier Drawing Board's founders, Steve Carr and Cey Adams, worried constantly about getting fired by Simmons, who would get upset if they used the color purple, or Cohen, who was "like a big hurricane that blows in and then blows out," recalled Carr, by 1995 they knew they were the best in the business. (Although Simmons never complained about them designing for Bad Boy, Carr and Adams tried to hide current Bad Boy projects from

Cohen. "If Lyor was coming in, we'd have to turn off our computers, because we'd have Puffy's shit on it," Carr recalled.)

To Lyor Cohen, Puffy Combs was still a formidable competitor,
even though they were friends. Cohen knew he needed a hit that
would eclipse Puffy's success with artists such as Biggie Smalls and
Craig Mack. One day in September, Lyor called Chris Lighty and ordered, "You have sixty days to do the new LL Cool J album." LL had
recently turned in material for his new album, but Cohen was deeply
disappointed with the songs. Only one of these, "Mr. Smith," would
end up on the final album.

"That should be the title of your album," Lighty said to LL when
they met at the studio to begin their sixty-day sessions. "Now you're
a man; they should know you as Mr. Smith." LL agreed, and the two
of them actually met their deadline—with the help of the Trackmasters, who produced "Hey Lover," which featured Boys II Men, who
were still hot back then, and Rashad Smith, who produced "Doin'
It."

The story of "Doin' It," a huge summer-of-1996 song, started
with a beat that Lighty had first heard on a record of a female artist
named LeShaun "Almond Joy" Williams, who began the track with
the words "Doin' it well." The moment Puffy got word of this hot
new beat that contained a reworked sample of Grace Jones's 1985 hit,
"My Jamaican Guy," he started competing with Lighty for it. "Puffy
wanted that beat for Biggie at the time. I was like, 'Hello, no! I need
this beat for LL,'" recalled Lighty, who finally outbid Puffy for
$30,000. "I wound up overpaying."

After writing lyrics to the beat, LL emerged from the studio and
asked where the girl was who would be doing the duet with him. But
Lighty still hadn't picked a girl to pair up with LL and asked the
woman responsible for the original song, LeShaun, to come down to
the studio that night. The chemistry between her and LL was instant.
Their very first take of the song ended up on the album.

At the last minute, the production team Trackmasters introduced
a fifteen-year-old Brooklyn rapper named Foxy Brown to Chris

Lighty and suggested they put her on the remix of LL's "I Shot Ya"
single. Although Foxy had connections in hip-hop—her cousin was
the famed hip-hop DJ Clark Kent—and two years earlier got signed
to Capitol Records under the moniker Big Shorty, she was still looking for her big break. "I thought it was a great idea," Lighty recalled
of putting Foxy on "I Shot Ya." Lyor, however, "just didn't get it,"
says Chris. "It was like [Foxy] showed everybody: I can be like the big
boys," says Julie Greenwald. Indeed, most people who first heard her
on the record didn't even realize that she was a woman; her voice was
deep, almost masculine.

In October, LL's second single "Hey Lover" was released as a single and video and hit big. The single would have been a great addition to Def Jam's tenth-anniversary box set, which the label was
preparing for an October release. To promote it, Kevin Liles proposed
a college tour, in which Def Jam artists would go around college
campuses, do a big event at the auditorium, an afterparty, and an in-
store. There was also the possibility of collaborating with the NAACP
to encourage students to register for the upcoming 1996 election. On
October 6, 1995, the Def College Jam Tour kicked off in Pennsylva-
nia at Cheyney University, but quickly ran into problems.

A Jacksonville, Florida, concert a few weeks later was canceled at
the last minute, provoking a minor riot and the disappearance of
$70,000 worth of sound equipment stolen by the promoter of the
show himself. A November 3 performance at Tennessee State University was halted after only ten minutes, with Method Man cut off
midrap. Students got agitated, threw bottles and debris at the police,
and booed. These disasters caused Def Jam to land on *Rap Sheet* magazine's infamous "Shit List" on November 6. "That was a fucking
money-pit loser," says Julie of the almost $300,000 tour. "We lost so
much money because we were in over our heads. We had so many
bands and so many expenses and guarantees."

The tour nearly cost Kevin Liles his job. "From that point, everybody said, 'Oh, Kevin's a big spender,' " he says. The idea began with
the best intentions. The year before, Kevin had organized a one-

night-only event at Howard University, which he called Def College Jam. "It was Onyx at their height, Biggie Smalls, Redman, and Method Man in a museum," Kevin remembers the evening. "It was one of the most special moments—just the energy! At that moment, I said, 'Fuck this, we're taking this around the country. We're gonna do it!' "

Liles saw the silver lining: "Nineteen ninety-five will go down in history as being a defining moment, because we [went] from Def Comedy to Def College and now to Def Poetry. People always did shows at college, but we were the first to come up with Def College Jam. It was a very expensive marketing tool."

Def Jam ran into other stiffs that year, such as twenty-one-year-old Jayo Felony's *Take a Ride,* released in mid-October. Distribution was through ILS records—Independent Label Sales—which didn't maintain any direct accounts with stores, usually selling to one-stops. "There was Polygram for all the good stuff, and then there was ILS: Mel-Low, Jayo Felony—a lot of the artists that they weren't sure of, that were a little more street," John Stockton points out. "ILS was more of an independent. We'd go to cities, and [the album] wouldn't even be in the stores. I think Kevin really cared about it, but it was just a lot of politics; it being an ILS project, it wasn't one of the priorities." *Take a Ride* was "a West Coast classic," says Stockton.

Def Jam had learned how to handle those "stiffs"—the first singles that didn't make any noise. "We go into defense mode," Julie explains. "Either you shut down a project, or you come with a second single. You have to really reshift, because you have to assess the situation: 'Was my first single the best single on the album? If so, what the fuck am I doing chasing a second single for?' " In Def Jam's history, only a few artists—mostly baby acts—have put out only one single.

Luckily, LL's album, *Mr. Smith,* which hit stores on November 21, the same day as Def Jam's tenth-anniversary box set, *Classics,* and made up for the stiffs. LeShaun Williams, the woman who sang on "Doin' It," was rejected by LL for the video because he felt she had gained too much weight during a recent pregnancy. LeShaun was so

CAROLINE TOREM-CRAIG

Together with Def Jam, LL Cool J experienced a second life with the success of *Mr. Smith* and his summer 1996 anthem, "Doin' It."

upset that she even led a protest outside of an LL concert at Radio City Music Hall. "I was fired because he said that I wasn't hot. I wasn't 'what they wanted to see,' " she told *MTV News.* "He pointed me towards the mirror and said, 'C'mon, look at yourself.' Touched my stomach. 'C'mon, B. They ain't checking for that. You know what I'm saying? The song is hot. Gotta be hot. Maybe you should take some time, go home to your family. You know, lose some weight.' "

But LL Cool J saw it differently. "All I wanted LeShaun to do is look her best," he explained, so when I presented her to the world as an artist, people would gravitate towards her that much more, and it would extend the life of her career. If I'd put that girl on television like that, I think in the long run she would have came to me and said, 'Why did you let me do that?' " Williams was so upset by the whole thing that she filed an official complaint against LL with the Equal Employment Opportunity Commission and planned on filing a civil suit against him, charging sex discrimination and breach of contract. The suit was eventually dropped.

Slick Rick, who had three songs on the box set, was waiting for his first parole hearing in two years. He was ready to show remorse. In 1993, the parole board had denied him parole, stating that he didn't show enough "recognition of wrongdoing." Throughout the ordeal, Def Jam, and especially Lyor Cohen, stood behind Rick. Cohen even wrote a personal check for Rick's medical exam, required by the Immigration authorities before Rick's parole hearing. ("Even to Lyor, there's a certain benevolence," as Steve Carr points out.)

•   •   •

Despite his earlier ambivalence, Lyor Cohen was suddenly on a mission to sign Foxy Brown and sent Chris Lighty out to "block" Puffy, who also wanted to sign her, and was "riding around in his Mercedes following her all over the city," recalled Lighty. Lyor sat on the stoop of Foxy's brownstone in Brooklyn, which Chris believed was not a reflection of genuine interest in her talents, but a competitive move against the other labels, which included Bad Boy and Elektra. "The glamour and glitz of Russell," as Lighty puts it, ultimately convinced Foxy to sign with Def Jam. "When you wanna close, and you need the close, and it's full-blown war, that's when you bring Russell out."

"She had the most amazing setup," says Julie Greenwald. "Because before her own single dropped, she was a guest artist on so many people's records that she dropped with such force, and she could hold her own." The first of these projects was *The Nutty Professor* soundtrack, released on June 4, 1996. Foxy was featured on two songs, both of them hits: "Touch Me, Tease Me" with Case and "Ain't No Nigga" with an MC named Jay-Z, a Brooklyn-born-and-bred rapper with a unique, fast rhyme flow reminiscent of Big Daddy Kane.

Jay-Z was putting out records on his own label, Roc-A-Fella, which he formed with partner Damon Dash, a Harlem-raised businessman, who started out managing Jay-Z through his now defunct company Dash Entertainment back in 1994. After some failed attempts at getting Jay-Z a major deal, they decided to pool their resources and form Roc-A-Fella Records. Around the same time, an Irv Gotti–managed group called Cash Money Click had a single out called "4 My Click," which featured Queen's rapper Mic Geronimo. Jay-Z also knew Geronimo's manager, Irving "Irv Gotti" Lorenzo. Gotti, a former DJ from Hollis, Queens, had gotten his start in the

CAROLINE TOREM-CRAIG

Although difficult and demanding, Foxy Brown brought a much needed dose of sex appeal to Def Jam in 1996.

music business at the independent label TVT as a producer/talent scout, where Ja Rule was signed as part of Cash Money Click. Gotti had moved his way up from producer to A&R at TVT Records, where he signed Queens MC Mic Geronimo, who had a hit in the winter of 1994 with "Shit's Real," which DJ Irv (Gotti) produced. Lyor Cohen caught the video one day on the Box and was immediately impressed.

Just like Run-DMC, the Click hailed from Hollis, Queens, and just as his instinct had told him in 1993 to sign an unknown Warren G., Cohen thought the leader of Click—Ja Rule—would be a good fit for Def Jam. "I had heard through the grapevine that Lyor was looking to sign Cash Money Click, so we scrambled and finally got to Lyor," recalled Ja. "At the meeting, Lyor was amped by Irv's energy." Although no deal was struck at that time—Ja Rule was still under contract with TVT—Irv Gotti's enthusiasm and talent-scouting abilities impressed Cohen. Soon, Gotti would play a role in Roc-A-Fella's deal with Def Jam.

By the spring of 1996, Damon Dash and Jay-Z had landed a distribution deal for Roc-A-Fella with Priority Records, and released his debut album, *Reasonable Doubt,* in June. It sold over three hundred thousand copies, and with Foxy Brown already on board, it would only be a matter of time before Def Jam and Roc-A-Fella would unite.

Unlike some of the previous female rap artists at Def Jam, such as

Bo$$, Foxy wanted to be sexy. "It was really important that she was a girl," says Greenwald. To that end, Foxy needed the works: hair, makeup, styling. "She had such expensive taste," recalls Julie, who would sometimes become Foxy's stylist, when Def Jam couldn't afford one, and take the young rapper on shopping trips. "She was a hot artist who wanted to look and act a certain way, and we had to step her game up. We took more pride in putting our money and efforts into our artists than ourselves. We threw one big party a year—the Christmas Party—but beyond that, it wasn't about us promoting us. If you have one dollar to spend, I used to say, 'No, I'm not gonna make a Def Jam T-shirt, I'll make a Redman T-shirt.' I'm not gonna spend my money just promoting Def Jam. Where does Def Jam get me? I used to argue and fight and make sure that the marketing dollars always went to the artists. Some people put their labels first, and some people put the artists first."

Although Def Jam could control where they put their money, they certainly couldn't control their artists' attitudes. And Foxy had one of the worst in the business. For the cover of her debut album, *Ill Nana,* Foxy Brown was scheduled to be shot by Norman Watson, the son of the world-famous photographer Albert Watson. Norman was based in England, where Foxy was going to do a promo show, so the photo shoot was planned in London. Steve Carr, who was art-directing the project, flew in with her.

"It was the night before the shoot, and we had Norman come over with the portfolios of the glam squad—makeup and hair people—a bunch of different ones for her to choose from," Carr recalls. "[Foxy], of course, is late, and comes in, and [Norman] starts trying to talk to her in a really sweet, nice way. And at that time, she was just so arrogant and so mean-spirited. She was looking through it, like, 'This is bullshit, this sucks. Where's all the black girls?' Although Norman tried reassuring Foxy that these were the top people in the field, Foxy continued being difficult, then got up and left. And he was like, 'Wow. That's not cool,' " recalls Steve of Norman's reaction. Steve tried to blame her attitude on jet lag. At 4 a.m.—with only two hours left before the photo shoot's call time—Steve's phone rang. It was Norman Watson. "I've never done this in my life, but I can't do this," he said. "I can't shoot her. I hate her. It'll come through in the pictures." Because this was a rare and expensive overseas shoot for Def Jam, Steve tried to change Norman's mind, but to no avail. "We ended up doing it back in New York with another photographer, who wasn't nearly as good," says Steve, who didn't see Foxy again until the rescheduled shoot. But Foxy's behavior was tolerated, as long as she sold records—and she did. On November 19, 1996, her debut album *Ill Nana* hit stores and within two weeks had climbed to number one on the *Billboard* charts.

Around that time, the relationship between Greenwald and Cohen suddenly soured. "I thought I was definitely walking out the door," she recalled. "He was destroying me. He was on a two-month tear where every day I could do no right." During one breakfast meeting with Kevin Liles and Cohen, things got especially tense. "Anything I said, he just tore me down," she recalls. Afterward, Greenwald called Cohen at the office to tell him that she was quitting. Lyor asked her to come by his office and talk about it. "He said he didn't realize [how his behavior was affecting her]. And he apologized." Julie told him how hard work had been for her lately. "I just don't understand what happened to us," she said. "It's horrible. I can't even work here anymore." "I'm sorry," said Lyor. "I didn't realize it got so bad. You can't leave." Greenwald decided to stay, and "we've just kinda grown together," she says.

•　　　•　　　•

On the weekend of March 9, 1997, much of the urban music industry congregated in L.A. for the *Soul Train* Awards—the only awards show that Russell Simmons once claimed he liked to attend. For Def Jam, the *Soul Train* Awards meant nonstop work. For the past four years, they had been hosting a showcase at the House of Blues during the *Soul Train* Awards weekend, "where whoever is current, or whoever's got records out, is performing, and that's the hot ticket," recalls David Belgrave, who was working the event that year. That

It's good to be . . . from left: Kevin Liles, Russell Simmons, Lyor Cohen and Julie Green-wald—the four pillars of Def Jam in the new millennium—at a charity event in 2003. In a few short months, Cohen, Greenwald, and Liles would no longer be at Def Jam.

year, Def Jam had their newest R&B artist, Case along with Warren G., and Montell Jordan performing.

By Saturday night, with the show over and most of the hectic activity behind them, the Def Jam staff—as well as the rest of the industry folks in town—could finally relax and enjoy the evening. That night, *Vibe* magazine hosted a party. "I had Inga [Foxy Brown] and her girls and Pretty Boy, her little brother, all up at the party," recalls John Stockton, who had introduced Foxy to West Coast rapper Kurupt (they would later date) at another party just a few nights before. The new couple were hanging out all night. There was a general feeling of celebration and high spirits. "They played [Biggie's newest hit] 'Hypnotize' like fifteen gazillion times," recalls David Belgrave of the *Vibe* event. "It was the first time that I was really having a good time." Although the party got broken up by fire marshals and police due to overcrowding and smoking hazards, spirits were high as everyone filed outside to get their cars from valet parking.

"We were all outside, and Case and I are running around like ten-year-olds playing tag, and just acting crazy," recalls John Stockton. "And then Puff and Big pull up, and we were talking to them. They pulled out; not longer than twenty seconds later, we heard the shots."

Foxy and her crew were standing no more than fifty feet from where the shooting took place. David Belgrave and his friends were right at the curb of the driveway when they saw the "commotion." "We just thought it was a fight, so we didn't even stop talking," recalls David.

Suddenly someone started screaming, "They shootin'! They shootin'!" Celebration turned to chaos as people started running. Like wildfire, word spread that Biggie had gotten shot. As soon as she found out, Foxy, who was good friends with Biggie, "wanted to go to the hospital," recalled Stockton. David Belgrave, meanwhile, decided to drive straight to the Le Montrose Hotel, which was the hip-hop industry's hotel of choice at the time, where he knew everyone would probably congregate. He wasn't prepared for the scene when he got to the hotel: "This was like the hip-hop version of whatever the hospital looked like when Kennedy got shot. People were zombies."

Def Jam released Warren's sophomore album, *Take a Look Over Your Shoulder,* on March 25, just two weeks after Biggie's death, when the hip-hop nation was still in mourning. The timing couldn't have been worse. "We tried to get them to not do that," says Wron G. "But they did it." "I was trying to outdo the one before that," Warren says. "And I think I did outdo the first one. But the sales wasn't the same. I don't know what happened. They didn't push it like they did my first one, but I wasn't tripping." The album had only one mild hit on it—"I Shot the Sheriff"—but it wasn't enough to carry it. "Nobody had that killer instinct because Biggie had died," said Wron G. "[Warren] wasn't ready to promote that album. Biggie was dead now. We started doubling the security. I wouldn't use the word *depression,* but he was sorrowful. Everybody was thinking ill."

In the wake of B.I.G.'s untimely death, hip-hoppers—especially on the East Coast—needed a new hometown hero, someone with as much charisma and talent as B.I.G. The found their hero in Jay-Z, and so would Def Jam. *Reasonable Doubt,* his debut, was now gold, and with Foxy Brown a success, Irv Gotti put a bug in Cohen's ear. In Jay-Z, Def Jam could have the total package: street credibility backed up with commercial appeal; a talented vocalist with his own style and a tremendous work ethic. Like Biggie Smalls, Jay-Z claimed that he never wrote down his rhymes, recording all of his raps from memory. He called it "a gift from God."

Def Jam ended up competing for Jay-Z with their old parent company, Sony, who "showed up and tried to throw their wallet in the way," as Simmons recalled. Epic Records, a subsidiary of Sony, came close to closing a deal with Damon Dash, Roc-A-Fella's founder, but Cohen "aggressively pursued [Dash]," recalled Todd Moscowitz. Conflicted, Dash met with Cohen and explained to him how difficult it was to make a decision: Epic, after all, was offering him a higher, more lucrative deal. "In a matter of that conversation, [Cohen] managed to scoop the deal back from Epic," says Moscowitz. "Lyor was best at getting the deal and moving the talent."

On April 8, 1997, Roc-A-Fella finalized their deal with Def Jam, in which the label would be given complete autonomy and even limited association with their parent company. "Because we're the 'mighty Def Jam,' we always kind of wanted Roc-A-Fella to breathe," as Julie Greenwald explains. "Damon and Jay [were] like, 'We're Roc-A-Fella, we're trying to build something here.' " Just like Def Jam, Roc-A-Fella started out as an independent and, like Def Jam, signed with a major label for a distribution deal within two years of its existence.

And like Def Jam, Roc-A-Fella was a success out of the box. Jay-Z's Def Jam debut, *In My Lifetime, Vol. 1*—a completely modern collection of radio-ready tracks, with few references to past styles—was released on October 21, 1997, and quickly went gold. The album had street edge, but with pop sensibilities, and even featured a guest appearance by Puffy. In marketing Jay-Z, Def Jam's plan was to "increase his visibility and make him that crossover artist without sacrificing his full street credibility," as Def Jam's product manager Jazz Young explained. Def Jam saturated the marketplace with Jay-Z–related materials, including retail and street posters, flyers, and TV spots for two weeks before and two after the release of the album. In addition, painted stencils were used to mark city streets with Jay-Z's logo and name.

Cohen would sign another artist with an Irv Gotti connection, a

CAROLINE TOREM-CRAIG

Just like Def Jam and Columbia in the mid-eighties, Roc-A-Fella's Damon Dash (*left*) and Jay-Z were allowed to maintain their creative autonomy from Def Jam. But not without its share of damage control. Pictured here at the infamous party at the Kit Kat Klub in New York City, when Jay-Z stabbed Lance "Un" Rivera, in October of 1999.

gritty Yonkers, New York, rapper named DMX. Gotti passed on to Cohen a mix tape that DMX had rapped on—Ron G.'s *Mix Tape 23*—a track called "Watcha Gonna Do?" which already had some street buzz. After an impromptu audition for Cohen at a Yonkers recording studio, DMX signed with Def Jam, and Gotti was given an A&R job. "He is a troubled soul," says Cey Adams of DMX. "But he is easily one of the most talented people to come along in hip-hop in the last ten years. You can tell he lived a life that you never want to experience. There's something in his eyes, there's a weird fire in his eyes."

DMX quickly established himself as not just one of the most talented new artists of the year, but also one of the most uncompromising. When MTV asked him to a change a hook to his first single, "Where My Dogz At," for the video, he simply refused. "[MTV] said the song is too scary," recalled Julie Greenwald, who had the task of convincing DMX to change his mind. "X, it's really great, because the song is so big, and we can get it on MTV, I just need you to flip these lyrics," she begged him one night at the studio. "Real dogs sniff blood," DMX replied. "What?" Greenwald asked, confused. He repeated the sentence and left her to figure it out. After leaving the studio, she called Cohen. "Did you get him to flip his lyrics?" he asked. "Oh, no, real dogs sniff blood," Julie replied. "They will find his record."

True to their word, MTV didn't play that video. They didn't play the video for DMX's next single, "Stop Being Greedy," either. Radio was also reluctant. "But the right stations were playing it," says Greenwald. "Maybe he had five hundred spins, which is nothing, but it was five hundred of the right spins, and the most urgent spins you'd ever seen in your entire life." That's exactly what pulled people to DMX: his urgency. "He was so different," Julie says. "He was this dude who at first you wonder if he's scary, is he nice, what is he? He's bald and he's growling. And he's very in your face, but he was always very sweet. He's got a very sensitive side to him, and it's like when he first came in, he didn't give a fuck, he just wanted to make the records he wanted to make."

In the tradition of their long-form commercials—Redman in the abandoned lot, Onyx in the barbershop—Def Jam created one for DMX, which produced major buzz and paved the way to a new era of hip-hop advertising. The commercial opened with a shot of "shiny, happy people," as Julie calls them, followed by a sudden shot of lions ripping meat, then going back to the shiny, happy people. "It was the craziest TV commercial," recalls Julie. "It was the first time we bought sixty-second spots."

If his popularity grew from the underground with his first two singles, after Def Jam released the commercial and DMX's third single—"Get at Me Dog" on February 10—the rapper was welcomed into the mainstream with his debut, *It's Dark and Hell Is Hot,* released on May 19, 1998. Few Def Jam insiders had predicted DMX's success, and Julie wasn't one of them. "I would love to take credit for that, but nope," she says. "Very few people thought, 'Oh my God, this is gonna be the one.' Lyor did, Irv Gotti did. Irv's definitely brought us the hits."

In June of 1998, DMX went on the road as one of the headliners for the monthlong Survival of the Illest Tour, which became one of

the many campaigns—following the success of Month of the Man—
"where we would group all the Def Jam acts and try to make our
money go," as Julie Greenwald pointed out. "We put them all out in
the fourth quarter." After years of inflated venue-insurance rates,
concerned fans, and low ticket sales, hip-hop tours were doing well
again. Puff Daddy had started the trend the previous year, when he
took his Puff Daddy & The Family world tour on the road, with
Mase, Lil' Kim, the Lox, Busta Rhymes, Jay-Z, and Foxy Brown.

Joining DMX for Survival of the Illest were Onyx and the Def
Squad. Only four years earlier, Onyx were "saving Def Jam," as
Sticky Fingaz put it, but now they were hoping the label would save
them. Their third—and what would become their final—album on
Def Jam, *Shut 'Em Down,* barely went gold. "Our unity with [Jam
Master] Jay was broken, our unity with the label was broken," says
Sticky, who came by the office one day and threw a tantrum. "I
flipped out, pulling plaques off the wall, throwing shit around, mad,"
he remembers. Sticky doesn't blame the label for being greedy—
that's how labels are *supposed* to act, he says, it's the nature of the business. "They're sharks! That's what they do."

•   •   •

"The Brain," "The Taste," and "The Action." For as long as he's
been a part of Def Jam's inner circle, Kevin Liles has liked to refer in
those terms to Lyor Cohen, Julie Greenwald, and himself, respec-
tively. "Lyor would think of something, see if it worked with Jules,
we would all sit together, and I would say, 'Well, this is how we
should execute that,'" Liles explains. "The three of us are just such a
great dynamic, it's unbelievable," Greenwald agrees. Their chemistry,
trust for one another, and respective strengths that worked in unison
would help take Def Jam to unprecedented heights in the late 1990s.
Together, they would devise marketing campaigns, strategic partner-
ships, and anything else to propel the Def Jam brand into the new
millennium with force.

On July 14, 1998, at only thirty years old, Liles was named president of Def Jam—a giant leap from his previous position as the label's general manager/VP. Liles would be responsible for overseeing Def Jam's daily operations and the search for new talent. Liles had had that vision for himself from the beginning: "When I officially came in, in 1995, I had already started preparing to be president. I never asked for the title, but I always acted the part."

One of his first projects as president was Jay-Z's second Def Jam album, *Hard Knock Life, Vol. 2,* released in September of 1998. It was an ex-

A rare moment with the two kingpins of Def Jam: DMX and Jay-Z.

plosion. On October 31, the album was number one in America, ahead of Lauryn Hill, Shania Twain, and 'N Sync. It stayed there for five consecutive weeks, setting a *Billboard* record as the first rap album to do so. "You just can't be a rapper out there; you have to make rap *songs,*" Hank Shocklee points out. "That's one thing I have to give Jay-Z credit for. He was a rapper that couldn't make good rap songs until he met with Jermaine Dupri and they made [*Hard Knock Life's*] 'Money Ain't a Thing.' Jermaine showed him how to make a song, and once Jay got the formula, he took it into overdrive. Then he stopped trying to be a rapper and became more of a songwriter."

In November, Method Man and Redman both celebrated the success of their albums—Method Man's *Tical 2000: Judgement Day,* and Redman's *Doc's da Name 2000*—reaching number one, thanks in large part to Def Jam's marketing campaigns. "Nothing around here sneaks under the radar, everything gets a huge push," Julie

Greenwald pointed out. "We don't put out as much as other record companies, but the ones we put out with, we have to do right. That's why when we don't sell, it hurts so much, because it's like we spend so much money and so much time and so much resources on it. We don't do the throw-it-out-there-and-see-if-it-sticks. And we'd rather do it that way."

But employees at the company knew from November of 1998 that a big merger was coming. Seagram's—the Canadian beverage and entertainment conglomerate that owned MCA, Interscope, Universal, and Geffen Records—was closing a deal to buy the huge Polygram conglomerate for an astounding, unprecedented $10.4 billion. Interscope, Geffen, and A&M would be positioned as one group—composing a West Coast power base dubbed the Interscope Records Group. It would be led by a management team topped by Interscope chief Jimmy Iovine. On the East Coast, Motown, Def Jam, and Universal Records would be grouped in a Universal Music Group structure. Polygram Group Distribution chief Jim Caparro was tapped to run the Mercury and Island Records labels.

Ten years earlier, Sony had bought CBS Records for $2 billion and it was the biggest industry news of the year. Now, the stakes were higher, and Def Jam was set to gain much more from this sale.

On December 10, 1998, Seagram's acquired Polygram. For the staff and the artists, this would mean only one thing: in several weeks, or several months, thousands would be laid off, with many musical acts jettisoned, which would "rock the music industry," as *Variety* wrote. Seagram's would be absorbing some record labels whole and simply discarding others. Universal Music Group emerged from the wreckage as the world's largest recording company, a market-share behemoth. This giant would control one-third of the industry's sales, pushing Warner Music out of its long-held top spot. Artists and staff would be reduced to mere pegs in the game, as departments would be streamlined, thus saving the corporation $300 million. Many industry insiders commented that the sale was a "hostile takeover" by Seagram's, which bought Polygram "lock, stock, and barrel."

It was the first megamerger in the history of the music industry. Seagram's was purchasing Polygram's Mercury, Island, Motown, A&M, and Def Jam Records. Labels with long, colorful histories would be reduced to name only, with no choice but to cut their artist rosters significantly. When it came to "reevaluating," artistic merit was no consideration. Seagram's goal was to figure out which artists had been, and would continue to be, the most profitable. Around three thousand jobs and more than two hundred acts were expected to be cut from the newly formed Universal Music Group.

Some artists tried to get out before they were kicked out. Warren G., whose album sales had by now dipped significantly since his *Regulate* heyday, remembers, "hearing like a gang of people was gonna be dropped. Before I was gonna let the company try to drop me, I was gonna leave. I wasn't trying to have no company drop me. I didn't want that under my belt." After some resistance from Cohen, Warren was finally let out of his contract.

In the midst of the impending merger, Def Jam was lining up its holiday releases: DMX's *Flesh of My Flesh, Blood of My Blood* album—his second in less than a year—on December 22, 1998. It became the bestselling album in the nation, selling 670,000 copies during Christmas week. DMX, the troubled young man from Yonkers, edged out Garth Brooks and his *Double Live* album, which had been sitting at number one for five weeks. (He was the first artist in Soundscan history to have two number one albums in the same year.)

It was the perfect conclusion to a banner year, and the beginning of a two-year winning streak at Def Jam. "The reason I think we had a banner year," says Kevin Liles, "was because we decided to build the brands and give [successful] executives opportunities." He is quick to differentiate these label deals from RAL. "This time, it wasn't the artists that we were giving the opportunity to," says Liles, "it was people who we felt understood the business, not just the art of it. We groomed Irv for three, four years before we gave him that opportunity. Dame had his own company [Roc-A-Fella], and we sort of worked with them for a year prior to [giving them a label deal in

1997]. And then Ruff Ryders, they were Irv's friends, and we hung out a lot with them. Also, at that time I started to grow in a more acting-owner role. It felt so good that people believed in me, like I believed in Lyor and believed in Russell."

•   •   •

Employees and artists at Polygram Music Group knew for a few months that the big day was coming. Finally, and dreadfully, it happened on "Black Thursday"—January 21, 1999. There had been other days like it in the music industry, most notably "the Friday Massacre," in August of 1982, when CBS Records had fired three hundred employees and closed nine of its U.S. sales branches. But this was worse. The hardest hit were A&M, Geffen, and Mercury, which let go over three hundred acts—some of them profitable—and ten times as many employees. Once home to such rock powerhouses as Guns N' Roses, Geffen became a skeleton operation with a few A&R executives. "It's a painful thing to watch," remarked founder David Geffen.

"It's a Wall Street world now. Get ready," said Al Cafaro, who got fired as the president of A&M Records, one of the first labels to get cleaned out. For the staff at A&M, one of the oldest and most esteemed labels in history, the sale was so traumatic that the flag bearing the company's logo was hung at half-mast on the day of the layoffs. Mercury Records lost 60 of its 150 employees and was expected to downsize at least 110 of its 140 acts over the following eight months. Motown Records became a ghost of its former self, with only 7 out of its original 75 employees remaining.

But not only the labels would suffer as a result of the merger; consumers would soon discover that some of their favorite artists were now harder to find in record stores.

By February of 1999, Russell Simmons was rumored to be selling off the remaining 40 percent stake in Def Jam to Seagram's Universal Music Group, which already owned 60 percent of Def Jam, for an expected $250 million. The decision to sell was carefully thought out.

Greenwald and Cohen talked about trying to "ride out" the merger and remain independent a little longer. But ultimately, the deal just sounded too good, and the timing was right. "We could come to this other company and take it over," she said to Cohen. "Don't you wanna try something new and different? It would be great to stay small and not become corporate, but the money was so good, that, yo, we gotta take it." The sale was completed by April of 1999, and with it, Def Jam now became the black-music arm of the newly re-structured unit, Island Def Jam. Cohen became its copresident, along with John Reid, both of whom reported to IDJ's chairman, Jim Ca-parro. Cohen collected $100 million from the sale and was now liv-ing as lavishly as his marquee acts, with a home on the Upper East Side and private-plane trips to the Hamptons. As copresident, Cohen would now be overseeing not just rap acts but Island Def Jam's rock acts, such as Sum 41, Saliva, and Nickelback—something that he had always wanted to do. Julie Greenwald and Kevin Liles would con-tinue to work with him side by side as vice president of marketing and president of Def Jam, respectively. Each also got a nice check from the sale.

Russell Simmons, meanwhile, would retain his title as chairman of Def Jam. Having married his longtime girlfriend Kimora Lee back in December of 1998, he moved back to his native New York from L.A., into a duplex penthouse loft in the Wall Street area, purchased from Keith Richards for $2 million. Rick Rubin's American Records—which had dropped *Def* from its name back in 1993—was folded into Universal Music Group as well, as a result of the merger of its own parent company, Geffen, with A&M and Mercury into In-terscope Geffen A&M. Although he continued to operate American Recordings out of L.A., Rick would now be flying to New York City more often for company meetings with his new boss, Lyor Cohen. The two had put old grudges behind them and were now close friends.

In its own dysfunctional way, the original Def Jam family was back together again.

CHAPTER 14

Starting Over

The new incarnation of Island Def Jam was starting off with a bang. Ja Rule's debut album *Venni, Vetti, Vecci* was released on June 1, 1999, Def Jam's first major release under the newly formed Universal Music Group and the first release under Irv Gotti's newly formed Murder Inc. label, which Island Def Jam financed. The setup for the album was flawless: Ja Rule made appearances on several high-profile songs, including Blackstreet's "Girlfriend/Boyfriend," and Jay-Z's monster hit "Can I Get A . . . ," which was one of the biggest rap songs of 1998.

Like Death Row's Suge Knight, Gotti picked the name of his label for shock value. It would go on to haunt him five years later. Twenty-three-year-old Ja Rule, like Russell Simmons, was from Hollis, Queens, and there had already been major buzz on the young rapper, who'd rapped in a Coca-Cola commercial even before he'd released his single "Holla Holla," which would climb as high as No. 11 on the Hot R&B Singles & Tracks chart. By June 19, his debut album had shot up to number one on the Top R&B Albums chart, and to No. 3 on the *Billboard* two hundred chart, directly behind the Backstreet Boys and Ricky Martin.

Def Jam, high off their incredibly successful 1998 year and perhaps emboldened by the impending new millennium, got more ambitious than ever. In August of 1999, Def Jam announced that it would do something completely unprecedented in the music industry—it would release five new albums in the weeks between Thanksgiving and New Year's. Record companies traditionally avoid that period because it is too late to profit from the holiday-season sales. Because it had worked with DMX's *Flesh of My Flesh,* Def Jam decided to try to repeat

CAROLINE TOREM-CRAIG

His gruff voice drew comparisons to Tupac early on, but Ja Rule quickly developed his own identity and massive hits like "Put It on Me" for Def Jam and his imprint, Murder Inc.

that magic. Along with LL Cool J's album on November 3, Def Jam planned to release a new CD by Method Man on December 7, and by Redman on December 14; and another new album on December 21. The fifth album would be by a new artist named Sisqo.

"Dru World Order," as Def Jam referred to it, was announced in August of 1999 for the group Dru Hill, who recorded for Island Records before the Universal Music Group merger and whose four members had each signed separate production deals with Def Soul/Def Jam. Sisqo, the group's twenty-three-year-old lead singer, would be spearheading the project with a planned November solo CD release, followed by a solo CD by the other three members: Jazz, Nokio, and Woody. The big finale for the Dru World Order would be the release of Dru Hill's new album in November of 2000. "This will be a historical, groundbreaking endeavor," Kevin Liles gushed.

"Our goal is to have the number one and number two albums at the end of 1999, and the number one and number two albums in the first week of 2000," said Liles to the *L.A. Times.* Some industry members agreed that it could work. "It worked last year big time, and with these artists back-to-back it could be monstrous," said Violet Brown, urban-music buyer for the Wherehouse chain. Others were more skeptical. "Up to Christmas the traffic is massive," said Best Buy vice president Gary Arnold. "But after that it really diminishes, and that could mean losing sales over the long haul."

On November 3, 1999, Def Jam launched another R&B label, Def Soul. While the idea for Def Soul was a collaborative effort among Cohen, Kevin Liles, and Director of A&R Tina Davis, the formation of the new imprint was mainly overseen by Liles. "Our problem was, radio stations were saying, 'I'm already playing seven of your Def Jam records,' so I'm thinking, 'Maybe I gotta create something else,' " Liles explained. "People always give us the stigma of we are a rap label, so we came up with this brand called Def Soul. We are now brand-builders."

Def Soul's first release, Montell Jordan's album *Get It On . . . Tonite,* hit stores on November 9, followed by Sisqo's *Unleash the Dragon* at the end of November. For the occasion, Sisqo dyed his close-cropped hair a shocking silver color. "I'm going to save R&B," he chimed to the press. "The world is going to be saying, 'I want to be like Sisqo,' just like they did with Michael [Jackson]." But not everyone thought his master plan was going to work. Releasing three more solo albums from the other members of Dru Hill, followed by a group album, seemed too lofty an idea for some critics. "Music doesn't always lend itself to predictable mathematics," one reporter mused. "In reality, this venture has the potential to be Sisqo's last stand."

Indeed Def Jam's plan didn't entirely pan out. Instead of releasing separate albums from Redman and Method Man, a joint album called *Blackout* hit shelves on September 28, 1999. Jay-Z and DMX, however, did release their new albums within days of each other before the new year. On December 21, DMX released his third album, *And Then*

There Was X, which immediately shot up to the number one spot in the country, selling over seven hundred thousand copies in its first week. It was followed by Jay-Z's fourth album, *Volume 3: The Life and Times of S. Carter,* on December 28, and that album also debuted at No. 1, placing DMX at No. 2. Indeed, just as Liles had hoped, Def Jam had the No. 1 and No. 2 albums of the new millennium in the country.

By March of 2000, Sisqo's "Thong Song" was the most played record in Def Jam's history and helped push his *Unleash the Dragon* album into the Top 5 on the charts, while selling 2.1 million copies. But his goal for Dru World Order wasn't quite materializing as he and Kevin Liles, president of Def Soul/Def Jam, had hoped. By April, there were still no solo albums from the other members of Dru Hill, and there was certainly no group album anywhere in sight. On April 16, Sisqo would be performing on the *Soul Train* Awards, but the other members would decline to join him onstage, as had been the original plan. "I'm really down right now," he said before the show. "I'm just going through the motions."

By May of 2000, DMX had sold an astounding 10 million records since his debut in 1998—a total of three multiplatinum records. He had also coheadlined two of the most successful hip-hop tours ever: the Hard Knock Life Tour in the summer of 1999 and the sold-out forty-city Ruff Ryders/Cash Money Tour with fellow Ruff Ryders Eve and The Lox. DMX helped Def Jam, combined with Def Soul, gain the highest market share of urban music in the United States.

Meanwhile, Ja Rule's sophomore album, *Rule 3:36,* was finished, and Def Jam was setting it up for an October 3 release. The follow-up to his 1999 platinum release, *Venni, Vetti, Vecci,* displayed the same ferocious growling and intensity heard on the classic club joint "Holla Holla." The video to the new album's danceable first single, "Between Me and You," would be taking over TVs everywhere in September. Ja Rule recorded all of *Rule 3:36* in Los Angeles. Influences on the album range from artists Barry White to Joan Osborne, whose philosophical "One of Us" gets revamped ghetto-style by the gritty MC.

CAROLINE TOREM-CRAIG

"Irv has definitely brought us the hits," says Julie Greenwald of the founder of Murder Inc. (renamed The Inc. in 2004). Irv Gotti started out as an A&R rep but quickly established himself as a mogul star-maker.

After Gotti's huge success with Ja Rule, Island Def Jam paid him to form a joint venture with Murder Inc. He and Island Def Jam would each own 50 percent of Murder Inc. Gotti and Cohen were closer than ever. "Lansky"—after Meyer Lansky, a founding father of the original Murder Inc. mob— was how Gotti affectionately referred to his boss.

After opening a branch in Germany—the capital of European hip-hop—known as Def Jam Germany, which would be located in Berlin and sign hip-hop and R&B artists from Germany, Def Jam also expanded into the South, with the creation of Def Jam South and the signing of Atlanta rapper Ludacris in early 2001. "We knew that he wasn't just gonna sell from the Northeast," explains Greenwald. Once Def Jam noticed that his first single off the album, "Southern Hospitality," started getting buzz in the South, "he got on a bus and spent two months doing the most extensive promo tour just in the South, which is so different from us," says Greenwald. "He was going to places like Biloxi, Memphis, Chattanooga. It was awesome, because it really gave us a road map into the South, and he obviously cemented himself as a Southern artist, but now it's so much more of a big, broad national artist."

For Cohen, 2001 couldn't have ended on a higher note. In December, forty-one-year-old Cohen took over Island Def Jam and would now be reporting directly to Universal Music Group chief

With Def Jam South, and its star artist Ludacris, Def Jam tapped into a profitable market—just as they did with the formation of Def Jam West in 1992—and this time, with even better results.

Doug Morris. Most industry insiders had said it was only a matter of time before Cohen would grab the reins from his boss, Jim Caparro, who resigned as the chairman of Island Def Jam with two years left on his contract in November. "I'm done, the company is built," Caparro said. In early December when Cohen took over as chairman, Island Def Jam was said to be the most profitable label at Universal Music Group, earning an estimated $100 million in profits in 2001. Along with hip-hop successes like Ja Rule, DMX, and Jay-Z, Island Def Jam had also broken several big rock acts, including Sum 41 and Nickelback.

Cohen would now be on the same level as his rumored rival Jimmy Iovine, the head of Interscope Geffen A&M, another label under Universal Music Group, and home to powerhouse artists like No Doubt and Eminem. Cohen and Iovine reportedly clashed when the latter tried to lure several Island Def Jam artists, such as Sisqo, to Interscope. Cohen retaliated by offering an executive job to Fred Durst, the lead singer of Limp Bizkit, one of Interscope's biggest groups. (By the following year, the two executives' differences were patched up, and Cohen would call Iovine a "good friend.")

Cohen would also now have an opportunity to sign and oversee rock acts. His roots in rock went back to his first meeting with Simmons at the Mix Club back in 1983, when Cohen booked Social Distortion and Red Hot Chili Peppers along with Run–DMC. "Lyor was very passionate for years about starting a rock label, or at least incorporating it into Def Jam," says Scott Koenig. "But no one would believe in him."

No sooner did Cohen take over the label than he promoted his right-hand woman, Julie Greenwald, to president of Island Records, the rock and pop arm of Island Def Jam, on January 7, 2002. In addition to her new post, Greenwald—who had served as senior vice president of marketing for Island Def Jam—was named executive vice president of Island Def Jam, a title she was to share with Kevin Liles, who remained the president of Def Jam/Def Soul. "I was a hip-hop chick for seven years," points out Greenwald. "And now I'm the rock chick. It ended up changing my life."

With Cohen as its leader, Island Def Jam only got hotter, as three of its acts—Ludacris, Nickelback, and Ja Rule—debuted in the nation's Top 10 album chart on the week of January 17, 2002. Cohen was proving that he could excel at running a diverse roster of artists, not just hip-hop, and Island Def Jam's forty-nine Grammy nominations that year were further proof.

On January 28, Cohen announced the upcoming release of *Best of Both Worlds,* another incredible venture that would pair R&B's biggest seller, R. Kelly, with his hip-hop counterpart, Jay-Z, for a joint album. Cohen and Barry Weiss, president of Jive Records, R. Kelly's label, agreed that Island Def Jam would promote and market the album in the United States and Canada, while Jive would release it throughout the rest of the world. "We are thrilled to kick off the new year with such a musically and culturally important project," Cohen told the press, while Liles concurred, "This is clearly more than just an album—it's a movement. One album, one tour, one movement, all from our culture."

But if Cohen was an expert at concocting clever cross-marketing campaigns in hip-hop and R&B, doing the same in the realm of pop and rock would prove more challenging. This was not the same music that he and Julie Greenwald were used to testing, first and foremost, on club DJs. Cohen decided to follow the same approach he had used during the past three years at Island Def Jam: releasing fewer albums per year, and using street-level, word-of-mouth promotion. Sum 41 toured small U.S. venues months before the band was introduced on television and radio.

On May 9, 2002, Cohen announced that Island Def Jam would be signing pop singer Mariah Carey to a $28 million deal. Within a month, Carey relocated to the island of Capri to record her debut album, where Cohen visited her for three days, "swimming in the Blue Grotto, and eating for four hours." Carey's upcoming album was one of the question marks hanging over Island Def Jam. Cohen's international strategy was also being examined. The offices in the UK, Germany, and Japan had signed no significant acts, and Cohen admitted that he had "been frustrated by the international strategy" and that he needed "to give it way more sunlight and water."

Still, Cohen's big advantage was that his Island Def Jam was part of the most dominant record company in the world, Universal Music Group, which had cornered 30.6 percent of the U.S. market in CD sales in 2002. In fact, while most music labels were losing sales due to online swapping and other piracy, UMG was thriving, with acts like Eminem, Nelly, and Ashanti dominating the charts and selling millions of albums.

Over the course of his career, Kevin Liles had always been given freedom by Cohen to develop projects to keep the label "hot" and to develop the next ten years of Def Jam. Liles negotiated an unprecedented alliance between the world's leading independent video-game publisher, Electronic Arts (EA), and Def Jam in September of 2002. *Def Jam Vendetta,* the first game in a series, was scheduled to hit stores in March of 2003. In this hip-hop street-fighting game, the characters were actual Def Jam artists like Ludacris, Method Man, and DMX. EA would be paying Def Jam's parent company, Universal Music

Group, a licensing fee for the music titles it used, as well as a royalty rate to Def Jam for utilizing the label's brand name.

"I just said, 'If Russell's doing the clothes and the movies and the comedy, I wanna do games!' " Liles recalled. "So I started to think about growing the logo—again, let's become another household name in another way. Lyor said, 'We're a service company.' I said, 'Lyor, I read this book by Ray Kroc of McDonald's. Ray Kroc said, "Most people would say McDonald's is a hamburger company. No, it's a real estate company. Because most of our buildings are in prime real estate areas, so we make more money off the real estate than we make off selling hamburgers." '

" 'We're no longer a record company, we're no longer a service company. We're a *lifestyle* company that happens to sell records,' " Kevin said to Lyor. " 'Like McDonald's is a real estate company that happens to sell hamburgers.' " What Kevin meant by "lifestyle company" was that Def Jam was like a "travel agent" to hip-hop culture. "So if you wanna know what's the funniest shit, watch *Def Comedy Jam,*" he explains. "If you wanna know what the upcoming movement is, *Def Poetry.* If you wanna know what the hot new game is, Def Jam interactive."

"That's why I credit him [Cohen] with any success that I have now," says Liles. "Because he allowed me to make the mistakes early on. And didn't penalize me for making mistakes; he encouraged me to make them and learn from them."

•   •   •

In January of 2003, Vivendi Universal—the parent company of the Island Def Jam Group—was served with grand-jury subpoenas by federal agents at the company's New York offices. The murder of Jam Master Jay in October of 2002, allegedly over drugs, had seemingly given new urgency to an eighteen-month-long federal investigation into Murder Inc.'s ties to the drug world. Island Def Jam was ordered to turn over royalty records, invoices, and other data that could help authorities link Irv Gotti with reputed former drug kingpin Kenneth "Supreme" McGriff.

Authorities believed McGriff might have financed Murder Inc., and that Gotti might have been laundering money for McGriff. The subpoena was issued weeks after federal agents raided Murder Inc. offices and confiscated computers and files. Murder Inc. moved out of the Def Jam offices shortly after the raid (their contract was unaffected)—although Def Jam claimed that the move had nothing to do with the federal charges. Soon after, the label dropped *Murder* from their name and kept it simply as The Inc.

Both McGriff and Gotti denied any wrongdoing, while Lyor Cohen kept mum. Cohen and Gotti had always been close, just one floor apart at IDJ's headquarters on Eighth Avenue, and Cohen served on the executive board of Murder Inc.

More legal trouble was to come. In May, Cohen lost a case to independent label TVT Records, which sued him and IDJ for blocking the release of early Ja Rule material (the rapper was once signed to the indie, but became a platinum success at Def Jam). TVT won a huge award, some of which Cohen was held personally liable for.

The lawsuit had shaken Cohen. More than ever, he drew strength from his staff, whom he addressed via e-mail on May 6, 2003: "I just want you all to know that we are going to appeal this decision and fight. I can't thank you enough for all of your endless support. It means the world to me that I work with such a loving staff. Again, please don't worry about me, keep your heads up and let's get back to breaking artists and selling records."

When the music industry started buzzing in November of 2003 about Lyor Cohen's possible departure from his post as the head of Island Def Jam Records for another label, the idea seemed unfathomable. "[Def Jam] is like his child," Brett Ratner said in the summer of 2003. "He'll do anything to protect it."

But Cohen, who had been with the label since 1985, was not the same young, blindly ambitious, and temperamental executive who'd once thrived on Def Jam's cultivated chaos. At forty-three, he had mellowed into a devoted family man. Running the company had, for him, become more than stressful; because of the TVT decision and the Murder Inc. investigation, it was also a liability.

From left: Lyor Cohen, Foxy Brown, Lady May, and L.A. Reid, then president of Arista Records, at an event in April of 2002. Few would have predicted that within a year, the man on the far right would take over Cohen's job.

With his Island Def Jam contract approaching its expiration date, Cohen started thinking about quitting. He had not had a bona fide hit in nearly a year. Mariah Carey's album, *Charmbracelet,* had failed to meet its hyped-up expectations. Ja Rule's recent album was a flop, and Jay-Z, Def Jam's crown jewel, was talking about going into retirement. Cohen wanted a new challenge—he was even considering starting his own independent label with the money he would receive from the $120 million sale of Phat Farm in January of 2004 (Cohen was a partner in the clothing line with Simmons).

So when Warner Bros. Records came calling in the fall of 2003, Cohen saw a golden opportunity. He could be an even bigger fish in a big pond. Warner had recently been purchased by a group of investors for $2.6 billion, making it the biggest independent record label in the world. Although their offer to Cohen was actually lower than the $10 million he would get from Universal Music Group for re-signing, Cohen knew that he would be joining old friends at Warner, two men who had been in his corner for many years: Roger Ames and Edgar Bronfman, chairmen of the Warner Music Group.

Back in 1994, Ames had helped Polygram aquire 60 percent of Def Jam and sign them to a new distribution deal. Five years later, Bronfman—then head of the newly formed Universal Music Group—purchased the remaining 40 percent of Def Jam. He and Cohen worked together until 2000, when Bronfman sold all of his assets in UMG to the French company Vivendi.

After all the speculations, Cohen's final day at Def Jam came abruptly. On Monday, January 26, 2004, he simply packed up his office and left. There was no two-week notice. The decision, recalled close friend and former Def Jam road manager Sean Carasov, "was really hard on him—and everyone around him." His departure added yet another, somewhat sad, twist to the Def Jam story. For a man who'd been "obsessed" with the concept of family—in business and his personal life—leaving Def Jam felt like a father abandoning his child.

But he did not leave alone. Julie Greenwald, Cohen's right-hand woman for over ten years and the president of Island Records, was hired in April of 2004 as the president of Warner's Atlantic Music Group.

In Cohen's place, L. A. Reid—an entirely different type of executive—was hired as Island Def Jam's chief executive. He took over Julie Greenwald's old corner office, where he liked to play his music so loud that it shook the walls of the art department next door. Reid's background was almost entirely in pop-crossover R&B music like TLC and Toni Braxton; he had little credibility in the hip-hop world. A cofounder of LaFace Records with Babyface, Reid had taken over Clive Davis's position at Arista in 2000, but was fired less than three years later because the label had reported losses of up to $200 million. (In the music industry, profits from a few big sellers, like the ones Reid had with Usher, Outkast, Pink, and Avril Lavigne, can easily be eaten up by the numerous stiffs.)

Exactly two years earlier, Cohen had said that his "greatest fear is for some idiot ending up being my successor and not handling the artists, the Island Def Jam brand, and the logo with the sensitivity and care they need." Indeed, concerns about Reid's reimaging of Def Jam were immediate. Many people wondered aloud if Reid had the sensibilities needed to run the gritty Def Jam label. Even Russell Simmons, who had sold the label years ago, wrote an open letter to the music community, published on allhiphop.com, in which he expressed his worries about "whether the legacy that Def Jam established will be maintained" under the new order, which was already falling into place. In August, Reid fired Kevin Liles, the president of Def Jam, because, as Simmons pointed out, "Kevin didn't know how to report to L.A. He was trained to be independent." Liles almost immediately joined his former Def Jam dream team—Julie Greenwald and Lyor Cohen—at Warner Bros. as the new vice president of the Warner Music Group.

With his boss, Doug Morris, CEO of Universal Music Group, giving Reid complete creative license ("Do what you have to do to make yourself proud. You are L. A. Reid," Morris reportedly said), Reid quickly started filling up the Def Jam roster with new talent, signing the St. Louis–based production duo Trackboyz, who had worked on hits for Nelly and D-12. Reid spent hours with Def Jam staffers, going through upcoming releases from artists like Joe Budden, whom he considered "too wordy."

Reid promised to turn Def Jam into the factory of diverse "hits and stars" that it was in the eighties. If Kevin Liles preferred to have Def Jam operate as a lifestyle brand that happened to sell records, Reid was going to flip that approach upside down, focusing more on churning out popular music.

Still, Reid was not planning on removing the street from the label entirely. Jay-Z, who had officially announced his retirement from rap in 2004, was named the new president of Def Jam in December of 2004. It was a novel idea that somehow fit perfectly with the entire Def Jam ethos: that the heart of hip-hop was always the DJ and the MC, and as long as those two elements remained authentic, then the label would continue to persevere.

The Def Jam Recordings founded in Rick Rubin's dorm room was clearly a faint echo of the giant conglomerate it had become. But then again, Def Jam had been built on the idea of transforming and challenging itself. Lyor Cohen once said, "You won't find the Harvard Business School example at Def Jam. We did what we had to do to survive." Well, Def Jam not only survived, it thrived.

Notes and Sources

Most of the material for this book came from the hundreds of hours of interviews I conducted from May 2003 until January 2005 with the following, in alphabetical order:

Cey Adams, Bill Adler, Tom Araya/Slayer, Carmen Ashhurst, Sunny Bak, Arthur Baker, David Belgrave, Bo$$, Sean Carasov, Steve Carr, Lyor Cohen, Lisa Cortes, Cut Creator, Chuck D., Nikki D., Drew Dixon, George Drakoulias, Doctor Dre, Adam Dubin, Karen Duran, Chuck Eddy, Mike Espindle, Peter Fletcher, Rocky Ford, Glen E. Friedman, Warren G., Wron G., Bobbito Garcia, Nick Gold, Julie Greenwald, Eric Haze, Michael Holman, Jeff Jones, Kaspa, Scott Koenig, Sheryl Konensburg, Julie Lanke, Brian Latture, Cara Lewis, Chris Lighty, Kevin Liles, Thomas Lytell, Ric Menello, Todd Moscowitz, Don Newkirk, Faith Newman, Pete Nice, Prince Paul, Tonya Pendleton, Darryl Pierce/L.A. Posse, Ricky Powell, Steve Ralbovsky, Brett Ratner, Ruben Rodriguez, Tony Rome, Dante Ross, Rick Rubin, MC Serch, Sam Sever, Hank Shocklee, Danny Simmons, Russell Simmons, Dwayne Simon/L.A. Posse, Slick Rick, Heidi Smith, Bill Stephney, Sticky Fingaz, John Stockton, Tashan, Al Teller, Angela Thomas, Leyla Turkkan, Tracey Waples, Lindsey Williams.

Additional source material came from previously published and unpublished material, including periodicals, websites, books, and employee archives.

Part One: Debut, 1982–87

Chapter 1: The Maverick

4   "menacing aura of a character in an urban psycho-killer film": Robert Hilburn, *Los Angeles Times,* April 16, 1989.

9   Rubin's parents: "King of Rap," *Village Voice,* November 4, 1986.

12–13   Beastie Boys, The Young and the Useless, and RATcage Records: Beastiemania.com.

13   "They had the potential": Ibid.

13   "*I* could do this better": Stanley Mieses, "Pipe Dreams and Sweet Dreams," *Record,* December 1985.

Chapter 2: **The Visionary**

15-16   "J.B. called my house late one night": "The Life and Def of Russell Simmons," essay by Robert Ford. November 1993.

18-19   Starting Run-DMC: Bill Adler, *Tougher Than Leather* (Consafos Press, 1987).

Chapter 3: **Coming Together**

28   On a weekend in December of 1983: Adam Horovitz, *Beastie Boys: Sounds of Science,* CD liner notes (Capitol, 1999).

32   Fresh Fest became one of the top-grossing tours of the summer: "Swatch Watch Tour grosses $3.5 mil in 27 performances," *Amusement Week,* December 22, 1984.

37   "Come celebrate the stars of Rush Productions": Invitation, Bill Adler Archives.

41   "Packed tighter than Afrika Bambaataa's": "The King of Rap," *Village Voice,* November 4, 1986.

41   "unfit for living": Ibid.

Chapter 4: **Dorm Room to Boardroom**

46   "the mogul of rap": "If a Big Beat Zaps You out of a Nap, the Music Is Rap," Meg Cox, *Wall Street Journal,* December 4, 1984.

50   budgeted at $3 million: "Schultz Lensed 'Groove' in 26 Days for $3,000,000," *Variety,* November 6, 1985.

51   Filming began in March of 1985 at Silvercup Studios: Charles E. Rogers, "Behind the Scenes on the Set of *Krush Groove,*" *Black Beat,* April 1985.

51   for the first time in movie history: Ibid.

51   Known as Big Red: Fredric Dannen, *Hit Men* (Vintage Books, 1990).

52   the Jonzun Crew, an electrofunk duo: Andy Kellman, "Jonzun Crew," Globaldarkness.com.

52   profits at CBS had skyrocketed: Dannen, *Hit Men.*

53   *"I'm the king of the Paramount!" Seattle-Post Intelligencer,* April 11, 1985.

53   "We made the *worst* of it": Ibid.

53   "unfortunate," *Daily News,* May 31, 1985.

53   "embarrassingly amateur": *Seattle Times,* April 11, 1985.

57   Madonna, who did her first showcase at No Entiendes: Andrew Morton, *Madonna* (St. Martin's Press, 2001).

61   touted as one of the most lucrative of all custom deals: "King of Rap," *NY Talk,* October 1985.

63   looked ultracorporate and even "ominous": Walter Yetnikoff with David Ritz, *Howling at the Moon* (Broadway Books, 2004).

67–68   On October 23, Warner Bros. held a premiere party: *Krush Groove* party invite, Bill Adler Archives.

68   "the film grossed $11 million": Internal Rush Productions memo from Bill Adler to a promoter, March 14, 1986.

68   three separate theaters in New York reported mêlées: Mike Brennan, "200 Stitches for Teen in 'Rap' Movie Riot," *New York Post,* November 4, 1985.

68   "Kids are so excited to see their heroes": "Krush Rep: Bad Rap?" *New York Newsday,* November 7, 1985.

70   Rush Productions immediately sent out a press release: "Beasties
            Bounced from Black Rock!" Rush Productions press release, January
            6, 1986.

Chapter 5: (Dysfunctional) Family

74   "dynamic, crucial, exciting" "Falling on Def Ears": *Blues & Soul,* Feb-
            ruary 11-24, 1986.
74   "I was real small for my age, plus I was blind in one eye": Scott Brodeur,
            "The Misadventures of Slick Rick," *The Source,* March 1995.
75   "Def Jam at the Apollo": Rush Productions press release, March 19, 1986.
79   compared to the Sex Pistols: *East Village Eye,* May 1986.
82   Rubin had replaced the original drums with "these big rock drums":
            Adam Yauch, *Beastie Boys: Sounds of Science,* CD liner notes (Capitol,
            1999).
84   made them look more like "mouldy wood paneling": *Now-Toronto*
            magazine, December 1986.
85   a lawsuit charging Osbourne: Patrick Goldstein, "CBS: A Case of
            Heavy-Metal Poisoning?" *Los Angeles Times,* October 1986.

Chapter 6: Invincible

100   "tearing up"—industry-speak for doing well—retail: *Hits,* November
            24, 1986.
100   At the last minute, they pulled a song called "The Scenario": Anthony
            DeCurtis, *Rolling Stone,* February 12, 1987.
100   ran a big ad in *Billboard* magazine, proclaiming themselves "the most
            daring label": Clea Simon, *Boston Rock,* July 1986.
101   Jackson deemed the Beasties' version a downgrade: *Black Radio Exclu-
            sive,* October 31, 1986.
101   "If I ever meet Wacko Jacko": Havelock Nelson, "The Beastie Boys:
            Three Naughty Rappers," *Black Beat,* April 1987.
101   L.A.'s KROQ FM station, who played it for a month: *New York Post,*
            April 28, 1987.
102   "I think B-boys are gonna love Juice": Bill Forman, "Raised on Rap,"
            BAM, June 6, 1986.
103   The *Voice* profile "credited him with everything but freeing the slaves":
            Creem, March 1987.
103   "I don't even own a Stones record": *East Village Eye,* December 1986.
103   "King of Rap": "The King of Rap," *Village Voice,* November 4, 1986.
107   "It's totally ridiculous": Scott Mehno, "Miami Nice," *East Village Eye,*
            May 1986.
114   "A twenty-one-foot penis that comes out of a box!": *New Music Express,*
            May 23, 1987.
115   "Please come back and throw more ice cubes. Love and Kisses": Per-
            sonal note from Joan Rivers to the Beastie Boys, January 19, 1987, Bill
            Adler Archives.
119   Brass Monkey had more than doubled, and consumers' traditional age
            expanded to include younger drinkers: *Adweek,* April 20, 1987.
120   dealers started leaving the ornaments off cars until delivery: "Mercedes
            Stars in a Beastie Fad," *Auto Week,* April 20, 1987.

121   Registering a song was actually as simple as: Donald S. Passman, *All You Need to Know About the Music Business* (Simon & Schuster, 1991).

Part Two: Growing Pains, 1988–93

Chapter 7: Together Forever?
131   The single would become the first hip-hop record: *Hits* magazine, August 1988.
136   declared "one of the most influential records" of the year: Robert Hilburn, *Los Angeles Times,* January 10, 1988.
137   the record label had been purchased by the Japanese technologies giant: "Sony History," www.sony.net.
138   Also known as phencyclidine: "A Drug Feared in the '70s Is Tied to Suspect in Killing," *The New York Times,* October 21, 2003.
139   "he liked to smoke weed, get into fights": LL Cool J, *I Make My Own Rules* (St. Martin's Press, 1997).
140   Def Jam was "in a state of total disarray": Internal memo from Bill Stephney to Russell Simmons, January 31, 1988, Bill Adler Archives.
142   he wasn't sure "if they'll ever make another record": *New Music Express,* April 16, 1988.
142   Rubin wanted to take a small advance for the sake of independence: *Black Radio Exclusive,* January 1989.
143   "It's as fun as *RoboCop*": "Rush to Judgement," *Hits,* August 22, 1988.
143   Def Jam was being challenged by a new crop of hip-hop labels: "Rap Breaks Through to Majors," *Billboard,* February 20, 1988.
145   Cohen picked Sosua in the Dominican Republic: "E. K. Smith and Lyor Cohen," *Manhattan Register,* May 4, 1988.
146–47   Although the group had accused Profile: *Billboard,* April 1997.
148   Everyone from Santa Claus to Freddy Krueger had a 1-900 line: "Smooth Operators," *Daily News,* April 16, 1989.
150   "Vile, vicious, despicable, stupid, sexist, racist, and horrendously made" was one typical reaction: Richard Harrington, *The Washington Post,* September 17, 1988.
151   *Tougher Than Leather* stayed in the black, grossing $20 million: David Hinckley, "Things That Go Bump," *Daily News Magazine,* August 5, 1990.

Chapter 8: Rush Communications
154   "I love Lyor like a brother, but": Internal memo from Bill Adler to Russell Simmons, August 3, 1988.
158   "We're splitting Black Gold off from Def Jam": "Def Jam Bows Black Gold, Signs 5 Acts to R&B Label," *Billboard,* November 12, 1988.
162   The Beasties had demanded "three times as much money" for the new album: *New Music Express,* November 3, 1989.
162          $20 million lawsuit filed by Def Jam against Capitol Records: *Billboard,* January 21, 1989.
162   "I hate this, I really hate this situation": Simmons said to a reporter, *New Music Express,* November 1989.

163   "We know that we also need the help of the staffs who work the rock and pop acts": Internal memo from Russell Simmons to Tommy Mottola, February 7, 1989, Bill Adler Archives.

165   Described Def Jam as a "seething rubble": *New Music Express,* March 11, 1989.

166   Trans America, a major insurance carrier for rap shows: "Insurer Cancels Coverage of Rap Show": *Billboard,* December 24, 1988.

166   "Any ban on insurance for rap shows": Ibid.

Chapter 9: **Damage Control**

171   No sooner did the film hit theaters: Steve Hochman, *Los Angeles Times,* December 1989.

171   "self-hating Jewish trash": *New York Post,* January 4, 1990.

171   "My first instinct was to can Public Enemy": Walter Yetnikoff, *Howling at the Moon* (Broadway Books, 2004).

172   "They're garbage": Marie Moore, "Slick Rick: Tales from the Stark Side," *Word Up!* July 1989.

173   "I've heard crowds booed Sugar Ray Leonard": Sony Music Entertainment, LL Cool J presentation, January 2, 1991.

174   "The worst advice I ever gave him": Ibid.

174   Someone in LL's entourage was arrested and charged with rape during the Minnesota date: *The Associated Press,* August 13, 1989.

178   In Canada, the MuchMusic video station: *Toronto Star,* February 21, 1990.

180   "Fucking Jew bastard," Griff reportedly screamed at Serch: "Griff Lashes Out at 3rd Bass in Manhattan Office," *East Coast Rocker,* February 21, 1990.

180   "I don't like Professor Griff and I hate what he stands for": Rush Management press release, February 12, 1990.

181   "Does this mean my contract with Def Jam Records is over?": L. Lajoan Jenkins PR, February 12, 1990.

Chapter 10: **RAL**

183   It was a more lucrative deal: *Billboard,* March 31, 1990.

183   "Are the papers signed yet?" *Vanity Fair,* July 1992.

184   But for now he had seven: Ibid.

184   "I want a film company big enough": Veronica Webb, "The Making of a Mogul," *Paper,* April 1990.

185   Cher had left behind all of her furnishings when she'd moved: *Jet,* May 28, 1990.

185   "He just added some phones": Ibid.

185   "Hip-hop died when Russell bought Cher's apartment": *Vanity Fair,* July 1992.

185   Within a month, Russell was a partner: David Hinckley, "Things That Go Bump," *Daily News Magazine,* August 5, 1990.

185   "I want to be compared to powerful people": *Paper,* April 1990.

186   didn't even keep an appointment book: *Manhattan, Inc.,* February 1990.

187   The Spectrum in Philadelphia: *The New York Times,* April 28, 1990.

187   Despite all the controversy: Columbia Records press release, July 3, 1990.

188   Rick pulled up beside them, on the corner of: Ibid.
188   "I just panicked": Ibid.
188   "I should have just stopped and pulled over or whatever": *The Source*, March 1995.
189   Simmons paid Rick's bond: *Daily News*, October 16, 1990.

Chapter 11: **Hard-Core**
210   Serch performed with Nas at the nightclub Shelter: *College Music Journal (CMJ)* flyer, October 28, 1992, Angela Thomas archives.
213   An HBO sitcom was also being negotiated: *The Source*, March 1993.
213   Even Russell "worried" about how well Pete's album would sell: *The Source*, June 1993.
217   But with the creation of Broadcast Data Systems: *Fast Company*, November 1993.

Part Three: **Fast Company,** 1994–2004

Chapter 12: **The Lyor Show**
233   The deal would include film projects: "Def Jam to Leave Sony, Plan to Move to Polygram," *Billboard*, May 14, 1994.
240   *No Pressure* was really "a compilation," since there were so many guest stars: *Beatdown*, October 1993.
243   "There will be a formal dress code": Bad Boy Records invitation to Puff Daddy's birthday party, November 8, 1994.
244   In November of 1994, Polygram's acquisition: "Polygram Buys Half of Def Jam," *Billboard*, November 26, 1994.
250   LL later admitted that his "acting sucked" in the film: LL Cool J, *I Make My Own Rules* (St. Martin's Press, 1997).
250   "as a way of demonstrating public support for Rick and applying pressure to the judicial system," he explained: Internal memo from Bill Adler to Lyor Cohen, March 1995.
251   Slick Rick's parole board review was scheduled for December of 1995: Adler Communication press release, May 4, 1995.
251   "Rick was quiet, sober, and serious": personal letter from Allen Ayers, Jr. to Judge Vomaska, April 27, 1995, Bill Adler Archives.
251   "They're an irresponsible crackhouse of a record company": *Toronto Star*, December 22, 1995.
255   "as crazy as a bag of angel dust": Russell Simmons speaking in *The Show* (Sony Pictures, 1995).

Chapter 13: **Sexy Again**
258   There was also the possibility of collaborating with the NAACP: *Rap Sheet*, November 10, 1995.
258   the disappearance of $70,000 worth of sound equipment: Ibid.
260   LeShaun led a protest outside of an LL concert: www.artistdirect.com.
267   "showed up and tried to throw their wallet in the way," as Russell Simmons recalled: Russell Simmons with Nelson George, *Life and Def* (Crown, 2001).

272   On December 10, 1998, Seagram's acquired: *Variety,* December 10, 1998.

273   Labels with long, colorful histories would be reduced to name only: *York Daily Record,* April 2, 1999.

273   edged out Garth Brooks and his *Double Live* album: "Def Jam Plans a Happy New Year," *Los Angeles Times,* August 15, 1999.

275   purchased from Rolling Stone Keith Richards for $2 million:*Jet,* April 26, 1999.

Chapter 14: Starting Over

277   release a new CD by Method Man on December 7, and by Redman: "Def Jam Plans."

277   "This will be a historical, groundbreaking endeavor": "Super Group Dru Hill Announces Formation of 'Dru World Order,' " *Business Wire,* August 9, 1999.

278   "In reality, this venture has the potential to be Sisqo's last stand": Jermaine Hall, "King of the Hill," *Oneworld,* January 2000.

279   Def Jam had the No. 1 and No. 2: "Def jam/Roc-a-Fella Delivers No. 1 and No. 2 Albums of New Millennium," *Business Wire,* January 6, 2000.

279   "I'm just going through the motions": *Los Angeles Times,* April 16, 2000.

281–82   Island Def Jam had also broken several big rock acts: New York *Daily News,* December 14, 2001.

282   Cohen would call Iovine a "good friend": *Times Union,* May 9, 2002.

283   "One album, one tour, one movement": *Business Wire,* January 28, 2002.

283   "swimming in the Blue Grotto": *Times Union,* May 9, 2002.

288   "the Island Def Jam brand, and the logo with the sensitivity": Ibid.

288   Joe Budden, whom he considered "too wordy": *Newsweek,* August 14, 2004.

Def Jam Recordings, U.S. Discography

Def Jam Recordings has arguably the most impressive and prolific catalog of any hip-hop label. Every effort has been made to compile the most thorough and accurate listing of Def Jam's single and album releases in the United States from November, 1984—when Russell Simmons and Rick Rubin officially partnered to form Def Jam Recordings—through December, 2003, when Lyor Cohen resigned as the chairman of Island Def Jam.

1984	Title	Artist	Catalog No.
Singles	"I Need a Beat"	LL Cool J	001
1985			
Singles	"Rock Hard" b/w "Party's Getting Rough" and "Beastie Groove"	Beastie Boys	002
	"Def Jam/Cold Chillin' in the Spot"	Jazzy Jay	003
	"Drum Machine"	MCA and Burzootie	004
	"I Want You" b/w "Dangerous"	LL Cool J	005
	"This Is It"	Jimmy Spicer	006
	"It's the Beat"	Hollis Crew	007
	"I Can't Live Without My Radio"	LL Cool J	008
	"She's on It"	Beastie Boys	44-05292
	"Can You Feel It?/ Knowledge Me"	Original Concept	44-05342

1985	Title	Artist	Catalog No.

1985 Singles Cont.

	"Rock the Bells"	LL Cool J	44-05349
Albums	*Radio*	LL Cool J	CK-40239

1986
Singles	"Hold It Now, Hit It"	Beastie Boys	44-05369
	"Bottom Line"	Big Audio Dynamite	44-05370
	"The Word/Sardines"	The Junkyard Band	44-05922
	"The Rain" b/w "Your Song"	Oran "Juice" Jones	44-05930
	"It's the New Style" b/w "Paul Revere"	Beastie Boys	44-05958
	"Chasin' a Dream" b/w "Got the Right Attitude"	Tashan	44-05960
	"Bite'n My Stylee" b/w "Pump That Bass"	Original Concept	44-05961
	"Curiosity"	Oran "Juice" Jones	44-05968
	"Read My Mind"	Tashan	44-06737
Albums	*Oran "Juice" Jones*	Oran "Juice" Jones	CK-40367
	Reign in Blood	Slayer	CK-69406
	Licensed to Ill	Beastie Boys	314-527-351

1987
Singles	"Public Enemy No. 1"	Public Enemy	44-06719
	"I'm Bad" b/w "Get Down"	LL Cool J	44-06799
	"I Need Love"	LL Cool J	44-06511
	"Have You Seen Davy?"	Davy DMX	44-06811
	"You're Gonna Get Yours"	Public Enemy	44-06861

1987	Title	Artist	Catalog No.

1987 Singles Cont.

	"Miuzi Weighs a Ton" b/w "Rebel Without a Pause"	Public Enemy	44-06861
	"Jammin' to the Bells"	Chuck Stanley	44-06874
	"Cold Spendin' My Money"	Oran "Juice" Jones	44-06960
	"Feel for You/Davy's Ride"	Davy DMX	44-07463
	"Hazy Shade of Winter"	Bangles	38-07630
	"Are You My Woman?" b/w "Bring the Noise"	The Black Flames & Public Enemy	44-07545
	"Fight For Your Right (to Party)"	Beastie Boys	44-06548
	"Go Cut Creator Go"	LL Cool J	44-07476
	"Make You Mine Tonight"	Chuck Stanley	38-07425
Albums	*Yo! Bum Rush the Show*	Public Enemy	314-527357
	Davy's Ride	Davy DMX	314-40657
	Bigger and Deffer	LL Cool J	314-527353
	Less Than Zero	Various	314-527360
	GTP (Gangstas Takin' Over)	Oran "Juice" Jones	314-40955
	Finer Things in Life	Chuck Stanley	44-06020
1988 **Singles**	"Going Back to Cali"	LL Cool J	44-07563
	"Don't Believe the Hype"	Public Enemy	44-07846
	"Night of the Living Baseheads"	Public Enemy	44-08121

1988	Title	Artist	Catalog No.
1988 Singles Cont.			
	"Teenage Love"	Slick Rick	44-08139
	"Ooh Girl"	Davy DMX	44-07575
	"Charlie Sez"	Original Concept	44-07899
Albums	*Straight from the Basement of Kooley High*	Original Concept	44-29781
	It Takes a Nation of Millions to Hold Us Back	Public Enemy	314-527-358
	The Great Adventures of Slick Rick	Slick Rick	314-527-359
1989 **Singles**	"Sleep Talk"	Alyson Williams	44-68193
	"Children's Story"	Slick Rick	44-68223
	"I'm a Girl Watcher"	Papa Ron Love	44-68783
	"Steppin' to the A.M."	3rd Bass	44-68802
	"I Desire"	Newkirk	44-73109
	"Big Ol' Butt"	LL Cool J	44-68864
	"Gas Face"	3rd Bass	44-73121
	"Welcome to the Terrordome"	Public Enemy	44-73135
	"Sweat You"	Newkirk	44-73175
	"My Love Is So Raw"	Alyson Williams feat. Nikki D.	44-68794
	"It's Like Magic"	Blue Magic	44-68789

1989	Title	Artist	Catalog No.

1989 Singles Cont.

	"I Need Your Lovin' "	Alyson Williams	44–73142
	"Brooklyn Queens"	3rd Bass	44–65583
	"I'm That Kind of Guy"	LL Cool J	44–68792
	"Hey Young World"	Slick Rick	44–68951
	"Black Steel in the Hour of Chaos"	Public Enemy	44–68216
Albums	*The Black Flames*	The Black Flames	CK–44030
	Def Jam Classics, Vol. 1	Various	314–527362
	Raw	Alyson Williams	314–527363
	Walking with a Panther	LL Cool J	314–527-355
	Funk City	Newkirk	OK–45379
	The Cactus Album	3rd Bass	314–527361
	To Be Immortal	Oran "Juice" Jones	CK–45321

1990

Singles	"Jinglin' Baby (Remix)"	LL Cool J	44–73147
	"Brothers Gonna Work It Out"	Public Enemy	44–73391
	"Product of the Environment"	3rd Bass	44–73441
	"The Boomin' System"	LL Cool J	44–73458
	"Can't Do Nuthin' for Ya Man"	Public Enemy	44–73612
	"Gold Digger"	EPMD	44–73633
	"Around the Way Girl"	LL Cool J	44–73610

1990	Title	Artist	Catalog No.

1990 Singles Cont.

	"911 Is a Joke"	Public Enemy	44-73179
	"Half"	No Face	44-73464
	"Two-Minute Brother"	Bytches With Problems	44-73574
Albums	*Fear of a Black Planet*	Public Enemy	314-523446
	Def Jam Classics, Vol. 2	Various	314-523531
	Kickin' Afrolistics	The Afros	CK-46802
	Mama Said Knock You Out	LL Cool J	CK-46888
	Business as Usual	EPMD	CK-47067
1991 **Singles**	"Radioactive"	Downtown Science	44-73685
	"Daddy's Little Girl"	Nikki D.	44-73697
	"Pop Goes the Weasel" b/w "Derelicts of Dialect"	3rd Bass	44-73702
	"Mama Said Knock You Out"	LL Cool J	44-73703
	"Hip-Hop Junkies"	Nice & Smooth	44-73738
	"Hang on Kid"	Nikki D.	44-73812
	"Portrait of the Artist as a Hood" b/w "Green Eggs and Swine"	3rd Bass	44-73918
	"If I Was/This Is a Visit"	Downtown Science	44-74052
	"How to Flow"	Nice & Smooth	44-74092
	"Wasted"	Nikki D.	44-74054

1991	Title	Artist	Catalog No.
1991 Singles Cont.			
	"Can't Truss It"	Public Enemy	44–73870
	"In There"	The Don	44–73727
	"6 Minutes of Pleasure"	LL Cool J	44–73821
	"Small Thing"	Newkirk	44–73848
	"By the Time I Get to Arizona"	Public Enemy	44–74358
	"I Shouldn't Have Done It"	Slick Rick	44–74730
Albums	*Derelicts of Dialect*	3rd Bass	CK–47369
	Daddy's Little Girl	Nikki D.	44–403121
	Ain't a Damn Thing Changed	Nice & Smooth	314–523478
	Apocalypse '91 . . . The Enemy Strikes Back	Public Enemy	314–523479
	The Ruler's Back	Slick Rick	314–523480
	Wake Up the Party	The Don	314–523505
	Livin' Large	Various	314–523530
	Downtown Science	Downtown Science	314–47092
	Runs In the Fam-Lee	Fam-Lee	44–736724

1992			
Singles	"Throw Ya Gunz"	Onyx	42–74766
	"Sometimes I Rhyme Slow"	Nice & Smooth	44–74166
	"Cake and Eat It Too"	Nice & Smooth	44–74364
	"I Don't Give a Fuck"	Bo$$	44–743374

1992	Title	Artist	Catalog No.
1992 Singles Cont.			
	"Crossover"	EPMD	44-74172
	"Time 4 Sum Akshun"	Redman	42-74794
	"Blow Your Mind"	Redman	44-74424
	"Here It Comes"	MC Serch	44-74414
	"Rat Bastard"	Pete Nice & Daddy Rich	44-74785
Albums	*Business Never Personal*	EPMD	OK-52848
	Return of the Product	MC Serch	OK-52964
	Whut? Thee Album	Redman	314-523518
	Greatest Misses	Public Enemy	314-523487
1993			
Singles	"Slam"	Onyx	42-74882
	"Recipe of a Hoe"	Bo$$	44-74967
	"Deeper"	Bo$$	44-74737
	"Tonight's Da Night"	Redman	44-74958
	"Back Seat of My Jeep"	LL Cool J	44-74983
	"Stay Real"	Eric Sermon	44-77141
	"Ghetto Jam"	Domino	44-29340
	"How I'm Comin' "	LL Cool J	44-74810
	"Pink Cookies in a Plastic Bag"	LL Cool J	44-74983
	"Kick the Bobo"	Pete Nice & Daddy Rich	44-74883
Albums	*Bacdafucup*	Onyx	314-523447
	14 Shots to the Dome	LL Cool J	314-523488

1993	Title	Artist	Catalog No.

1993 Albums Cont.

	Born Gangstaz	Bo$$	314-523503
	Domino	Domino	314-529340
	No Pressure	EPMD	314-523460
	Dust to Dust	Pete Nice & Daddy Rich	314-564880

1994

Singles	"Return of the Hip-Hop Freaks"	Nice & Smooth	42-28537
	"Old to the New"	Nice & Smooth	44-853239
	"Bring the Pain"	Method Man	44-85396
	"Regulate"	Warren G.	44-858960
	"Gang Stories"	South Central Cartel	42-77367
	"Sweet Potato Pie"	Domino	44-77349
	"Give It Up"	Public Enemy	44-854091
	"Rockafella"	Redman	42-853967
	"It's a Boy"	Slick Rick	44-741211
Albums	Regulate . . . G-Funk Era	Warren G.	314-523335
	Jewel of the Nile	Nice & Smooth	314-523336
	Muse Sick-n-Hour Mess Age	Public Enemy	314-523362
	Tical	Method Man	314-523839
	Dare Iz a Darkside	Redman	314-523846
	Behind Bars	Slick Rick	314-523847
	N Gatz We Truss	South Central Cartel	314-529344

1995	Title	Artist	Catalog No.
1995 **Singles**	"Loungin' "	LL Cool J	314-575062
	"I'll Be There for You/ You're All I Need"	Method Man	42-518792
	"How High"	Redman/ Method Man	314-579925
	"50/50 Luv"	BG Knocc Out & Dresta	314-579717
	"Somethin' 4 Da Honeyz"	Montell Jordan	42-856963
	"I Got Him All the Time (He's Mine)"	MoKenStef	42-851705
	"This Is How We Do It"	Montell Jordan	42-851469
	"Sittin' in My Car"	Slick Rick	314-575865
	"Hey Lover"	LL Cool J	314-577495
	"BG Thang"	Mel-Low	314-577423
Albums	*Mr. Smith*	LL Cool J	314-523845
	Def Jam 10 Year Anniversary Box Set	Various	314-523848
	This Is How We Do It	Montell Jordan	314-527179
	The Show, soundtrack	Various	314-529021
	Prophecy	Capleton	314-529264
	This Is the Shack	Dove Shack	314-527933
	Azz Izz	MoKenStef	314-527364
1996 **Singles**	"Touch Me, Tease Me"	Case	42-385462
	"Doin' It"	LL Cool J	314-576121
	"Whateva Man"	Redman	314-574026

1996	Title	Artist	Catalog No.
1996 Singles Cont.			
	"More to Love"	Case	314-575653
	"I'll Be"	Foxy Brown	314-574061
Albums	*Case*	Case	314-533134
	The Nutty Professor	Various	314-531911
	Ill Nana	Foxy Brown	314-533684
	All World	LL Cool J	314-534125
	Muddy Waters	Redman	314-533470
	More . . .	Montell Jordan	314-533191
1997 **Singles**	"Get Me Home"	Foxy Brown	314-574061
	"Bring Back Your Love"	Christion	314-571593
	"Just Another Case"	Cru	314-573857
	"I Shot the Sheriff"	Warren G.	314-574095
	"Sunshine"	Jay-Z	314-528702
	"4,3,2,1"	LL Cool J	314-568321
	"Big Bad Mamma"	Foxy Brown	314-571441
	"I Gotta Know"	Playa	314-56882
	"Cheers to You"	Playa	314-568214
	"Let's Ride"	Rell	314-575774
Albums	*In My Lifetime, Vol. 1*	Jay-Z	314-536-392
	Da Dirty 30	Cru	314-537-607
	Phenomenon	LL Cool J	314-539186

1997	Title	Artist	Catalog No.

1997 Albums Cont.

	How To Be a Player	Various	314-537-973
	Ghetto Cyrano	Christion	314-536281
	Back In Business	EPMD	314-536973
	Take a Look Over Your Shoulder	Warren G.	314-537234

1998
Singles

	"Hot Spot"	Foxy Brown	314-566499
	"I'll Be Dat"	Redman	314-566-699
	"Faded Pictures"	Case	314-566494
	"Slippin' "	DMX	314-566881
	"Let's Ride"	Montell Jordan	314-568475
	"Love for Free"	Rell	314-568842

Albums

	El Niño	Def Squad	314-558343
	It's Dark and Hell Is Hot	DMX	314-558-227
	Flesh of My Flesh, Blood of My Blood	DMX	314-538-864
	Hard Knock Life: Vol. 2	Jay-Z	314-558902
	Rush Hour, soundtrack	Various	314-558-663
	The Professional	DJ Clue	314-558891
	He Got Game	Public Enemy	314-558231
	Doc's Da Name 2000	Redman	314-558977
	Tical 2000: Judgement Day	Method Man	314-558920

1999	Title	Artist	Catalog No.

1999
Singles

	Title	Artist	Catalog No.
	"Breaks Up to Make Up"	Method Man feat. D'Angelo	314-563405
	"Happily Ever After"	Case	314-563631
	"What's My Name?"	DMX	314-562540
	"Holla Holla"	Ja Rule	314-566959
	"Can I Get A"	Jay-Z	314-567683
	"Get It On . . . Tonight"	Montell Jordan	314-562-280
	"Hard Knock Life"	Jay-Z	314-566977
	"I Can't"	Foxy Brown	42-870801
	"Vivrant Thing"	Q-Tip	314-562170
	"Da Goodness"	Redman	314-566831
	"When Will U See"	Rell	314-562302
	"Street Talkin' (I Own America)"	Slick Rick	314-562-185
	"Da Rockwilder"	Method Man & Redman	314-562440
Albums	*Personal Conversation*	Case	314-538-871
	Venni, Vetti, Vecci	Ja Rule	314-538-920
	Blackout!	Method Man/ Redman	314-546-609
	And Then There Was X	DMX	314-546-933
	Chyna Doll	Foxy Brown	314-558933
	Violator, The Album, Vol. 1	Various	314-558941
	Vol. 3: Life and Times of S. Carter	Jay-Z	314-546813

1999	Title	Artist	Catalog No.
1999 Albums Cont.			
	Get It On . . . Tonight	Montell Jordan	314-546714
	Coming of Age	Memphis Bleek	314-538991
	Unleash the Dragon	Sisqo	314-546816
	Art of Storytelling	Slick Rick	314-558936
2000 **Singles**	"Who We Be?"	DMX	314-572720
	"Oh Yeah"	Foxy Brown	314-572-836
	"Thong Song"	Sisqo	314-568-890
	"The Truth"	Beanie Sigel	314-562-662
	"Dance for Me"	Sisqo	314-588700
	"Party Up"	DMX	314-562605
	"What You Want"	DMX	314-562958
	"Put It on Me"	Ja Rule	314-572751
	"Big Pimpin' "	Jay-Z	314-562833
	"Hey Papi"	Jay-Z	314-562862
	"Girl Next Door"	Musiq Soulchild	314-572748
	"Got to Get It"	Sisqo	314-562455
	"Back for the First Time"	Ludacris	314-548138
	"Remember Them Days"	Beanie Sigel	314-562-823
Albums	*Aijuswanaseing*	Musiq Soulchild	314-548289
	The Truth	Beanie Sigel	314-546621
	Belly	Various	314-558925

2000	Title	Artist	Catalog No.
2000 Albums Cont.			
	DJ Clue Presents: Backstage	Various	314–546641
	Rule 3:36	Ja Rule	314–542928
	Dynasty: Roc La Familia	Jay-Z	314–548203
	G.O.A.T.	LL Cool J	314–577021
	Mirror Mirror	Kelly Price	314–542472
	The Professional 2	DJ Clue	314–542325
	The Understanding	Memphis Bleek	314–542587
2001 **Singles**	"Area Codes"	Ludacris	314–588-671
	"Southern Hospitality"	Ludacris	314–52131
	"Is That Your Chick?"	Memphis Bleek	314–15111
	"What's Your Fantasy?"	Ludacris	314–588817
	"Who We Be"	DMX	314–572721
	"We Right Here"	DMX	314–539710
	"Always on Time"	Ja Rule	314–583446
	"I Cry"	Ja Rule	314–572850
	"Izzo (H.O.V.A.)"	Jay-Z	314–588815
	"Missing You"	Case	314–572750
	"Girls, Girls, Girls"	Jay-Z	314–543810
	"I Just Wanna Love U (Give It to Me)"	Jay-Z	314–572666

2001	Title	Artist	Catalog No.
2001 Singles Cont.			
	"Let's Get Dirty"	Redman	314-572917
	"Smash Sumthin'"	Redman	314-572995
	"Can I Live"	Sisqo	314-572917
	"Pain Is Love"	Ja Rule	314-586440
	"Beanie"	Beanie Sigel	314-572935
	"BK Anthem"	Foxy Brown	314-529138
Albums	*Broken Silence*	Foxy Brown	314-548834
	The Blueprint	Jay-Z	314-586396
	Pain Is Love	Ja Rule	314-586437
	The Great Depression	DMX	314-586450
	Malpractice	Redman	314-548381
	Unplugged	Jay-Z	314-586617
	Word of Mouf	Ludacris	314-586446
	The Reason	Beanie Sigel	314-548838
	Open Letter	Case	314-548626
2002 **Singles**	"Foolish"	Ashanti	314-588986
	"Baby"	Ashanti	44-063851
	"Livin' It Up"	Ja Rule	314-588814
	"Luv U Better"	LL Cool J	44-063956
	"Hey Ma"	Cam'Ron	44-063958
	"Oh Boy"	Cam'Ron	314-582864
	"My Block"	Scarface	314-582865

2002	Title	Artist	Catalog No.
2002 Singles Cont.			
	"Move Bitch"	Ludacris	314-582948
	"Roll Out"	Ludacris	314-582948
	"N.S.E.W."	Disturbing Tha Peace	314-15732
	"Candy"	Foxy Brown	314-588858
	"Last Temptation"	Ja Rule	44-063490
	"Happy"	Ashanti	314-582935
Albums	*Ashanti*	Ashanti	314-586830
	The Blueprint 2: The Gift and The Curse	Jay-Z	44-063381
	The Last Temptation	Ja Rule	44-063487
	Cradle 2 Tha Grave	Various	44-06361
	Come Home with Me	Cam'Ron	314-586876
	10	LL Cool J	44-063219
	Golden Grain	Disturbing Tha Peace	44-063205
2003			
Singles	"Pump It Up"	Joe Budden	44-077895
	"From Me to U"	Juelz Santana	44-077056
	"Where the Hood At"	DMX	B0000C9061
	"X Gon' Give It to Ya"	DMX	44-077904
	"99 Problems"	Jay-Z	B0001ZXMHZ
	"Stand Up"	Ludacris	JB0001
	"Yeah Yeah You Know It"	Keith Murray	B00009YXG7
	"Rain On Me"	Ashanti	B0000DIXN9
	"Rock Wit U"	Ashanti	B00009VZ88

2002	Title	Artist	Catalog No.
Albums	*Joe Budden*	Joe Budden	B00009KEDN
	Blood In My Eye	Ja Rule	B0000DJYR8
	Grand Champ	DMX	B0000C421G
	The Black Album	Jay-Z	B0000DZFL0
	The Blueprint 2.1	Jay-Z	44-077296
	Soulstar	Musiq Soulchild	44-011920
	Chicken N Beer	Ludacris	44-055370
	Chapter II	Ashanti	B00009VRDI
	2 Fast 2 Furious	Various Artists	44-042602
	He's Keith Murray	Keith Murray	B000093ILS
	M.A.D.E.	Memphis Bleek	B0000Z80D0

Acknowledgments

This book would not have been written if it wasn't for the seventy-plus people who volunteered their time to be interviewed. Pulling out long-shelved memories can sometimes be a daunting process, which is why my gratitude to these people is so profound, particularly to: Cey Adams, Bill Stephney, Sean Carasov, Ric Menello, Scott Koenig, Steve Ralbovsky, Rick Rubin, who also connected me to another tremendous source, Jeff Jones, Tracey Waples, Hank Shocklee, Drew Dixon, Bo$$, Steve Carr, and Chuck D. Thank you to Russell Simmons and Lyor Cohen, who generously took time out of their incredibly busy schedules to share their memories with me.

I am especially indebted to Angela Thomas, Adam Dubin, and Bill Adler, who in addition to being interviewed numerous times also gave me complete access to their amazing archives.

An enormous, heartfelt thank you to Brett Ratner, who not only wrote the terrific introduction to this book, but was one of my best interviewees. I am grateful beyond words.

My research assistant Darren "Dee Tee" Teruel was a tremendous help in locating many individuals, setting up interviews (as well as doing the great interview with Tom Araya of Slayer), providing feedback and support.

Thank you to Sean Carasov, Glen E. Friedman, Sunny Bak, Janette Beckman and Caroline Torem-Craig for providing the rare photographs.

Thank you to my sister Julie Gueraseva, who designed the jacket for the book, read all of my drafts, helped me transcribe interviews, and crisis managed, among many other contributions. I couldn't have done any of this without her.

Thank you to my editor Melody Guy and her assistant Danielle Durkin (my second editor) for this tremendous opportunity and for being so supportive.

Thank you to my agent, Kate Garrick at DeFiore and Company. I can't believe it's been four years since we started this journey with a ten-page proposal. I'm glad you've been there for me every step of the way.

Thank you to my parents for the love, and to my mother for reading drafts of the manuscript and offering helpful suggestions.

My education played a huge part in my development as a writer. I thank my alma matter, Smith College, for opening my mind and instilling in me a love for the written word.

Index

Page numbers in *italics* refer to illustrations.

About the Author

STACY GUERASEVA has been writing about music and culture since 1995 for national publications that have included *Interview,* *Vibe,* and *XXL.* She is the former editor in chief of Russell Simmons's *Oneworld* magazine and juror for the annual Hip-Hop Odyssey (H2O) film festival. Ms. Gueraseva graduated from Smith College with a bachelor's degree in American Studies. A native of Moscow, Russia, she currently lives in Brooklyn, New York. You can visit her at www.defjambook.com

About the Type

This book was set in Bembo, a typeface based on an old-style Roman face that was used for Cardinal Bembo's tract *De Aetna* in 1495. Bembo was cut by Francisco Griffo in the early sixteenth century. The Lanston Monotype Machine Company of Philadelphia brought the well-proportioned letter forms of Bembo to the United States in the 1930s.